DATE DUE

~~JUN 14 '97~~			
~~DE 1 '99~~			
9/3/02			

DEMCO 38-296

The Monograph

The volumes within the *Tall Buildings and Urban Environment* series correspond to the Council's group and committee structure. The present listing includes all current topical committees. Some are collaborating to produce volumes together, and Groups DM and BSS plan, with only a few exceptions, to combine all topics into one volume.

PLANNING AND ENVIRONMENTAL CRITERIA (PC)
Philosophy of Tall Buildings
History of Tall Buildings
Architecture
Rehabilitation, Renovation, Repair
Urban Planning and Design
External Transportation
Parking
Social Effects of the Environment
Socio-Political Influences
Design for the Disabled and Elderly
Interior Design
Landscape Architecture

DEVELOPMENT AND MANAGEMENT (DM)
Economics
Ownership and Maintenance
Project Management
Tall Buildings in Developing Countries
Decision-Making Parameters
Development and Investment
Legal Aspects

SYSTEMS AND CONCEPTS (SC)
Cladding
Partitions, Walls, and Ceilings
Structural Systems
Foundation Design
Construction Systems
High-Rise Housing
Prefabricated Tall Buildings
Tall Buildings Using Local Technology
Robots and Tall Buildings
Application of Systems Methodology

CRITERIA AND LOADING (CL)
Gravity Loads and Temperature Effects
Earthquake Loading and Response
Wind Loading and Wind Effects
Fire
Accidental Loading
Safety and Quality Assurance
Motion Perception and Tolerance

TALL STEEL BUILDINGS (SB)
Commentary on Structural Standards
Methods of Analysis and Design
Stability
Design Methods Based on Stiffness
Fatigue Assessment & Ductility Assurance
Connections
Cold-Formed Steel
Load and Resistance Factor Design (Limits States Design)
Mixed Construction

TALL CONCRETE AND MASONRY BUILDINGS (CB)
Commentary on Structural Standards
Selection of Structural Systems
Optimization
Elastic Analysis
Nonlinear Analysis and Limit Design
Stability
Stiffness and Crack Control
Precast Panel Structures
Creep, Shrinkage, & Temperature Effects
Cast-in-Place Concrete
Precast-Prestressed Concrete
Masonry Structures

BUILDING SERVICE SYSTEMS (BSS)

HVAC/Energy Conservation
Plumbing and Fire Protection
Electrical Systems

High-Tech Buildings
Vertical & Horizontal Transportation
Environmental Design
Urban Services

The basic objective of the Council's Monograph is to document the most recent developments to the state of the art in the field of tall buildings and their role in the urban habitat. The following volumes can be ordered through the Council.

Planning and Design of Tall Buildings, 5 volumes (1978-1981 by ASCE)

Developments in Tall Buildings–1983 (Van Nostrand Reinhold Company)

Advances in Tall Buildings (1986, Van Nostrand Reinhold Company)

High-Rise Buildings: Recent Progress (1986, Council on Tall Buildings)

Second Century of the Skyscraper (1988 Van Nostrand Reinhold Company)

Tall Buildings: 2000 and Beyond, 2 volumes. (1990 & 1991, Council on Tall Buildings)

Council Headquarters
Lehigh University, Building 13
Bethlehem, Pennsylvania 18015 USA

Building Design
for Handicapped
and Aged Persons

Data

sons / Council on Tall
5 ; Gilda M. Haber, chairman
Thomas O. Blank ... [et al.].
1 environment series)

Includes bibliographical references and indexes.
ISBN 0-07-012533-3
1. Architecture and the handicapped. 2. Architecture and the
aged. I. Haber, Gilda M. II. Blank, Thomas O., date.
III. Council on Tall Buildings and Urban Habitat. Committee 56.
IV. Series. V. Series. Monograph (Council on Tall Buildings and
Urban Habitat)
NA2545.A1B84   1992
720'.42—dc20   92-7210
                                                              CIP

1 2 3 4 5 6 7 8 9 0   DOC/DOC   9 8 7 6 5 4 3 2

ISBN   0-07-012533-3

*For the Council on Tall Buildings and Urban Habitat, Lynn S. Beedle is
the Editor-in-Chief and Dolores B. Rice is the Managing Editor.*

*For McGraw-Hill, the sponsoring editor for this book was Joel Stein, the
editing supervisor was Peggy Lamb, and the production supervisor was
Donald F. Schmidt. This book was set in Times Roman. It was
composed by McGraw-Hill's Professional Book Group composition unit.*

Council on Tall Buildings and Urban Habitat

Steering Group

Council on Tall Buildings and Urban Habitat

Contributors

Boundary Layer Wind Tunnel Laboratory (U. Western Ontario), London
H. K. Cheng & Partners Ltd., Hong Kong
Douglas Specialist Contractors Ltd., Aldridge
The George Hyman Construction Co., Bethesda
Johnson Fain and Pereira Assoc., Los Angeles
LeMessurier Consultants Inc., Cambridge
W. L. Meinhardt & Partners Pty. Ltd., Melbourne
Obayashi Corporation, Tokyo
PSM International, Chicago
Tooley & Company, Los Angeles
Nabih Youssef and Associates, Los Angeles

Contributing Participants

Adviesbureau Voor Bouwtechniek bv, Arnhem
American Institute of Steel Construction, Chicago
Anglo American Property Services (Pty.) Ltd., Johannesburg
Artech, Inc., Taipei
Atelier D'Architecture De Genval, Genval
Austin Commercial, Inc., Dallas
Australian Institute of Steel Construction, Milsons Point
B.C.V. Progetti S.r.l., Milano
Bechtel Corporation, San Francisco
W.S. Bellows Construction Corp., Houston
Alfred Benesch & Co., Chicago
BMP Consulting Engineers, Hong Kong
Bornhorst & Ward Pty. Ltd., Spring Hill
Bovis Limited, London
Bramalea Ltd., Dallas
Brandow & Johnston Associates, Los Angeles
Brooke Hillier Parker, Hong Kong
Campeau Corp., Toronto
CBM Engineers, Houston
Cermak Peterka Petersen, Inc., Fort Collins
Connell Wagner (NSW) Pty. Ltd., Sydney
Construction Consulting Laboratory, Dallas
Crane Fulview Door Co., Lake Bluff
Crone & Associates Pty. Ltd., Sydney
Crow Construction Co., New York
Davis Langdon & Everest, London
DeSimone, Chaplin & Dobryn, New York
Dodd Pacific Engineering, Inc., Seattle
Englekirk, Hart, and Sobel, Inc., Los Angeles
Falcon Steel Company, Wilmington
Fujikawa Johnson and Associates, Chicago
Gutteridge Haskins & Davey Pty. Ltd., Sydney
T.R. Hamzah & Yeang Sdn Bhd, Selangor
Hayakawa Associates, Los Angeles
Hellmuth, Obata & Kassabaum, Inc., San Francisco
Honeywell, Inc., Minneapolis
INTEMAC, Madrid
International Iron & Steel Institute, Brussels
Irwin Johnston and Partners, Sydney
Johnson & Nielsen, Irvine
KPFF Consulting Engineers, Seattle
Lend Lease Design Group Ltd., Sydney
Stanley D. Lindsey & Assoc., Nashville
Lohan Associates, Inc., Chicago
Martin & Bravo, Inc., Honolulu
Enrique Martinez-Romero, S.A., Mexico
McWilliam Consulting Engineers, Brisbane

Mitchell McFarlane Brentnall & Partners Intl. Ltd., Hong Kong
Mitsubishi Estate Co., Ltd., Tokyo
Moh and Associates, Inc., Taipei
Mueser Rutledge Consulting Engineers, New York
Multiplex Construction (NSW) Pty. Ltd., Sydney
Nihon Sekkei, U.S.A., Ltd., Los Angeles
Nikken Sekkei Ltd., Tokyo
Norman Disney & Young, Brisbane
O'Brien-Kreitzberg & Associates, Inc., Pennsauken
Ove Arup & Partners, Sydney
Pacific Atlas Development Corp., Los Angeles
Peddle Thorp Australia Pty. Ltd., Australia
Peddle, Thorp & Walker Arch., Sydney
Perkins & Will, Chicago
J. Roger Preston & Partners, Hong Kong
Projest SA Empreendimentos e Servicos Technicos, Rio de Janeiro
Rahulan Zain Associates, Kuala Lumpur
Ranhill Bersekutu Sdn Bhd, Kuala Lumpur
Rankine & Hill, Wellington
RFB Consulting Architects, Johannesburg
Robert Rosenwasser Associates, PC, New York
Emery Roth & Sons Intl., Inc., New York
Rowan Williams Davies & Irwin, Inc., Guelph
Sepakat Setia Perunding (Sdn.) Bhd., Kuala Lumpur
Shimizu Corporation, Tokyo
South African Institute of Steel Construction, Johannesburg
Steel Reinforcement Institute of Australia, Sydney
Steen Consultants Pty. Ltd., Singapore
Stigter Clarey & Partners, Sydney
Studio Finzi, Nova E Castellani, Milano
Taylor Thompson Whitting Pty. Ltd., St. Leonards
BA Vavaroutas & Associates, Athens
Pedro Ramirez Vazquez, Arquitecto, Pedregal de San Angel
VIPAC Engineers & Scientists Ltd., Melbourne
Wargon Chapman Partners, Sydney
Weidlinger Associates, New York
Wimberley, Allison, Tong & Goo, Newport Beach
Wong & Ouyang (HK) Ltd., Hong Kong
Woodward-Clyde Consultants, New York
Yapi Merkezi Inc., Istanbul
Zaldastani Associates, Inc., Boston

Other Books in the Tall Buildings and Urban Environment Series

Planning and Environmental Criteria

Building Design
for Handicapped
and Aged Persons

Council on Tall Buildings and Urban Habitat
Committee 56

CONTRIBUTORS

Thomas O. Blank
Alexander Chen
Reuben Eldar
Th. M. G. Guffens
Gilda M. Haber
James D. Harrison
Donald N. Henning
Leonard F. Heumann

Satoshi Kose
Khee Poh Lam
James N. Macdonald
Wolfgang F. E. Preiser
Miriam Shtarkshall
Jonathan D. Sime
James G. Small

Editorial Group

Gilda M. Haber, Chairman
Thomas O. Blank, Editor

McGraw-Hill, Inc.

New York St. Louis San Francisco Auckland Bogotá
Caracas Lisbon London Madrid Mexico Milan
Montreal New Delhi Paris San Juan São Paulo
Singapore Sydney Tokyo Toronto

AUTHOR ACKNOWLEDGMENT

This Monograph was prepared by Committee 56 (Design for the Disabled and Elderly) of the Council on Tall Buildings and Urban Habitat as part of the *Tall Buildings and Urban Environment Series*.

Special acknowledgment is due those individuals whose contributions and papers formed the initial contribution to the chapters in this volume. These individuals are:

Thomas O. Blank, Chapter 1
Satoshi Kose, Chapter 2
Alexander Chen, Chapter 3
Donald N. Henning, Chapter 4
Th. M. G. Guffens, Chapter 5
Reuben Eldar, Chapter 6
Miriam Shtarkshall, Chapter 6
Khee Poh Lam, Chapter 7

James D. Harrison, Chapter 7
Leonard F. Heumann, Chapter 8
Gilda Moss Haber, Chapter 9
Jonathan D. Sime, Chapter 10
James N. Macdonald, Chapter 11
Wolfgang F. E. Preiser, Chapter 12
James G. Small, Chapter 12
Thomas O. Blank, Chapter 13
Gilda Moss Haber, Chapter 14

CONTRIBUTORS

The following is a complete list of those who have submitted written material for possible use in the Monograph, whether or not that material was used in the final version. The Committee Chairman and Editor were given quite complete latitude. Frequently, length limitations precluded the inclusion of much valuable material. The Bibliography contains all contributions. The contributors are: Thomas O. Blank, Alexander Chen, Reuben Eldar, Miriam Shtarkshall, Th. M. G. Guffens, Gilda M. Haber, James D. Harrison, Donald N. Henning, Leonard F. Heumann, Satoshi Kose, Khee Pho Lam, James Macdonald, Wolfgang F. E. Preiser, Jonathan D. Sime, and James G. Small. Acknowledgment is given to Philip Gartshore, Eddie Burke, and C. D. Zwierzchowski for their support.

COMMITTEE MEMBERS

Nigan Bayazit, Thomas O. Blank (Editor), Alexander Chen, John T. Christian, Arza Churchman, Henry J. Cowan, Enzo Cucciniello, John Deshon (Vice-Chairman), Gregory Dixon, Paulette Fried, Selwyn Goldsmith, Larry Grosse, Th. M. G. Guffens, Gilda Moss Haber (Chairman), Joan Harvey, Don Henning, Johann Kaiser, A. W. P. Kerr, Satoshi Kose, James N. Macdonald, Ronald L. Mace, Eric Marchant, R. Shankar Nair, Leon Pastalan, Jake Pauls, Wolfgang F. E. Preiser, Danielle Rimbert, John Salmen, Jonathan D. Sime, Gary Staffo, and Axel Stemshorn.

GROUP LEADERS

The committee on Design for the Disabled and Elderly is part of Group PC of the Council, "Planning and Environmental Criteria." The leaders are:

Bill P. Lim, Chairman
Richard M. Aynsley, Vice-Chairman
Yona Friedman, Vice-Chairman
G. Day Ding, Vice-Chairman
Walter Henn, Editor
Werner Voss, Editor

Foreword

This volume is one of a new series of Monographs prepared under the aegis of the Council on Tall Buildings and Urban Habitat, a series that is aimed at updating the documentation of the state-of-the-art of the planning, design, construction, and operation of tall buildings and also their interaction with the urban environment of which they are a part.

The original Monographs contained 52 major topics collected in 5 volumes:

Volume PC: *Planning and Environmental Criteria for Tall Buildings*
Volume SC: *Tall Building Systems and Concepts*
Volume CL: *Tall Building Criteria and Loading*
Volume SB: *Structural Design of Tall Steel Buildings*
Volume CB: *Structural Design of Tall Concrete and Masonry Buildings*

Following the publication of a number of updates to these volumes, the Steering Group of the Council decided to develop a new series. It would be based on the original effort, but would focus more strongly on the individual topical committees rather than on the groups. This would do two things. It would free the Council committees from restraints as to length. Also it would permit material on a given topic to more quickly reach the public.

This particular Monograph was prepared by the Council's Committee 56, *Design for the Disabled and Elderly.* Particular issues relating to the handicapped and the aged were not treated in the 1978-1981 Monograph series, and the Council took steps to treat this important topic by creating a special committee to deal with it. The result of the committee's efforts is this Monograph. It provides in the first part an international perspective as seen from Japan, the United States, Canada, The Netherlands, and Singapore. This unique international survey examines the myriad of design, construction, legislative, and management issues that must be taken into account in designing tall buildings to meet the special needs of the elderly and the disabled.

The second part deals with such critical topics as life safety, assisted escape, and access and egress for handicapped persons; nonevacuation techniques in compartmented fire-resistive buildings, guidance systems for the visually impaired, and safe, secure, and smart housing technology for the disabled and elderly.

The Monograph Concept

The Monograph series *Tall Buildings and the Urban Environment* is prepared for those who plan, design, construct, or operate tall buildings, and who need the latest information as a basis for judgment decisions. It includes a summary and condensation of research findings for design use, it provides a major reference source to recent literature and to recently developed design concepts, and it identifies needed research.

The Monograph series is not intended to serve as a primer. Its function is to communicate to all knowledgeable persons in the various fields of expertise the state of the art and most advanced knowledge in those fields. Our message has more to do with setting policies and general approaches than with detailed applications. It aims to provide adequate information for experienced general practitioners confronted with their first high-rise, as well as to open new vistas to those who have been involved with them in the past. It aims at an international scope and interdisciplinary treatment.

The Monograph series was not designed to cover topics that apply to all buildings in general. However, if a subject has application to *all* buildings, but also is particularly important for a *tall* building, then the objective has been to treat that topic.

Direct contributions to this Monograph have come from many sources. Much of the material has been prepared by those in actual practice as well as by those in the academic sector. The Council has seen considerable benefit accrue from the mix of professions, and this is no less true of the Monograph series itself.

Tall Buildings

A tall building is not defined by its height or number of stories. The important criterion is whether or not the design is influenced by some aspect of "tallness." It is a building in which "tallness" strongly influences planning, design, construction, and use. It is a building whose height creates different conditions from those that exist in "common" buildings of a certain region and period.

The Council

The Council is an activity sponsored by engineering, architectural, construction, and planning professionals throughout the world, an organization that was established to study and report on all aspects of planning, design, construction, and operation of tall buildings.

The sponsoring societies of the Council are the American Institute of Architects (AIA), American Society of Civil Engineers (ASCE), American Planning Association (APA), American Society of Interior Designers (ASID), International Association for Bridge and Structural Engineering (IABSE), International Union of Architects (UIA), Japan Structural Consultants Association (JSCA), and the Urban Land Institute (ULI).

The Council is concerned not only with buildings themselves but also with the role of tall buildings in the urban environment and their impact thereon. Such a concern also involves a systematic study of the whole problem of providing adequate space for life and work, considering not only technological factors, but social and cultural aspects as well.

The Council is not an advocate for tall buildings per se; but in those situations in which they are viable, it seeks to encourage the use of the latest knowledge in their implementation.

Nomenclature

The general guideline was to use SI metric units first, followed by U.S. Customary System units in parentheses, and also "old" metric when necessary. A conversion table for units is supplied at the end of the volume. A glossary of terms also appears at the end of the volume.

The spelling was agreed at the outset to be "American" English.

A condensation of the relevant references and bibliography will be found at the end of each chapter. Full citations are given only in a composite list at the end of the volume.

From the start, the Tall Building Monograph series has been the prime focus of the Council's activity, and it is intended that its periodic revision and the implementation of its ideas and recommendations should be a continuing activity on both national and international levels. Readers who find that a particular topic needs further treatment are invited to bring it to our attention.

Acknowledgment

This work would not have been possible but for the early financial support of the National Science Foundation, which supported the program out of which this Monograph developed. More recently the major financial support has been from the organizational members, identified in earlier pages of this Monograph as well as from many individual members. Their confidence is appreciated.

Professor Tom Peters of Lehigh University served as Group Advisor. Acknowledgment is next due the headquarters staff at Lehigh University with whom it has been our pleasure to be associated, namely, Jean Polzer (secretary) and Elizabeth Easley (student assistant).

All those who had a role in the authorship of the volume are identified in the acknowledgment page that follows the title page. Especially important are the contributors whose papers formed the essential first drafts—the starting point.

The primary conceptual and editing work was in the hands of the leaders of the Council's Committee 56, Design for the Disabled and Elderly. The Chairman is Gilda Moss Haber of the University of Maryland, Silver Spring, Maryland, USA. The Vice-Chairman is John Deshon of Edwards Bisset and Partners, Milton, QLD, Australia. Comprehensive editing was the responsibility of Thomas O. Blank, University of Connecticut, Storrs, Connecticut, USA.

Overall guidance was provided by the Group Leaders Bill P. Lim, Queensland University of Technology, QLD, Australia; G. Day Ding, California Polytech State University, San Luis Obispo, California, USA; Richard M. Aynsley, University of Auckland, Auckland, New Zealand; Yona Friedman, architect, Paris, France; Walter Henn, Technische Universität Braunschweig, Braunschweig, Germany; and Werner Voss, Werner Voss and Partners, Braunschweig, Germany.

Lynn S. Beedle
Editor-in-Chief

Dolores B. Rice
Managing Editor

Lehigh University
Bethlehem, Pennsylvania
1992

Preface

As the world proceeds into the second century of the skyscraper and toward a new millennium, several points about modern society that bear directly upon the relationship of handicapped and aged to tall buildings are clear:

1. Tall buildings are no longer confined to urban centers, but spread abundantly to outlying metropolitan centers of housing and commerce and into small cities.
2. Tall buildings will continue to be central to the social and economic life of industrialized and industrializing nations.
3. There is a global spreading of the effects of changes in any part of the world, brought about by instantaneous communication and computing technology and extending to social, economic, and political domains.
4. The entire world is "graying," with greatly expanding elderly populations, especially those over 75.
5. Medical technolgy is finding ways to keep people with severe disabilities alive and functioning even more quickly than it is finding ways to cure the disabling conditions, resulting in an increasing disabled population.
6. There is a growing insistence by disabled and elderly *both* for recognition of special social and environmental needs *and* for maximum autonomy, independence, and equal access.

This Monograph begins to address these far-reaching changes in the way the world works. The Monograph compiles information from around the world about the current state of affairs in design for the handicapped and aged so that what appears to work well can be adapted and extended, while what is not effective can be avoided. The goal is to make those concerned with tall buildings and urban habitat—research, design, development, construction, regulation, maintenance, management, and education—better able to deal with these changing conditions and requirements.

As part of the series sponsored by the Council on Tall Buildings and Urban Habitat, this Monograph, thus, is an important complement to the Monographs of most of the committees focused on the construction process and related professional issues.

Such a Monograph could not have been accomplished without the foresight of the Director and the Steering Group to include more than "nuts and bolts," concrete and steel in their purview. We appreciate the opportunity to add this dimension to the expansive work of the Council. The editors are especially grateful for the support, encouragement, advice, and technical assistance of the staff of the council, in particular Dolores Rice, and the Director of the Council, Lynn Beedle. We also wish to acknowledge the initial involvement of Arza Churchman as the first Vice-chairman of the Committee.

Most of all, we as editors acknowledge the efforts, patience, and expertise of the contributors, both those who participated in the first workshop of the Committee at the 1986 Chicago meeting of the Council on Tall Buildings and Urban Habitat and those who have joined the effort subsequently. The thirteen persons besides the editors who provided papers to elucidate their special areas of expertise have been crucial to providing the reader with a well-rounded view of many facets of buildings for disabled and elderly. Their sustained efforts have been particularly essential because the Committee is one of the newer ones of the Council, and the issues it addresses were virtually unrepresented in the original volumes. Further, only they, in their own countries and disciplinary areas, could be most effective at portraying the unique responses in specific instances to issues that are only now beginning to be addressed in an integrated, coherent, universally recognized fashion.

Gilda Moss Haber, Chairman
Thomas O. Blank, Editor

Contents

1

Introduction

What are the needs of disabled persons? How are they similar to or different from the needs of the population as a whole, or of the fastest growing segment of most industrialized societies, the elderly? Why are the design and placement of tall buildings in particular essential components of an equation that can add up to access to goods, services, housing, and leisure activities for all, including persons with disabilities? How have the special characteristics and needs of elderly and disabled populations been met by design guidelines, by architecture and planning, and by the management of buildings?

And how have different nations, with different cultural traditions, economic bases, and distributions of the disabled and elderly within their populations, dealt with these issues? Are there common themes or approaches that transcend national boundaries? How can those of different national backgrounds, disciplinary affiliations, and perspectives within society come together to ensure that all persons have maximum access to what their societies have to offer?

These are a few of the questions to be addressed in this Monograph, a contribution to the series exploring the broader issues that face those involved with high-rise design and construction, and with urban habitats in general.

In the early 1980s the Council on Tall Buildings and Urban Habitat established a committee that would be concerned with the relationship of design factors to the needs of persons with handicaps. The committee soon expanded its purview to include not only that group of users, but also the elderly, and is called the Committee on Design for Disabled and Elderly. This was done partly because, at least in very old age (85+), many persons have some limitation in free movement and in the use of that built environment, and partly because several types of housing are specifically designed for older persons. Furthermore, a significant portion of the housing designed especially for older persons is of medium or high-rise construction, making it a particularly good exemplar of special user design for larger, multistory buildings. Also, in the 1970s and 1980s both governments and developers became much more aware of the myriad problems involved in the use of built environments by disabled persons. This led to considerable emphasis on barrier-free designs (see, for example, Bednar, 1977).

1.1 SCOPE

The goals of the committee and, therefore, of this book parallel those of the Council as a whole. The first set of goals is to engender an exchange of ideas across boundaries seldom crossed. The scope of the committee's work is international in perspective and multidisciplinary in academic interests; it crosses boundaries often set up between academia, corporations, and governmental entities. Thus the book contains input from a number of countries, especially in Part 1, enabling the reader to make comparisons across the broad range of approaches developed within particular cultural traditions, geographical constraints, and population demographics. Many of the contributors themselves have commitments to several disciplinary orientations. and together the academic contributors represent psychology, sociology, family studies, engineering, architecture, planning, and management. Some are trained in and focused upon gerontology and the characteristics and needs of the elderly population; others are more broadly focused across all ages, but concerned specifically with disability and rehabilitation.

Furthermore, several contributors have positions within governments or quasi-governmental units, whereas others are situated in corporations or private nonprofit organizations interested in factors related to disability, health, and building design. Different chapters or sections within chapters are concerned with residential, commercial, or public uses. Sometimes the focus is directed to interior spaces at a relatively micro level of concern, sometimes to exterior spaces, site placement, and access to and from buildings. Overall, issues specific to high-rise design are included, but placed within a framework of interest that crosses all types of construction. Finally, both buildings specifically designed for older users or those with disabilities, and design factors of buildings for the broader population that relate to needs and accessibility for those population groups, are given equal attention.

In all of these ways, the reader is invited to make connections across these and other boundaries that often serve to inhibit free exchange of ideas and, therefore, often fail to address the goal of enabling the active involvement of all citizens as fully as might be the case. It is crucial to foster communication across widely divergent types of researchers and practitioners, since so many specific aspects are interdependent on others. The social character of a type of building, for example, can influence greatly the effectiveness or failure of design approaches that might, under other social conditions, be received very differently. Psychological characteristics and needs of users may be as important as physical needs in affecting usage. Determinations concerning codes and construction criteria are often based on research findings, but are developed within specific political arenas and in recognition of a host of economic, social, and design tradeoffs. Adequate exploration of building design thus requires communication across the widest possible set of boundaries.

A second goal, also shared with the Council as a whole, is to reach an understanding of high-rise buildings that places them within a broader social, psychological, and environmental context. That is, tall buildings, important in themselves, take on even greater significance when considered in light of their role in the mix of residential, commercial, and retail buildings that comprise any urban landscape. Thus in some places the focus is on specific building design and the particular issues of relating disabled and elderly persons to high-rise design. In other places, though, the focus is more broadly directed to the relationship of those categories of persons to *any* physical environment they need to use, whether it be a high-rise residential building, an individual home, a shopping center, a transportation service, or a governmental office.

A central assumption is the belief that no specific physical setting exists or has its effect in a vacuum, but rather that individual buildings and their settings together form the background for daily living. In that regard, the effects of one environment may be critical for the social and personal satisfaction and functioning of an individual bound closely to only that one environment. For most of us, though, including most persons with disabilities and most elderly persons, the effects of one environment form a part of a larger mosaic of effects. Thus we have as a third goal, making the reader more aware of the many ways physical settings combine to influence the everyday lives of their users.

1.2 WHY LOOK SPECIFICALLY AT THE DISABLED AND THE ELDERLY?

Certainly an important question to answer at an early stage concerns the focus on persons with disabilities and the elderly. There are several levels to consider. First, a significant portion of the population of all countries is handicapped in some way that is important in dealing with physical settings. Although there are many ways to define a focus on disability or handicap, the definitions of handicap or disability that guide the focus of this book are that a person with *disability* has limitations in the ability to control, manipulate, and move freely within at least some settings critical for fulfilling everyday needs. *Handicap* is in some ways the reverse of disability; it is the inability of physical environments or settings to allow all persons, including but not limited to persons with disabilities, to make full use of the setting. It is important to realize that all of us, to some degree, are handicapped, that is, none of us can control all aspects of the environments we encounter or move freely into any setting.

On the other hand, some persons clearly have a much greater degree of restriction than the norm, and it is those persons on whom most of this book focuses. Defined as above, it is estimated that 5 to 10% of the population of most countries is environmentally disabled. Specific percentages and more detail are contained in Chapters 2 to 7, which deal with different countries. The range and the variety of disabilities are enormous, creating major problems for policymakers and for those in the construction and design trades who are sensitive to the needs of the disabled.

Inclusion of the elderly is in some ways more complicated and in other ways easier to deal with. It is becoming increasingly important to consider the elderly at many levels in this latter part of the twentieth century. In almost all countries, the fastest growing segment of society is in the age groups beyond 60; in the United States and many other countries, the age group above 85 is the fastest growing of all. Insofar as older people have environmental needs and capabilities that differ from those of the younger, materials that focus on the impact of design and other physical environmental factors on that portion of the population are urgently needed.

Is the elderly portion of the population different from other age groups, with different needs and abilities? The answer to this question is an unequivocal "yes and no." In many regards, older persons are *not* distinctly different from others. They continue to live mostly in single-family homes in age-integrated communities and spend much of their time in activities similar to what they had done before and what younger people do. On the other hand, there are some systematic differences that are increasingly likely to appear as one moves into and through old age. Thus at the level of individuals, older persons may experience changes in the ways they approach the built environment. At the aggregate level, it appears that older age groups become more and more different from the more or less hypothetical "normal" person who forms the basis for most design and construction decisions. Many of these differences are in the same direction as the difference between the part of the population called "disabled" and the general population. (For further discussions of the factors to be addressed in the next few pages, the reader is referred to Blank, 1988; Hooyman and Kiyak, 1991; or most textbooks about gerontology.)

Together, these differences may make at least fairly large parts of the elderly population as well as most disabled persons more bound to and affected by particular characteristics of the physical environment; Powell Lawton has dubbed this *environmental docility* (Lawton, 1985). Environmental docility has two important implications, one negative and one positive. If some persons are more affected by physical design factors, they can be adversely affected by many "flaws" in design that either go unnoticed or are minor inconveniences for the majority of the population. Building deficiencies, busy intersections, many steps, poor lighting or placement of appliances, and other factors may magnify effects that make use of the environment more difficult or even impossible. An easy way to think about these effects is to imagine oneself shopping or doing some other important activity during a snowstorm. What happens to most of us who have normal strength, agility, and other aspects of ability to control environments in those conditions is similar to what many older persons and disabled persons face every day (Blank, 1982).

What are some of these differences? One level of difference, *normal* aging effects, includes the expectable changes in senses, musculature, and organ efficiency that inevitably accompany growing old. A second level within the elderly population, *pathological* aging, is the occurrence of disease states or injuries that are analogous to those which in a younger population would be called disability or handicap. These include diseases or injuries that lead to paralysis, gross visual or auditory impairment, abnormalities or breakage of bones, and the like.

There are complex changes involved in normal aging and in the incidence of disability or pathological aging, and many reference sources in gerontology, rehabilitation, and physical or occupational therapy provide detailed accounts of both disabling conditions and the processes of normal and pathological aging. Within this scope, however, it is important to note several factors briefly. For example, decline in sensory acuity, or sharpness, inevitably begins in early and middle adulthood; by age 65, most individuals have one or more declines in ability that are sufficiently severe that they inhibit full use of one's physical environment. Speed of movement, from the conduction of nerve impulses to gait and reaction time, also declines. Flexibility of muscles, bones, and organs lessens. The reduced flexibility or increased rigidity leads to a variety of dysfunctions, including decreased strength, agility, and rate of recovery after exercise, slowing of the rate of function of organs, and risk of osteoporosis. Falls are likely to become more frequent and to be more dangerous.

The accumulation of inevitable changes is likely to reduce an older person's ability to respond fully and precisely to stimulation from the environment. At the same time it must be remembered that the difference between the levels of ability of a young person and an older one is more often not that extreme. Frequently the ability of most older persons is still adequate to deal in the same basic way with the environment (that is, it is above the threshold required for performance).

Normal aging, in and of itself, is not likely to produce major changes in the relationship of person to environment. In combination with pathological aspects of aging, however, it can exacerbate effects of the disease or injury state in comparison to what it would be in a younger person. Also, when the optimal level of performance is needed—for example, when negotiating a steep stairway with inadequate lighting, as may be the case with a power failure in a high-rise building—the effects of normal aging may themselves be dangerous and frightening.

Of course, disability is often age-blind. Disabilities can and do result from congenital diseases and diseases that develop in childhood or early adulthood, from a variety of injuries, or from violence. Unlike normal aging and many pathological states, many of the causes of disability in later life occur suddenly. While all disabilities may make use of the built environment difficult, those which occur suddenly do not allow for the individual to develop processes and mechanisms of accommodation and adaptation that often moderate the effects of a more gradual loss of function.

1.3 MODEL—INTERRELATIONSHIP TO ENVIRONMENTAL USE

In considering the implications of normal aging, pathological aging, and disability on the ability to deal with physical environments, a model of the relationship between persons and environments can be helpful. One of the most popular of several models is called the *ecological model,* which was introduced by Lawton and Nahemow (1973). Although it was developed and has been applied mostly to residential settings, it has a more general range of applicability. Rather than being a precise delineation of the person-environment relationship, it is a heuristic model that can give both a broad overview of that relationship and a rough approximation in individual cases that may be used for determinations about intervention in a particular living situation. Because the model is described in a number of available sources (Blank, 1988; Hooyman and Kiyak, 1991; Lawton, 1985; Lawton and Nahemow, 1973) and in more detail in Chapter 3, only enough will be described at this point to make clear how one may attack issues of relating disability and aging to design factors.

The ecological model is based on three concepts: dealing with persons, environments, and the relationship of the two. At the level of the individual, the model states that each individual has a level of personal environmental competence. This is a composite of individual abilities, resources, skills, physical status, health, and psychological ability to be attentive or attuned to one's environment. Although the measurement or determination of components of personal competence has proven to be elusive, it is certainly the case that, often at a glance, we can see that some people are very capable or competent in being able to manipulate or control their environments and others are much less capable. Indeed, part of the definition of disability is a relatively low level of competence in dealing with one's environment.

At the level of the environment, Lawton and Nahemow use a concept from motivation theory but adapt it to their own purposes. They state that each environment or setting has a certain amount of demand—*press*—that it places in those who inhabit it; that is, some environments are difficult to deal with or adapt to and some are easy. Again, the measurement and the detailed determination of environmental press in a global sense are difficult, because there are literally thousands of aspects of the environment that can be rated on the amount of demand. The expectations of others and social pressures may be at very different levels from physical aspects; indeed, other people may be either inhibitive of control and expression of personal competence, or they may themselves be resources that make a difficult-to-deal-with environment much easier. Lighting may be excellent, for example, but the ambient temperature may be so high or low that the environment becomes demanding. Size, visual characteristics, noise, time pressure, variety of stimulation, and many other factors may all be operating in the same direction or, more likely, some may be high in press or demand while others are low.

To relate environmental press fully to personal competence would require knowing in what areas a person is capable or disabled. In other words, some aspects of the environment are going to be differentially demanding, depending on the characteristics of those who are trying to use the environment. Visual stimulation or lighting, obviously, will not adversely affect a blind person but will greatly affect one with a moderate level of visual deficit in comparison to the effect on a person with average vision. In other words, the individual with perhaps the lowest personal environmental competence—the blind person—will be unaffected by an aspect of environmental press that greatly affects the slightly disabled person of moderate competence and slightly bothers the person of relatively high competence.

As the examples show, use of the model in a precise sense is difficult. As they also show, however, the general point of the model is critical. Insofar as we can array environments from difficult to simple—and we can do so in at least a very crude way—and can array personal competences from very high to very low—as also seems reasonable—we can examine whether a particular person's competence is "matched" to the environment. When it is matched, Lawton and Nahemow refer to *environmental fit*. They further point out that the relationship of person to environment is critical to both functioning and the emotional state. Individuals who fit with their environment of the moment can perform capably in it and are likely to be satisfied with it. Those who are further away from an optimal level of fit act in dysfunctional ways and are likely to be unhappy, frustrated, and negative. Lawton and Nahemow make clear that both the settings that are too difficult and those that are too easy have adverse effects.

What does this have to do with design for disabled and elderly persons? A considerable amount. Disability, by definition, means that a person's level of competence, at least in regard to some elements of the environment, is considerably below that of most people. Likewise, even normal aging, not to mention the greater likelihood of at least one chronic disease state in later life, is quite likely to result in a lower level of personal competence, both in individuals in relation to their youth and in group terms when older age groups are compared to younger ones.

Thus these groups are less likely to adapt easily to and be fully functional in a wide range of environments. They either need special accommodations, or must rely on prosthetics, or they simply must avoid certain environments that are likely to be overly demanding. Conversely, the fact that a setting that is too simple can also be deleterious means that the physical environments designed to compensate for assumed lack of competence can actually be harmful to older or disabled person who *are* competent. For example, placement of a person who is mobility-impaired but mentally intact and has adequate senses, in an institutional setting that compensates for mental incompetence, inability to do one's own grooming and toileting, and visual problems by limiting activity and providing only simplified, visually jarring information, will be both functionally limiting and likely to induce frustration.

In summary, disability and some aspects of both normal and pathological aging are likely to make these subpopulations have different capabilities and needs in terms of the built environment. These persons may be more affected by their physical settings and less capable of easily manipulating a setting or even leaving it. As a result, their relationship to the environment is worthy of careful examination, separate from the more general body of knowledge about person-environment relations and the effects of architectural and construction choices. However, disability and the effects of aging are manifold. Most people who are disabled in one area are normal or above normal in others. Furthermore, as we will see throughout the following chapters, disabilities and the magnitude of aging effects are of such widely varying orders and categories that it is inappropriate to talk about designs for the aging or disabled. A much finer grained analysis of environmental demand and personal levels of competence is required to be able to produce and implement designs that are useful for at least some segments of the elderly and disabled populations without adversely affecting others. This makes the development of regulations and the implementation of general barrier-free goals extraordinarily complex. That complexity is seldom reflected in existing legislation, as we shall see in subsequent chapters.

1.4 WHAT IS DONE FOR THE DISABLED AND THE ELDERLY?

Two points should be made. First, there are several excellent detailed publications on design that take into account aspects of normal aging, pathological aging, and both physical and mental disabilities (see, for example, ANSI A1171.1, 1980; Bednar, 1977; Calkins, 1988; Green et al., 1975; Hoglund, 1985; Laurie, 1977; Raschko, 1982). This Monograph is not meant to supplant those but to supplement them. Thus the reader interested in specific details of design for a particular disability should consult those other sources as well.

Second, a number of governments and agencies have acted vigorously to make environments more responsive to individuals and groups with lower levels of environmental competence. In particular, barrier-free designs have been developed, and in some places legislation has been passed in an attempt to ensure that all persons, regardless of their disability, can have access to public buildings, shopping, and residential life.

These efforts are to be applauded and emulated in other countries. The presentation of what has been done and what legislation has been effective is one of the goals of this Monograph. However, critical issues that have not been adequately addressed in more than a handful of demonstration projects must be kept in mind. The main emphasis has been placed on barrier-free design, which is usually translated into design that allows access to and within buildings for persons in wheelchairs. Indeed, the international sign for access incorporates the logo of a wheelchair. A secondary emphasis has been placed on access for persons with visual problems, especially to facilities, elevators, and information sources within buildings. Far less emphasis has been placed on other sorts of disabilities.

In fact, even barrier-free designs have been found to have negative effects for some categories of persons with mobility deficits as well as for those with other disabilities such as visual deficits. For example, curb cuts and ramps have been incorporated in most recent construction of curbs, streets, and public access buildings in urban areas. In fact, in some countries ramps are required by legislation for every public building (see Chapters 3 and 4). When constructed properly, curb cuts and ramps aid greatly in ensuring access for wheelchair-bound persons, but the downward slopes make them very difficult to negotiate with a walker. Thus persons reliant on walkers would actually be better off without those "barrier-free" improvements. Persons with vision problems are also placed at a disadvantage, especially if the boundaries of the ramp or curb cuts are not marked in bold, contrasting color or texture schemes. Even a person with normal aging may be unable to differentiate clearly between the sloping ramp or curb cut and the surrounding level surfaces. Again, what produces a less demanding environment for some types of disabilities may make a more demanding environment for another category. Often design choices are in conflict. A major issue to consider is how best to cope with that unpleasant fact of life.

1.5 MAJOR ISSUES AND THEMES

In large part, the issues treated in this Monograph flow from the questions asked at the beginning of this chapter. A number of issues will emerge over and over again, but the overarching theme is the great variety of both needs and abilities of the populations to be served and the responses to those populations across the world.

Seven smaller themes derive from that overarching theme. These include (1) the value and problems of considering elderly and disabled persons as a unit when designing or evaluating buildings; (2) the variety of needs that are encompassed by the misleadingly simple term "disability" and the relationship of disabilities to the handicaps often built into environments; (3) the variety of responses that have been developed and how those fit with particular political systems, size of country, and locus within governmental requirements, voluntary guidelines, or privately developed innovations; (4) the variety of levels of focus, from individual units to entire buildings to neighborhoods; (5) the importance of considering the interplay of physical environmental, psychological, social, and economic factors along with personal physical competence rather than treating each as an independent concern; (6) the role technology has played and is likely to play in answering the call for better access to, life safety in, and use of the built environment; and (7) the flexibility required to respond to changing situations and needs of users.

Many of these themes will arise in virtually every chapter, whereas some chapters, especially those in Part 2, focus more fully on one or another. For example, Chapter 13 primarily considers the individual unit from a technological viewpoint. Chapters 10 to 12 are concerned with entire buildings, including both technologically sophisticated and more standard responses to emergency situations. Chapter 9 broadens the focus to include the surrounding community of housing for the disabled, whereas Chapter 8 is concerned with one sort of building, defined by its source of support (federally subsidized) and its population of interest (elderly).

For now, let us very briefly consider how each theme is being addressed herein and how each may be or is being included in the research and professional communities concerned with the built environment. The first theme of the relationship of elderly and disabled in terms of their physical environments is answered in the Monograph by a combination of chapters, most of which address concerns with both elderly and disabled persons. Several chapters deal more or less exclusively with one or the other group; together they complement the remainder of the chapters. For example, Chapter 8 is primarily concerned with housing specifically for older persons, Chapters 10 and 12 are concerned with disabled persons, while most other material is more general and includes both types of users. Furthermore, authors take a good look at housing and other settings specifically for the disabled and the elderly as well as at broader environmental issues encompassing all users.

An ability to examine similarities and differences in these populations is critical, yet seldom met in legislation or research. Some policies lump together the elderly and the disabled, often based on the erroneous assumption that being old is equated with being disabled in one or more ways. Theoretical models, on the other hand, have mostly been developed in reference to only one or the other group. For example, Lawton and Nahemow's ecological model, described earlier, was proposed and is identified as a model about the relationship of older persons to environments, even though it is more widely applicable. The same can be said for several other models of congruence or fit (for example, Kahana, 1982).

A second theme concerns the range of disabilities. A number of chapters, especially those which focus on particular countries, include relatively detailed considerations of how governmental standards apply across a range of disabilities. Chapter 13 considers how technology will respond to both mobility and sensory deficits. It should, however, be pointed out that an overriding image that emerges in many of the chapters is that many responses to disability have adopted simplistic approaches, usually concentrating only on mobility deficits, and then even only certain deficits (such as wheelchair users). Since this point has been made already in this chapter, it is merely restated as an example of an area that must be better addressed at research and policy levels.

The third theme is the variety of needs and responses across various countries. Countries included are very large and populous (the United States in Chapter 3), large and less densely populated (Canada in Chapter 4), very small and densely populated (Israel in Chapter 6, Singapore in Chapter 7), or of a medium size and density (Japan in Chapter 2, Netherlands in Chapter 5). The countries also represent both Western European, American, and Asian geographical regions and capitalist and socialist political systems. Representation of Third World Asian or African countries, Latin America, and Eastern Europe must be addressed in future volumes.

Many countries have adopted standards that are quite idiosyncratic, without much regard for international equivalence. We hope that this volume will encourage greater communication and further efforts at standardization. A very encouraging sign is the emerging working relationship and information sharing of several organizations devoted to research and practice in the built environment. These include the U.S.-based Environmental Design Research Association (EDRA) and the International Association for Physical Space. While none of these organizations is exclusively devoted to either disability or aging, each has a section, division, or network on either or both. Of course the Council on Tall Buildings and Urban Habitat has had a very broad international orientation; the Committee on Design for Disabled and Elderly encourages the expansion of international efforts in the areas of disability and gerontology.

Similar points can be made about the variety of levels of interest. Again, many disciplines have developed their own perspectives on dealing with disability (and less frequently aging), but communication has been less than adequate. The breadth of interests provides in the fourth theme a breadth of views and a number of attempts at integration that often have been missing. The organizations noted are multidisciplinary in orientation, to complement specific disciplinary organizations such as the American Psychological Association's Division on Population and Environment. Certainly, the problems and issues are of such a nature that only interdisciplinary and multidisciplinary efforts can begin to address them properly.

The fifth theme shifts focus to the multiplicity of ways physical environmental factors, psychological orientations, social constraints and supports, and economic aspects can interact to form a context for the expression of a person's competence to deal with the built environment. The use of models, such as Lawton and Nahemow's, in various sections of the Monograph is one of the ways we have tried to keep this interactive perspective in the reader's mind. As with many of the other themes, the reality of treatment and design has often isolated the ways these factors interrelate and form an ever-changing pattern of function and dysfunction. The necessity of going beyond isolation is especially critical when dealing with disability and aging, both of which are processes over time that result in a changing, probably increasing sensitivity to one's contexts and their effects (the environmental docility idea as a dynamic process).

The sixth theme turns toward the consideration of a major set of changes in the way the built environment interacts with the dynamics of individuals and social systems just noted. Highly sophisticated, highly technological design and construction techniques have always played a role in accommodating the needs of special users in the population. Some of these technological features have then, over time, filtered into the broader range of physical structures. Telephones, security systems, and air-conditioning are only a few examples of such items that are now commonplace in virtually all settings, at least in industrialized nations. The acceleration in technologies based on computerization, robotics, and detection of heat, motion, and other environmental conditions is likely to continue in coming years, making the future built environments significantly different from those of the near past.

Because disabled, and to a lesser degree elderly, persons are more dependent on their particular physical settings and may already reside in specialized housing, it is likely that sophisticated technologies which take mobility and sensory problems into account will be developed in and applied first to large buildings with specialized purposes. However, it is also likely that over time these technologies will become available in wider and wider ranges of buildings and even whole communities. Many chapters, especially Chapters 12 and 13, include at least passing consideration of the role that technology is likely to play in physical environments of the future; several focus on emergent technologies and innovative design approaches that can facilitate transfer to broader settings.

This set of changes fits nicely with the thrust of the seventh theme, flexibility. Designs that accommodate users rather than demanding that users adapt to the environmental demands are clearly necessary to meet the needs of individuals as they age or as disabling conditions may become more limiting over time (related to the previous discussion of the ecological model of person-environment fit). They are also essential to account for the wide variety of types and levels of disability described and contained in the statement of the first, second, and fifth themes. Even a well-designed, appropriate environment may become dysfunctional if it is unadaptable to changing needs or characteristics of its users or is too narrowly focused on providing for a limited range or type of disability. Further, since buildings are designed for extended periods of time, in which there may be dramatic changes in political, social, and economic contexts, it is important that they be able to change to serve the needs of all users, but especially those of that portion of the population that is environmentally docile and potentially handicapped by various facets of design.

Finally, it should be made clear that this Monograph will include both exploration of the relevance of certain issues and approaches to both elderly persons and those with disabilities. Other topics or issues are appropriate only to one or the other, since disability and aging are by no means equivalent. Most older persons, even most very old ones, have only minimal disability or inability to use structures in an effective way and live in normal housing among persons of all ages. Likewise, many disabled persons are not elderly. The overall approach of this volume will consistently clarify both the points of correspondence in building design and the clear distinctions.

1.6 PLAN AND STRUCTURE

This Monograph includes two major parts, each with a special goal and focus. Part 1 (Chapters 2 through 7) contains overviews of the design and history of specialized efforts to provide for persons with disabilities and older persons in a particular country or geographical area. Part 2 is topically oriented, with chapters on specific issues relevant to high-rise buildings and to disabled or elderly users. Special topics include fire and safety design factors (Chapters 10 to 12), technological support of disabled inhabitants (Chapters 12 and 13), adaptation of structures to accommodate persons with mobility or sensory deficits (Chapters 8 to 10 and 14), and social effects of high-rise housing for special populations (Chapters 8 and 9).

Given the diversity of views and backgrounds represented, there is considerable latitude in the manner and style in which specific topics are treated or the variety of settings in the various countries. Even definitions of disabled, handicapped, and elderly vary from chapter to chapter, following the usage in particular countries or disciplines. At the same time the reader is given a clear sense of direction and participation in an organized dialogue.

Country overview chapters contain an appropriate amount of discussion of the following topics:

1. Definitions of disabled and aged as they are contained in research, guidelines, and legislation in that nation

2. History of legislation and building design guidelines and efforts that affect persons with disabilities and the elderly

3. Needs of specific types of handicapped and older persons as they are addressed in a particular country

4. Provisions for those with sensory deprivation (such as signage)

5. Provisions for those with mobility deficits

6. Interior design factors (such as bathrooms, doors, windows, materials used)

7. Elevator design and function

8. Design and use of public spaces

9. Exterior design factors including siting, pedestrian aids
10. Transportation
11. Other factors unique to a country or area

Special topical chapters will include consideration of:

1. Relevance of the topic to disabled or elderly users
2. A review of the state-of-the-art knowledge concerned with that topic
3. A clear description of innovations or proposed solutions, with an emphasis on practical application
4. A discussion of the approach of the contributors to broader design and service issues

This Monograph clearly is only a beginning in answering the many questions and dealing with the themes proposed. Indeed, in many ways it leads to even more questions. The editors and special contributors hope that this volume will encourage you, the reader, to offer your own voice in the ongoing dialog about these important topics.

1.7 CONDENSED REFERENCES/BIBLIOGRAPHY

ANSI A117.1 1980, *American National Standard Specifications for Making Buildings and*
Bednar 1977, *Barrier-Free Environments*
Blank 1982, *A Social Psychology of Developing Adults*
Blank 1988, *Older Persons and Their Housing—Today and Tomorrow*
Calkins 1988, *Designing for Dementia*
Green 1975, *Housing for the Elderly: The Development and Design Process*
Hoglund 1985, *Housing for the Elderly: Privacy and Independence in Environments*
Hooyman 1991, *Social Gerontology: A Multidisciplinary Perspective*
Kahana 1982. *A Congruence Model of Person-Environment Interaction*
Laurie 1977, *Housing and Home Services for the Disabled*
Lawton 1973, *Ecology of the Aging Process*
Lawton 1985, *Housing and Living Arrangements for Older People*
Raschko 1982, *Housing Interiors for the Disabled and Elderly*

Part 1 – Design and History of Specialized Efforts in Different Countries

2

Barrier-Free Design in Japan

Barrier-free design of buildings is relatively recent in Japan as specific design guidelines for central and local government buildings have only been developed over the last 15 years. Thus slopes and elevators to cope with gaps and height differences for the disabled, especially for wheelchair users, have become popular. However, the barrier-free design is not mandatory for privately owned buildings, nor is the concept yet fully understood by architects and designers. Many inconsistencies exist among the barrier-free designed buildings. The true meaning of the elimination of a gap between two levels by a slope is not widely acknowledged, and quite often wheelchair users find more than several gaps left untreated before they can reach the slope. They are sometimes called approach steps, and this illustrates the extent of knowledge ordinary designers possess with regard to barrier-free design. This is partly due to the fact that such areas are beyond the direct control of building owners and designers. Rather, they are controlled independently under the direction of the Ministry of Transport, the Police Department, and other agencies.

Once large-scale buildings, including high-rise buildings with elevators, have been reached, they are generally accessible and usable by the disabled, except in case of an emergency. In those buildings emergency elevators are usually provided for use by the fire department, and they might be of great help. It is regrettable that this benefit is not well recognized or publicized to disabled users. The importance of egress issues cannot be overemphasized and is dealt with in more detail in Chapters 10 and 12.

In smaller and medium-sized buildings the situation is worse. Step differences normally exist, and elevators are sometimes designed to stop at access halls between two floors where they locate toilets. No emergency elevators are provided, and no area for temporary refuge is ready for use. The development of a general concept of life safety for the disabled and the aged is greatly desirable.

Some problems unsolved by the government guidelines are discussed in this chapter, including additional comments on recent developments.

2.1 INTRODUCTION

The Disabled Persons Welfare Law was approved in the Diet in 1949 and came into force on April 1, 1950. It was the first step toward the improvement of conditions disabled persons encounter at various aspects of life. At its initiation, the law limited the meaning of disability to visual handicap, auditory handicap, and handicap of upper and lower limbs. It was only in 1967 that handicap of internal organs was included as a disability. Mental disability is still treated separately, reflecting the social attitudes toward disability. This is changing only gradually, and a long way to "normalization" remains.

Official statistics suggest that in 1987 there were about 2.5 million physically disabled persons in Japan, which is 2.1% of the total population, whereas the disabled persons handbook indicates another 20% as many. None of the data include persons with mental disabilities. It is therefore difficult to estimate the true number of disabled persons. Figure 2.1 and Table 2.1 show the number of disabled persons aged 18 years and over by type of disability over a period of years (Social Welfare Bureau, 1987). As can be seen, the number is increasing rapidly. Figure 2.2 gives a more detailed picture of the disability types in 1987, including disabled children (Social Welfare Bureau, 1987; Ministry of Health and Welfare, 1987).

Figure 2.3 shows the number of disabled persons by age groups, also for 1987. This clearly illustrates that aged persons predominate among the disabled. The probability of becoming disabled is given in Table 2.2. The data show that 8.8%

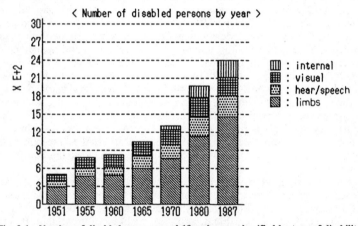

Fig. 2.1 Number of disabled persons aged 18 and over, classified by type of disability.

Table 2.1 Trends in number of disabled persons by type of disability (in thousands)

Year	Limbs	Hearing/speech	Visual	Internal
1951	291	100	121	—
1955	476	130	179	—
1960	486	141	202	—
1965	610	204	234	—
1970	763	235	250	66
1980	1127	317	336	197
1987	1460	354	307	292

< Type of disability in 1987 >

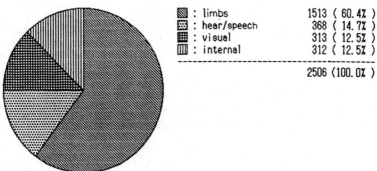

▧	: limbs	1513	(60.4%)
▨	: hear/speech	368	(14.7%)
▦	: visual	313	(12.5%)
▥	: internal	312	(12.5%)
		2506	(100.0%)

Fig. 2.2   Detailed distribution of disability types in 1987, including disabled children.

< Number of disabled persons by age group >

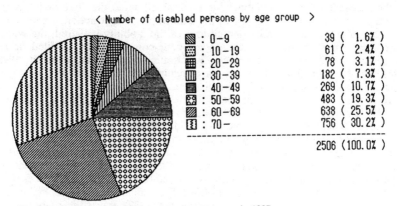

▧	: 0-9	39	(1.6%)
▨	: 10-19	61	(2.4%)
▦	: 20-29	78	(3.1%)
▥	: 30-39	182	(7.3%)
▤	: 40-49	269	(10.7%)
▩	: 50-59	483	(19.3%)
▨	: 60-69	638	(25.5%)
▣	: 70-	756	(30.2%)
		2506	(100.0%)

Fig. 2.3   Number of disabled persons by age group in 1987.

Table 2.2   Disabled population ratio among age groups (persons per thousand)

	Age group								
Year	0–17	18–19	20–29	30–39	40–49	50–59	60–64	65–69	70+
1965	3.7	3.9	4.1	7.1	15.8	24.8	38.9		63.9
1970	3.1	3.3	4.9	7.7	15.8	29.7	40.9	56.2	63.7
1987	3.0	2.2	4.9	9.1	15.7	31.7	56.9	72.9	88.0

Source: Ministry of Health and Welfare (1987).

of those aged 70 and over are disabled and 7.3% of those between 65 and 69. Among the causes that lead to the disability of upper and lower limbs, accidents (traffic, occupational, and domestic falls) and cerebral hemorrhage are increasing. It is perhaps worth noting that the aged are more liable to become victims of domestic accidental falls and cerebral hemorrhage. It is also remarkable that Japan is rapidly becoming one of the most aged societies in the world. It is estimated that in 2025 those aged 65 and over will comprise about a quarter of its population. Those aged 75 and over will outnumber those aged between 65 and 74 (National Population Institute, 1986). This means that in years to come the number of the disabled elderly will be quite large unless proper measures are taken to reduce the causes that lead to disability among the aged population.

2.2 BARRIER-FREE DESIGN—GOVERNMENT GUIDELINES

It was not until 1973 that the concept of barrier-free design was introduced to building designers of the government. In 1973 the government started to prepare for the accessibility of the buildings by the disabled under the directorship of the Government Building Department of the Ministry of Construction. At its initiation, the program was mainly oriented toward the mobility-impaired, the wheelchair users. In 1975 and 1976 the government compiled very detailed design guidelines, and these two guidelines (Government Building Department, 1975, 1976) have been used as references for designing public (central and local government) buildings accessible by the disabled. The Japanese National Railways (JNR) also issued a guideline for use in the design and construction of JNR facilities (Building Division of Construction Departments, 1977). In 1980 the government issued a supplementary memorandum identifying the types of buildings and the desirable measures that should be taken to meet the needs of the visually disabled. Since 1981 was the International Year of the Disabled, the government issued a brief pamphlet on design guidelines for the disabled (Government Building Department, 1981). A standard guide was also published under the sponsorship of the Building Guidance Division of the Ministry of Construction (Japan Federation of Architects and Building Engineers Association, 1982). It was the intent that the concept of barrier-free design would be widely acknowledged and used for private buildings as well as for government buildings.

The contents of the memoranda issued by the Government Building Department of the Ministry of Construction in October 1977 and December 1980 are given in Tables 2.3 and 2.4 (Government Building Department, 1981). The memoranda are very short, but they include the most basic points needed by wheelchair users and the visually impaired.

It is worth noting here that the Building Standard Law of Japan and its related regulatory rules, which should be taken as the basis for the barrier-free design guidelines and memoranda, do not state anything of the need for elevators or toilets. What they state is that one must comply with certain requirements if they are installed. For example, one is not required to have elevators for buildings that are lower than 31 m (103 ft). This means that one can design a medium-size office building of seven stories without any elevators.

2.3 EFFECTIVENESS OF DESIGN GUIDELINES IN PRACTICE

The guidelines mentioned are well followed in designing new government officc buildings and in rehabilitating existing buildings. These guidelines are primarily for government buildings, however, and their use in privately owned buildings is not mandatory.

Table 2.3   Memorandum on designing government buildings for disabled

A. Newly designed buildings

1. Circulation spaces in the confines of buildings should be designed for easy movement by wheelchair users.
2. A verbal communication system should be provided at the entrance of the building.
3. Entrance doors should be operated automatically where possible.
4. The width of internal doors to be used by the disabled should be 900 mm (35 in.) or larger.
5. Internal corridors should be as free of obstructions as possible.
6. The main stairs should have the dimensions of 160 mm (6.3 in.) rise and 300 mm (12 in.) going, with handrails on both sides where possible.
7. Elevators should be 1.4 m (4.6 ft) in width, 1.35 m (4.4 ft) in depth, with 0.8-m (2.6-ft) door openings or larger.
8. Offices with frequent use by the disabled should be on the ground floor.
9. At least one floor-standing urinary stool (as opposed to a wall-hung one) should be provided in each of the men's washrooms. Offices with frequent disabled visitors and large-size office buildings [about 3000 m^2 (32,300 ft^2) or larger] should have a separate toilet compartment for use by the disabled. If this in impossible, at least one western-type toilet should be provided in the men's washroom and in the ladies' washroom.

B. Rehabilitation of existing buildings

1. Design requirements A1 through A3 should be put into practice.
2. Internal doors narrower than 850 mm (33.5 in.) should be changed to 900 mm (35.5 in.) or wider if the doors are to be used by the disabled.
3. Toilets should be redesigned. As for the stool, one floor-standing stool in the entire building is satisfactory.

Source: Building Division of Construction Department (1977).

Table 2.4   Memorandum on designing government buildings for the visually disabled

The following provisions for the visually disabled are required in public employment security offices.
A. Circulation should be designed for easy use by the visually disabled.
B. Verbal communication systems installed at the entrance should be designed for easy access and use by the visually disabled.

Source: Government Building Department (1981)

In reality there are several problems. One of the most important problems is that there are discontinuities of grade along the route the disabled must use. It has been customary for Japanese designers to introduce changes in levels in order to identify the difference of spaces in function, for example. This is a violation of the guidelines, but the designers have been slow in recognizing this. So it sometimes happens that careful provisions have been made inside a building, but there is a gap between the road and the approach passage to the building through which it is difficult to pass, particularly for wheelchair users. The custom of taking off shoes is only preserved in dwelling units, where height differences are usually maintained by designers as a cultural tradition. This is causing much trouble to elderly users, and rethinking is in progress (Kose and Nakaohji, 1989).

Another problem is the contradictory needs of people with different types of disabilities, a major theme addressed in many chapters of this Monograph. For example, slope is widely recommended for wheelchair users, but it is not very good for those with canes or for the elderly in general, especially during descent. Perhaps the guidelines should be revised to recommend provision of both slopes and gentle steps for the disabled in order to give them the choice between two alternatives.

Unlike other countries where barrier-free design guidelines cover almost all kinds of buildings to be used by the general public (National Swedish Board of Planning and Building, 1981; Standards Association of New Zealand, 1985), as discussed in Chapters 3 and 4, Japan has never imposed barrier-free guidelines on private buildings. The government imposes on the private sector a requirement that companies should employ a certain ratio (around 2%) of people with disabilities as their workers, but nothing is explicitly stated about the physical environment that is desirable for them. The conditions of workplace, route of circulation, and so forth are to be prepared by the private sector. It is perhaps true that the government guidelines are consulted, but since the guidelines are in themselves a kind of compromise and lack the general concept of how the society should live along with the disabled, what is written is quite frequently ignored.

This introduces much inconvenience for the disabled in actual situations. For example, at our Building Research Institute a verbal communication system (intercom) is installed on one of the pillars of the car approach at the entrance door. The call button is in an odd place (at the opposite side) with difficult access from the car, and a slope on the pedestrian pavement is inconvenient for wheelchair users, even if they could come near the button. Furthermore, no receptionist is in the entrance lobby, and it will take time for one of the staff to meet the wheelchair-bound visitor. This mismatch makes it clear that the visitor should have asked the warden at the entrance gate.

In high-rise buildings there are usually elevators provided for use by the disabled. Perhaps the most important problem for high-rise buildings is the need of evacuation in case of an emergency, as discussed in Chapters 10 and 12. No explicit statement is given so far on how the disabled and the elderly should survive fires. In buildings 31 m (103 ft) or taller it is mandatory to install emergency elevators free from smoke and fire for use by the fire department. It is probable that those who have difficulty in managing emergency stairs could take refuge in the protected lobby area of these elevators and wait for help, or more use could be made of approaches for shelter within the building, as delineated in Chapter 11. The staff of the fire department are trained to act to first secure the safety of the occupants.

2.4 PROGRESS IN JAPAN

A move toward better barrier-free environment has been made recently by the local government of Kanagawa Prefecture. The Kanagawa government set up a working commission to issue a special local code on barrier-free design of buildings for public access (Working Commission Report, 1989). The local code will have its basis on the Building Standard Law, which permits establishing special requirements according to local needs.

Suggested recommendations include provisions for safety and ease of access to buildings (elimination of height differences), safety and ease of circulation in buildings (elimination of height differences and provision of wider doors), safety and ease of vertical circulation (elevators and stairs), and installation of accessible toilets. The buildings to be covered will be buildings with frequent access by the general public and larger-scale buildings. These requirements are in principle the same as the ones issued previously by the Government Buildings Department. What is unique is that this code will be implemented in line with the building permit, while previous barrier-free recommendations handled by local governments were under the initiative of welfare departments. The local government will have the right (in theory) to refuse the issue of a building permit if the proposed building does not comply with the barrier-free requirements. It will still take a year or two before the contents of special local codes are finalized, but it is expected that other local governments will follow Kanagawa Prefecture.

2.5 SPECIFIC DESIGN GUIDELINES

1 Circulation Spaces (Passages)

Circulation spaces within the confines of buildings should be designed for easy movement of wheelchair users and for easy use by the visually disabled. Elimination of level differences from the limit of the building site to the building entrance and safety precautions against falling during movement are needed, based on the principle of separation between pedestrians and vehicles. It is advisable to have heaters to melt snow and prevent icing in snowy or cold regions. For the visually disabled it is essential to be safe during movement. The application of braille flooring finishes is recommended where necessary.

Slopes. The effective width of passageways should be 1350 mm (53 in.); 900 mm (35 in.) is acceptable if wheelchair users have the priority to pass. Recommended inclination of the slope is $\frac{1}{20}$, or $\frac{1}{12}$ if the slope is protected from the rain. Steeper slopes are allowed if the total height difference is small. Wash should be $\frac{1}{50}$ or less with good drainage. The floor finish should be nonskid, and a snow-melting heater should be installed in snowy or cold regions. In applying braille flooring, proper color contrast against the flooring should be clear.

Crossing Between Pedestrian and Vehicles. If the passageway has level crossings with the vehicles, clear viewlines and a waiting area are important. Warning by floor finishes should be provided for visually disabled users. Signposting should be provided for auditory disabled users to arouse attention.

Gratings. The front casters of the wheelchair are about 145 mm (8 in.) in diameter and 22 mm (1 in.) in width. Gaps must be designed not to catch canes.

Braille Blocks. Braille blocks are applied for the benefit of visually disabled users. No standard exists of placement, color, or shape. Yellow blocks are generally used, however.

2 Verbal Communication System

Verbal communication systems (intercom or buzzer) should be provided at the entrance of the building. They should be designed for easy access and use by the visually disabled.

The verbal system is to be used when no receptionist is available, such as at night. If the verbal system is provided along the passageway, disabled visitors can tell that they have arrived. They will be assisted by the staff into the building.

System. The button height should be about 1100 mm (43 in.) for use by the wheelchair-bound. A wall-mounted intercom must be sensitive. Braille signs must be installed for the convenience of visually disabled persons. Access display lamps will help auditory disabled users.

Braille Maps. Brailled maps of the building placed beside the verbal communication system will assist visually disabled users to identify their whereabouts in the building.

3 Entrance

Entrance doors should be operated automatically where possible. The main entrance is the most busy access point and the door should be easy to use. Automatic sliding doors are the best solution, since they allow disabled users to enter buildings without any assistance. In snowy or cold regions, electric heaters are desirable to prevent the freezing of sensor mats or door railings.

Automatic Doors. Sliding doors are most desirable. An effective width would be 900 mm (35 in.) or more. Various sensing methods are available. A rubber mat switch is preferred as the movement of the user coincides with the door movement. The mat depth should be 1000 mm (39 in.) or greater to prevent the foot rest and front casters of wheelchairs from colliding with the door. If the door is along the emergency egress route, it should be backed up with batteries.

Sliding Door. A sliding door should be suspended from above, with easy hand grip, and should be clear. The detailed design should be considered against fingers getting caught. This type of door (nonautomatic) is suitable only for small facilities.

Swing Door. A door closer should be provided and adjusted. It should be made see-through, with careful precaution against colliding. Detailed design should be considered against fingers getting caught in between, or collision against the door edge. This type of door is suitable only for small facilities.

4 Internal Doors

The width of the internal door to be used by the disabled should be 900 mm (35 in.) or larger. Doors with no access by the disabled are exempt from this requirement. Reception counters should be grouped into one large room. The entrance to the room should be designed with automatic doors or without doors. Doors should be 900 mm (35 in.) or wider, including swing doors. Doors to machine rooms, storage facilities, and so on, are exempt from this requirement. The method of door opening can be selected in relation to the frequency of use.

Sliding Door. The door width should be 1000 mm (39 in.) or wider in order to assure 850 mm (33 in.) effective width (see Subsection 3).

Swing Door. If swing doors are used for openings with frequent disabled users, glass windows and lever handles should be provided for the benefit of users (see Subsection 3).

5 Corridors

Internal corridors should be as free from obstructions as possible. Uneven wall finishes should be avoided for the benefit of users who walk along the corridor. If an extruding part such as a pilaster is unavoidable, it should be guarded or the edge be made less sharp to avoid injury by collision. In determining the width of a corridor, the passage of wheelchair and walking-stick users must be taken into consideration in addition to the building regulations and planning requirements.

Width of Corridor. Wheelchair passage and frequency must be considered.

Rounding of Corners. This is also effective for the wheelchair to make turns.

6 Stairs

The main stairs should have a rise of 160 mm (6 in.) or less and a tread of 300 mm (12 in.) or larger, with handrails on both sides where possible. The dimensional requirement is determined with reference to walking-stick users and the elderly. The tread surface must be of nonskid finish and the nosing edge must never be sharp. In smaller government office buildings the stairs might not be wide enough to have handrails on both sides. Gaps between balustrades and the shape of non-skid nosings should be designed carefully.

Handrails. Handrails should be supported from the underside and be easily graspable in shape and size. The surface finish of handrails and supports should be smooth to prevent injury. Handrails should be continuous without interruption, including landings, and both ends extended horizontally about 400 mm (16 in.) along corridor walls. The gaps between wall and handrails should be 50 to 60 mm (2 to 2.4 in.).

Balustrades. The pitch between balustrades should be 110 mm (4 in.) to prevent falling, and the base of balustrades raised 50 mm (2 in.) to prevent slipping of walking sticks.

7 Elevators

Elevators should be 1400 mm (55 in.) in width, 1350 mm (53 in.) in depth, with door openings 800 mm (32 in.) or larger. This size allows a wheelchair and four or five passengers in the cage at a time. It might be possible for a wheelchair to make a 180 degree turn in the cage if there are no other passengers. The operating panel height must be 1100 mm (43 in.) from the floor. As the main means of circulation in the building, the elevators need to be conveniently located, of sufficient size, and easy to operate.

Since it is not recommended to use elevators in case of emergency, alternative egress routes and proper assistance for the disabled must be considered (see Chapters 10 and 12).

Specifications. Minimum dimensions are prescribed by JIS A4301 (Japanese Standards Association, 1983). This allows the wheelchair user to operate the elevator when entering the cage. (The panel should be lowered.)

Special Design. Elevators designed for the disabled (wheelchair users, visually impaired) are available. Elevator doors with glass windows are available for auditory impaired users.

8 Offices

Offices that will be frequented by the disabled should be on the ground floor to ensure the most appropriate service. Should a case arise where the main rooms are on the upper floor, it is better to have a special room on the ground floor to meet the needs of the disabled persons.

Entrance. If the office is large, the doors should be automatic, as given in Subsections 3 and 4.

Circulation Routes and Lobby. Circulation planning for the visually impaired must be simple, with obstacles avoided.

Counters. Counter heights and clearance for footrests for wheelchair users must be taken into consideration.

9 Toilets

At least one floor-standing urinary stool (as opposed to wall-hung units) should be provided in each men's washrooms. Offices with frequent disabled visitors and large-size office buildings (about 3000 m^2 or larger) should have a separate toilet compartment for use by the disabled. If this is impossible, at least one western-type toilet should be provided in the men's washroom and in the women's washroom.

It is advisable to have handrails with the urinary stool installed on the ground floor. A separate toilet compartment for the disabled should be usable by the wheelchair users. It is also convenient for the walking impaired, the elderly, and pregnant women. The door should be automatic or sliding, and it must be unlockable from the outside in case of an emergency. It is desirable to have a call button near the stool.

If a special compartment is not available, a toilet bowl with handrails will meet most needs. It is better to improve ordinary toilets than to have a special separate one.

Toilet Bowl.   It is advisable to have the underside of the bowl cut off to facilitate access by the wheelchair.

Urinary Stool.   A floor-standing urinary stool is easy to use by the visually impaired, the elderly, and children.

Washbasin.   It is better to have a washbasin provided with handrails to support a walking-stick user. A heavy-duty washbasin will suffice, but in this case all washbasins should be of the same type to prevent breaking weaker ones. The height of the washbasins must be carefully decided to accommodate wheelchair users.

10   Telephones

The coin slot of telephones must be 900 to 1000 mm (35 to 39 in.) from the floor. This ensures easy operation of the telephones by wheelchair users. Access areas should be provided for wheelchairs.

A telephone with an amplifier could be provided for the auditory disabled, and easy dialing is helpful for the visually impaired.

11   Mailboxes

Mailboxes should be placed where easy access by wheelchair users is afforded.

12   Parking Lot

A parking lot for wheelchair users should be provided near the building entrance. It is better to have eaves to protect it from the rain. Care should be taken to avoid manhole lids and similar obstacles within this area.

2.6   CONDENSED REFERENCES/BIBLIOGRAPHY

Building Division of Construction Department 1977, *A Design Guide of Station Facilities*

Government Building Department 1975, *A Design Guide for Disabled Users, Part 1*

Government Building Department 1976, *A Design Guide for Disable Users, Part 2*

Government Building Department 1981, *Design Guidelines of Government Buildings with*

Japan Federation of Architects and Building Engineers Association 1982, *Design Standard*
Kose 1989, *Development of Design Guidelines of Dwellings for an Aging Society*
Ministry of Health and Welfare 1987, *Survey Report on Conditions of Physically Handi-*
National Population Institute 1986, *Revised Estimates of Japanese Future Population*
National Swedish Board of Planning and Building 1981, *Handicap Adaptation of Buildings*
Social Welfare Bureau 1987, *Survey Report on Conditions of Physically Handicapped*
Standards Association of New Zealand 1985, *Code of Practice for Design for Access and*
Working Commission Report 1989, *Ad-hoc Working Commission on the Kanagawa Prefec-*

3

Barrier-Free Design in the United States

The goal of barrier-free design is to provide an environment that supports the independent functioning of individuals so that they can get to, and participate without assistance in, everyday activities such as acquisition of goods and services, community living, employment, and leisure. The theoretical justification for barrier-free design lies in the press-competence model illustrated in Fig. 3.1, developed by Lawton and Nahemow (1973) and already described in Chapter 1. Though developed within the context of the aging process, the fundamental prin-

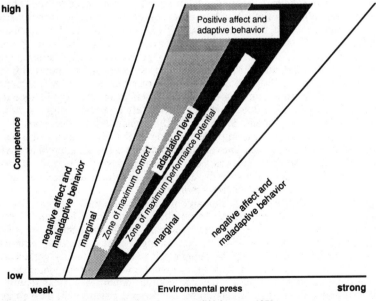

Fig. 3.1 Press-competence model. (*Lawton and Nahemow, 1973.*)

ciple has much broader applications. Specifically, an individual's behavior is a function of his or her competence and the environmental press of the situation. Competence is multidimensional in scope, encompassing a range of concerns such as biological health, sensory and motor capabilities, and social skills. Environmental press is determined by the individual and is measured in terms of the stress it induces or the support it offers. As shown in Fig. 3.1, the interaction of any level of individual competence (vertical axis) with any degree of environmental press (horizontal axis) results in adaptive behavior and affect, which ranges from adaptive and positive affect to maladaptive and negative affect. Within this range, a state of equilibrium, or adaptation level, is defined. This level represents a range of competences where the environmental press on the individual is perceived as neither too strong nor too weak.

Figure 3.1 also demonstrates how physical design can result in negative affect and maladaptive behavior depending on the competence of the individual. A barrier-filled environment, offering little support, creates a strong environmental press for the individual with a low level of competence, resulting in negative affect or maladaptive behavior. Alternatively, a highly supportive environment, such as facilities designed for those with severe physical impairment, can result in negative affect and maladaptive behavior for the individual with relatively high degrees of competence. In this instance, the highly supportive environment is perceived as overly supportive by the individual, thereby compromising feelings of self-worth. The model suggests that maximizing adaptive behavior and affect requires appropriate adjustments in the level of competence, such as the use of prosthetics, or changing the degree of environment press, such as creating a barrier-free environment, whenever there is a lack of agreement between person and environment.

Though a national effort to create a barrier-free environment in the United States dates back to the early 1960s, it is only within the last few years that government sanctions have supported design standards for accessibility. This history, also assembled in the workshop proceedings of the Design for the Handicapped Committee at the Council on Tall Buildings' Third International Conference, parallels that described for other countries by other contributors to this volume (Council on Tall Buildings, 1987). However, total reliance on sanctioned physical design standards will be successful only if the underlying social and economic concerns regarding the creation of a barrier-free environment are addressed. A clear understanding of these issues is of special significance to designers, architects, and builders, who are ultimately responsible for the creation of an accessible environment. Specifically, the implementation of physical standards must be tempered with an understanding of the beneficiaries of a barrier-free environment, the implications of an accessible versus an adaptable environment, and finally, the economic costs of barrier-free design. Without this insight, the promulgation of design standards, even with government sanctions, will not be sufficient to ensure a barrier-free environment.

This chapter will clarify these fundamental issues and thus provide a basis for assessing current design standards. In addition, it will serve to focus future efforts to make a barrier-free environment a reality. The presentation is divided into several main sections followed by concluding remarks. The first sections detail the concerns regarding who the beneficiaries are, accessibility versus adaptability, and the costs of design. This in turn will be followed by a synopsis of the U.S. national effort to ensure a barrier-free environment. The final section will critique design standards promulgated by the federal government as well as the American National Standards Institute (ANSI).

ANSI is a nongovernmental national organization that distributes a variety of recommended design standards. Its first set of standards, ANSI A117.1, was adopted in 1961 and formed the technical basis for the first accessibility standards adopted by the federal government and most state governments. Since then the standard has undergone a number of revisions. The current edition of the ANSI standards, *Specifications for Making Buildings and Facilities Accessible to and Usable by Physically Handicapped People* (ANSI A117.1-1980) is the subject of this review and was based on research funded by the Department of Housing and Urban Development. It is generally accepted by the private sector and is often the basis for state and local building codes (ANSI, 1980).

Federal design standards have been promulgated as the Uniform Federal Accessibility Standards (UFAS, 1984) and, as in other countries, principally apply to federally funded or constructed structures. To maintain uniformity between federal requirements and those commonly applied by state and local governments, UFAS follow ANSI A117.1 closely in substance and format. Together, these standards provide the basis for public and private efforts to create a barrier-free environment.

Identifying the beneficiaries of a barrier-free environment will clarify differences in needs among different population groups. In addition, it provides a basis for estimating the number of individuals most likely to gain from a barrier-free environment. Who benefits is a question which seeks to clarify misunderstandings regarding the handicapped, the disabled, and the elderly as beneficiaries of a barrier-free environment.

3.1 WHO BENEFITS?

1 The Handicapped and the Disabled

ANSI helps distinguish the handicapped from the disabled. A handicapped person is one "with significant limitations using specific parts of the environment." Consequently, the concept of handicapped is linked to a person's interaction with the environment. The U.S. Department of Health and Human Services is more explicit by defining a handicapped person as:

> ...anyone who is hampered in his mobility or functioning (as compared with an able-bodied person) as a result of obstacles put in his way by the design of a building, the choice of hardware and equipment, and the arrangement of outside space.

Similarly, UFAS (1984) define the physically handicapped as:

> ...anyone who has a physical impairment, including impaired sensory, manual or speaking abilities, which result in a functional limitation in access to and use of a building or facility.

In contrast, a disabled person suffers from a "limitation or loss of use of a physical, mental or sensory body part or function" (ANSI, 1980). The concept of disabled is intrinsic to the person's physical capabilities and is independent of one's ability to function within the environment. It reflects a measure of a person's competence. Not everyone who is disabled is handicapped. A disability becomes a handicap only when the environment hampers the individual's ability to perform a specific task at a specific time and place (Raschko, 1982). If a handicap exists, it is not caused so much by the disability as it is by physical barriers (or environmental press) that were created by others, either knowingly or unknowingly, with or without involvement by the disabled individual (Bednar, 1977; Morgan, 1976). In this light, a handicapped population reflects societal attitudes toward the disabled. This is not surprising. The disabled are thought to stigmatize a facility in the minds of many nondisabled persons (De Jong and Lifchez, 1983). For example, housing managers for the elderly were found to be reluctant to accept handicapped tenants because they felt such people create a "depressing atmosphere" for other tenants (U.S. Dept. of HUD, 1977, p. 44). However, it is more likely that the "depressing atmosphere" is due to the unsuccessful efforts of the disabled individual to negotiate the environment, rather than simply to the presence of a person with a physical impairment. By eliminating barriers (reducing environment press) that prevent the disabled from interacting freely with their environment, barrier-free design serves two purposes. It enhances the independence and feelings of self-worth of the disabled individual (maximizes adaptive behavior and positive affect), as well as helping overcome prejudices directed toward the disabled. Barrier-free design will not reduce the number of disabled Americans, but it will reduce the number of persons functioning in an environment with an artificially imposed handicap (Morgan, 1976, p. 50).

As in other countries described in this volume, it is difficult to obtain an accurate estimate of the number of disabled in the United States and much more difficult to measure those who are handicapped by their environment. The available figures, however, provide insight into the number of individuals likely to benefit from efforts to achieve a barrier-free environment.

As noted in Table 3.1, the U.S. Bureau of the Census reports that there were

Table 3.1   Number and percent distribution of persons 16 years or over with work disability* or public transportation disability,† 1979 (millions of persons)

	Total	%
Work disability		
All persons (16–64 years)	144.7	100
Persons with work disability	12.3	8.5
Persons not in labor force	7.6	5.2
Persons prevented from working	6.3	4.3
Public transportation disability		
All persons (16–64 years)	144.7	100
Persons with public transportation disability	2.6	1.7
All persons (65 years and over)	24.2	100
Persons with public transportation disability	3.6	14.8
All persons (16 years and over)	168.8	100
Persons with transportation disability	6.2	3.6

*Persons are identified as having a work disability if they had a health condition which lasted 6 months or more and which limited the kind or amount of work they could do at a job.

†Persons are identified as having a transportation disability if they had a health condition which lasted 6 months or more and which made it difficult or impossible for them to use buses, trains, subways, or other forms of public transportation.

Source: U.S. Bureau of the Census (1980).

12.3 million people between the ages of 16 and 64 who had a worker disability, that is, a health condition which lasted 6 months or more and which limited the kind or amount of work they could do at a job. The Bureau also reported that there were 2.6 million individuals between the ages of 16 and 64 with a public transportation disability, that is, a health condition which lasted 6 months or more and which made it difficult or impossible for them to use buses, trains, subways, or other forms of public transportation.

The prevalence of chronic conditions provides another indicator of physical impairments which can hinder daily activities. As noted in Table 3.2, over 27 million people suffer from arthritis, almost 19 million have some form of hearing impairment, 18 million report having orthopedic impairments, while 9 million have some degree of impaired vision. These conditions can affect the type and degree of activity enjoyed by the individual. The National Health Interview Survey (NHIS) refines these data by focusing on individuals who are limited in activity due to one or more chronic conditions or impairments (Table 3.3). Almost 8 million Americans were unable to carry on a major activity, such as work, keep house, or engage in school or preschool activities. The NHIS estimates that there are almost 32 million individuals who suffer from some degree of activity limitation due to a chronic condition, representing almost 15 out of every 100 Americans.

2 The Handicapped and the Elderly

As one might expect, the housing needs of the elderly are often linked with the goal of barrier-free design. Housing for the disabled is often associated with housing for the elderly, and conversely housing for the elderly is often associated with housing for the disabled. A review of the health characteristics of the elderly suggests why such associations are made.

Table 3.2 shows that the prevalence of chronic conditions increases with age. Whereas 47.7 persons per 1000 between the ages of 17 and 44 suffer from arthritis, the comparable rate for those 65 and over is 464.7 per 1000. Similar differences exist among the other reported chronic conditions. Table 3.1 reports that

Table 3.2 Prevalence of the seven top chronic conditions in the United States for persons 65+, 1981 (millions of persons)

Condition	All persons	Total persons 65+	Rate per 1000 persons		
			17–44	45–64	65+
Arthritis	27.2	11.5	47.7	246.5	464.7
Hypertension	25.5	9.4	54.2	243.7	378.6
Hearing impairments	18.7	7.1	43.8	142.9	283.8
Heart condition	17.2	6.9	37.9	122.7	277.0
Orthopedic impairment of the back and other extremities	18.4	3.2	90.5	117.5	128.2
Chronic sinusitis	31.0	4.6	158.4	177.5	183.6
Visual impairments	9.1	3.4	27.4	55.2	136.6

Source: U.S. Senate and AARP, 1980.

while 3.6% of all persons 16 years and over suffer from a public transportation disability, less than 2% of those between 16 and 64 have this problem, while among the elderly the rate is almost 15%. Finally, Table 3.3 reports that more than one-third of the individuals with some activity limitation (31.5 million) were 65 years and over (10.7 million).

The needs of the elderly are not likely to diminish. By the turn of the century an estimated 16.4 million persons 65 years and older will suffer from some degree of activity limitation due to a chronic condition. In 1979 the comparable figure was 10.7 million. Indeed, by the year 2050, projections indicate that almost 32 million older adults will suffer from some type of activity limitation, exceeding the entire functionally limited population in 1979.

These patterns do not imply that barrier-free design is solely a concern of the elderly. Not all individuals who suffer chronic conditions or limitations in activity are elderly. For example, although 10.7 million elderly suffer from some limitation in activity, there are almost twice as many (20.7 million) nonelderly who suffer from the same limitations. As noted earlier, Table 3.2 summarizes the greater prevalence of motor and sensory disabilities among the elderly. Nonetheless, there remain almost 16 million Americans under the age of 65 who suffer from

Table 3.3   Number and percent distribution of persons by chronic activity limitation status* according to age; United States, 1979 (millions of persons)

Age Group	All persons†		With no limitation of activity	
	No.	%	No.	%
All ages	215.7	100	184.2	85.4
Under 17 years	58.3	100	56.0	96.1
17–44 years	90.7	100	82.7	91.2
45–64 years	43.4	100	33.0	75.9
65 years and over	23.3	100	12.6	54.0

Age group	With limitation of activity							
	Total		Limited, but not in major activity		Limited in amount or kind of major		Unable to carry on major activity	
	No.	%	No.	%	No.	%	No.	%
All ages	31.5	14.6	8.0	3.7	15.6	7.2	7.9	3.7
Under 17 years	23	3.9	1.1	1.8	1.1	1.9	.1	0.2
17–44 years	8.0	8.8	3.0	3.3	4.0	4.4	1.0	1.1
45–64 years	10.5	24.1	2.4	5.4	5.3	12.1	2.8	6.5
65 years and over	10.7	46.0	1.6	6.9	5.2	22.3	3.9	16.9

*The National Health Survey reports on three levels of activity limitation. People with the most severe chronic activity limitation include those who are "unable to carry on a major activity (the ability to work, keep house, or engage in school or preschool activities)." The intermediate category represents persons who are limited in amount or kind of major activity. The least severe limitation category includes individuals who are not limited in a major activity, but are otherwise restricted, such as in recreational activities. This table reports that 16.9% of individuals 65 years and over are unable to carry on a major activity.

†For official population estimated for more general use, see U.S. Bureau of the Census reports on the civilian population of the United States in *Current Population Reports.*

Source: From Feller (1982), Table 1.

arthritis, 11.6 million who have hearing impairments, 5.7 million who have visual impairments, and over 15 million younger individuals with an orthopedic impairment. Similarly, not all elderly are handicapped by their environment. Table 3.3 shows that more than half (54%) of all individuals 65 years and older do not suffer any activity limitation. It is not until age 75 that over 50% have some type of activity limitation, and only 22% of this group are limited to the point that they cannot carry on a major activity.

The goal of barrier-free design for the handicapped, therefore, should not be interpreted as solely meeting the housing needs of the elderly, nor should meeting the housing needs of the elderly be interpreted as solely meeting the goal of barrier-free design for the handicapped. The process of aging results in social, psychological, and economic changes, aside from physical changes, which distinguish the elderly from the nonelderly. Consequently the nature of supportive environment designed for the elderly handicapped will be different from the environment designed for the nonelderly handicapped. Indeed, a 1980 survey of HUD-sponsored multifamily rental projects found agreement among managers and tenants that the nonelderly handicapped and the elderly make incompatible neighbors (U.S. Dept. of HUD, 1977, p. 37).

Even with this insight, the focus on the elderly and the handicapped provides a myopic view of those who would benefit from a barrier-free environment. Barrier-free design standards intuitively address the needs of the severely disabled, but must also address the needs of all individuals who are hindered in their daily activities by the environment. Children and pregnant women are examples of groups who benefit from barrier-free design. Further, families of individuals unable to freely interact with the environment are also often denied access to opportunities. For example, an individual who shares the companionship of someone who lacks full access to travel does not necessarily have unlimited travel opportunities. His or her obligation to the handicapped individual will influence the choice of activity (Snyder, 1983).

3.2 ACCESSIBILITY AND ADAPTABILITY

From a user standpoint, the goal of barrier-free design is access. An accessible environment is one that a disabled person can approach, enter, and use. Such an ideal has an obvious intuitive appeal. However, designing for complete accessibility has both social and economic constraints. In practice, designing for accessibility must be directed to the most severely disabled in order to guarantee that all will benefit. For example, if a person in a wheelchair can move around a building freely or exit it easily, so can an individual on crutches. However, if a person on crutches can move around a building freely, it does not guarantee that a person in a wheelchair will have the same freedom. Unfortunately, to build the necessary support environment for the severely disabled can result in design strategies which are inappropriate to the needs of the less disabled. Builders would consider such an approach as "overbuilding" and economically inefficient. Cost-sensitive builders would build only a limited number of accessible units, reserving them for people with any type of disability. Less disabled users would find the environment for the severely disabled as overly supportive, compromising their dignity and attaching an unwarranted stigma to their disability. This mismatch between competence and press results in maladaptive behavior. Compounding the problem is the dynamic nature of the person-environment action. For example, as people age, the type of design support needed to ensure an accessible environment changes. A disability may become more severe or additional disabilities may occur. The press-competence model is dynamic. Individuals who may have found environments accessible may no longer find this to be true over time.

Similarly, buildings age or depreciate, suffering from wear and tear. This will affect their ability to meet the accessibility needs of the population for whom they were originally designed. As noted in Table 3.4, over 40% of older homeowners (65 years and over) and almost 50% of older renters live in housing units built prior to 1939. In contrast, less than 10% of older renters or homeowners live in units built during the 1970s. Consequently, many of the older population live in the nation's older housing stock. Further, the majority of older householders is aging in the same housing unit. In 1980, 50% of older homeowners had moved into their homes in 1959 or earlier. Consequently, individuals may find that the original environment that once was accessible no longer is, due to personal changes or external circumstances. Design should address the dynamic person-environment interaction.

Adaptability is therefore an integral part of barrier-free design. The UFAS (1984, Sec. 3.5) define adaptability as:

Table 3.4 Age of householder by year structure was built for owner-occupied and renter-occupied units (thousands of units)

| Year structure was built | Owner-occupied units | | | | | |
| | 15–44 | | 45–64 | | 65+ | |
	No.	%	No.	%	No.	%
1979–3/1980	914	5.3	267	1.6	61	0.7
1975–1978	2946	17.0	1012	6.1	251	2.8
1970–1974	2707	15.6	1470	8.9	448	4.9
1960–1969	3582	20.7	4003	24.0	1255	13.6
1950–1959	2861	16.5	4358	26.2	1961	21.3
1940–1949	1451	8.4	1869	11.2	1473	16.0
1939 or earlier	2876	16.6	3701	22.2	3789	41.1
Total	17347	100.1	16680	100.2	9237	100.4

| Year structure was built | Renter-occupied units* | | | | | |
| | 15–44 | | 45–64 | | 65+ | |
	No.	%	No.	%	No,	%
1979–3/1980	62	1.4	15	1.0	6	0.6
1975–1978	227	4.9	57	3.6	23	2.3
1970–1974	322	6.9	87	5.5	39	3.9
1960–1969	794	17.1	225	14.1	107	10.5
1950–1959	1085	23.3	303	19.0	168	16.5
1940–1949	853	18.3	279	17.5	182	17.8
1939 or earlier	1322	28.4	632	39.6	497	48.7
Total	4665	100.3	1598	100.3	1022	100.3

*Represents rental units in attached structures only.
Source: U.S. Bureau of the Census, 1980.

...the ability of certain building spaces and elements such as kitchen counters, sinks, and grab bars, to be added or altered so as to accommodate the needs of either disabled or nondisabled persons or to accommodate the needs of persons with different types or degrees of disability.

Adaptability, thus, provides for equalizing the mismatch between the individual and the environment without requiring the individual to relinquish occupancy. It reflects the need to adjust for changing levels of competence and environmental press.

An adaptable environment would require new construction to have a basic design that would permit individuals to alter a standard dwelling quickly to meet individual needs. Figure 3.2 contrasts accessible versus adaptable design with respect to the location of grab bars at bathtubs, as recommended by the UFAS (1984, Fig. 34). Specifically, accessible design (Fig. 3.2*a*) provides for the explicit placement of grab bars for bathtubs with the seat at the head of the tub. In contrast, adaptable design (Fig. 3.2*b*) requires the builder to provide reinforced areas for the possible placement of grab bars (if needed). Further, if needed, the adaptable design allows the user greater flexibility on the final placement of the bars, allowing one to customize their use to the individual need. Such an approach would result in a more efficient use of resources, since the construction would be flexible enough to meet the changing needs of the individual, yet address the

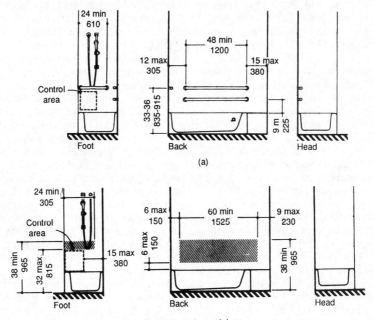

NOTE: The hatched areas are reinforced to receive grab bars.

(b)

Fig. 3.2 Location of grab bars of bathtubs with seat at head of tub. (*a*) **Accessible design.** (*b*) **Adaptable design.** (*UFAS, 1984.*)

builder's concern of spending unwarranted sums of money for a few potential cases.

Unfortunately, newly constructed adaptable housing would require broadly defined specifications, and thus would fall short of the provisions needed for housing those with severe disabilities (Byerts, 1978). For example, the UFAS definition of adaptability provides little guidance as to the extent of the accommodation. It is unclear exactly what spaces and elements need be altered, or exactly to what extent the alterations should occur. The difference between accessibility and adaptability highlights the static and dynamic nature of barrier-free design and raises the specter of costs associated with the implementation. The next section reviews the issue of cost in more detail.

3.3 COST

Perhaps the most controversial issue surrounding barrier-free design is cost. Builders are viewed as being reluctant to spend potentially unwarranted amounts of money for so few potential users. Critics note that the needs of future residents often appear to be compromised in the production of the setting. The loss in the building process "appears to be related to current accounting practices which focus on production efficiencies (first costs) rather than lifetime value and life-cycle costs of a building" (Howell, 1980, p. 11).

The evidence, however, suggests that the additional cost necessary for barrier-free construction is relatively small and that "both public and private construction budgets should be able to meet the additional costs with little or no apparent hardship" (De Jong and Lifchez, 1983, p. 10). In new construction the cost can be very low. Accessibility can be designed into the job, without requiring major deviations from the original building design. Estimates vary, but for most projects the additional cost should vary between 1.5 and 5% of the total construction costs (Robert Scharf Associates, 1981; Spradlin, 1982). However, new construction represents only a small proportion of the total housing stock. The 1980 Census reported over 43 million owner-occupied one-unit structures (detached). Of these, less than 3% were built between 1979 and March 1980, more than 75% were built before 1970, and almost one-quarter were built prior to 1940. Comparable figures exist for rental units as well. The evidence is clear. The environment is comprised of an aging housing stock. Consequently, though the cost of accessibility or adaptability is relatively minor, the overall impact of restricting policies toward newly built structures will also be minor, at least in the short run. The cost of barrier-free design revolves around existing structures and the individuals who are living in them, not around new structures and the individuals who will live in them. As one might suspect, the cost of alterations will vary. However, the evidence suggests that those likely to be in need are least likely to be able to afford an accessible environment.

For example, the median income of all residents who owned their home (single-unit detached) was $21,319 in 1980. However, residents living in homes built prior to 1940 had a median income of $16,383. Those living in units built during the 1940s had a median income of $17,427. In contrast, owners of homes built during the 1970s had a median income of at least $24,000. Since older units are likely to house older individuals, in other words those likely to be considering modifications, these figures are significant. The cost of alterations may be outside the available resources of the occupant. Widening doorways to accommodate a person in a wheelchair and installing a bathroom on the ground floor so that a heart patient would not have to climb stairs are typical major alterations. As will be seen later, such costs can be substantial to families with limited financial resources.

The cost of retrofitting existing facilities will depend on how easily the building can be made accessible or adaptable. The following provides examples of cost estimates for accessibility. The reader is advised to look at further data for a more detailed summary (Robert Scharf Associates, 1981). Notably, these costs are intended to be used only as guides for estimating the approximate costs of modifying buildings to accommodate the handicapped. The estimates rely on the predominant wage scales found in the urban northeastern United States of a decade ago. They include overhead and profit, labor, taxes, insurance, and sales tax. They also take into account incidentals such as painting, patching temporary protections, and low productivity (because work is performed in existing and occupied buildings). Design fees are not included in the costs. In addition, a set of factors are provided to adjust the specific estimates for a given region.

To provide an appropriate framework for viewing these costs, the specific ANSI standard or UFAS guideline to be met is initially stated. It is then followed by the 1981 cost estimates. The standards chosen for review reflect a variety of modifications for single-family as well as multifamily structures and address the needs of not only those with a mobility handicap but also those with visual disabilities and hearing disabilities. They are not meant to be comprehensive, but are provided to demonstrate the variations in costs associated with accessibility.

Wheelchair users require minimal maneuvering space to assure accessibility. ANSI standards and UFAS guidelines (Fig 3.3) require that the minimum clear width of an accessible route be 915 mm (36 in.) except at doors (ANSI, 1980, Sec. 4.3.3; UFAS, 1984, Sec. 4.3.3). Further, if an accessible route has less than 1.5 m (60 in.) clear width, then passing spaces of at least 1.5 by 1.5 m (60 by 60 in.) should be located at reasonable intervals, not to exceed 61 m (200 ft) (ANSI,

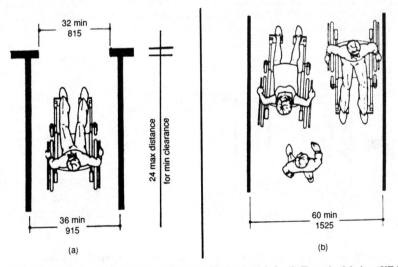

Fig. 3.3 Minimum clear width for wheelchairs. (a) Single wheelchair. (b) Two wheelchairs. (UFAS, 1984.)

1980, Sec. 4.3.4; UFAS, 1984, Sec. 4.3.4). Doorway thresholds create an additional obstacle. The standards and guidelines suggest that thresholds not exceed 19 mm (¾ in.) in height for exterior sliding doors or 12.5 mm (½ in.) for other types of doors (ANSI, 1980, Sec. 4.13.8; UFAS, 1984, Sec. 4.13.8).

Expanding interior corridors can cost from $40 to $56 per linear foot, depending on the material used. Widening ramps can cost approximately $13 per square foot; widening sidewalks can cost from $3.75 to $22 per square foot, depending on the material; while the costs of expanding drywall openings and replacing doors of inadequate width are estimated at $498 per set. The cost of replacing thresholds is estimated to vary from $31 to $48 per unit.

Access to parking facilities also is a problem, as addressed in Fig. 3.4. Parking spaces for disabled people are recommended to be at least 2.5 m (96 in.) wide with an adjacent access aisle of at least 1.5 m (60 in.) (ANSI, 1980, Sec. 4.6.3; UFAS, 1984, Sec. 4.6.3). In addition, passenger loading zones are to provide an access aisle of at least 1.2 m (48 in.) wide and 6 m (20 ft) long adjacent and parallel to the vehicle pull-up space. If curbs exist between the aisle and the pull-up space, then a curb ramp should be provided (ANSI, 1980, Sec. 4.6.5; UFAS, 1982, Sec. 4.6.5). Repainting parking stripes to create an accessible space is estimated to cost $19 per space. To remove a concrete curb and install a concrete curb ramp is estimated at $520.

Controls and operating mechanisms, such as light switches and dispenser controls, are integral parts of a barrier-free environment. It is recommended that such mechanisms be "operable with one hand and shall not require tight grasping, pinching, or twisting of the wrist" (ANSI, 1980, Sec. 4.27.4; UFAS, 1984, Sec. 4.27.4). The installation of lever handles in a bathroom is estimated to be $45 per set, while to replace a door lockset with lever-type handles is estimated to be $110 per unit.

Tactile warnings on walking surfaces are recommended as an aid to the visually impaired, specifically, tactile warning textures on walling surfaces consisting of "exposed aggregate concrete, rubber, or plastic cushioned surfaces, raised strips, or grooves. Textures should contrast with that of the surrounding surface" (ANSI, 1980, Sec. 4.29.2). Similarly, doors that lead to areas that may prove dangerous to a blind person "should be made identifiable to the touch by a textured

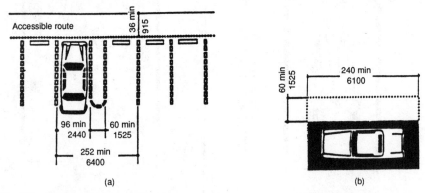

(a)   (b)

Fig. 3.4 (a) Dimensions of parking spaces. (b) Dimensions of access aisle at passenger loading zones. (*UFAS, 1984.*)

surface on the door handle. This textured surface may be made by knurling or roughening or by a material applied to the contact surface" (ANSI, 1980, Sec. 4.29.3; UFAS, 1984, Sec. 4.29.3). Estimates indicate that to install textured finishes to a floor within 1 m (3 ft) of a hazardous area will cost $36 per area, the installation of texture on door handles is $18, while to replace a door handle with a knurled handle is estimated to cost $115.

In a similar manner, visible and audible signals are recommended to be provided at each elevator entrance to indicate which car is answering a call [ANSI 1980, Sec. 4.10.13; UFAS, 1984, Sec. 1190.100(h)]. The cost of installing such devices is estimated as $560 per elevator cab.

Considerably greater expenses are possible, especially if structural, electrical, and vertical lift equipment must be modified. For example, the cost of constructing a new toilet room which is accessible is estimated to be $5300. Installation of an exterior elevator addition to an existing building (which may be necessary to assure that the elevator is accessible on all floors) is estimated to require a fixed cost of $68,000 plus an additional $5200 per stop. Residence-type elevators have become quite popular. The installation price for a typical residential elevator is approximately $11,000 (Spradlin, 1982).

Because of the expenses involved, disabled individuals may be virtual prisoners in their homes. Current policy addresses the issue by emphasizing accessibility of new or recently constructed structures. However, this is a long-term strategy. As yet a short-term policy to meet the immediate needs of disabled individuals has not been developed.

3.4 ISSUES OF BARRIER-FREE DESIGN

Much deserved attention has focused on the environmental needs of the disabled, the elderly, and the handicapped. Focusing on specific population groups simplifies the task for builders, designers, and architects, since characteristics and needs can be clearly identified. However, such an approach should not be interpreted as the final framework for assessing the benefits of a barrier-free environment. The issue of barrier-free design is not one of inconvenience to a select population. A safer, easier environment for the physically disabled benefits everyone. Ultimately, barrier-free design is for everyone, and not for a specific group. Builders, designers, and architects who voice concern over costs relative to the benefits of barrier-free design should bear this in mind.

The attention paid to the disabled, the elderly, and the handicapped serves a greater purpose by helping to clarify the fundamental issues surrounding barrier-free design. The distinction between the handicapped and the disabled defines the link between the person and the environment. A handicapped individual is a reflection of the interaction between an individual with a physical impairment and his or her environment. As such, concern over the handicapped is a concern over the environment. In this light, builders, designers, and architects have a clear responsibility for ensuring a barrier-free environment.

The distinction between the handicapped and the elderly is one of dignity. The presumption that all elderly are handicapped, or that all handicapped are elderly, is an oversimplification of the needs of both groups and is a disservice to both. Builders, designers, and architects are ultimately responsible for ensuring that the specific environment is appropriate to the specific individual. Barrier-free design is designing for the individual. This is emphasized more thoroughly within the context of accessibility and adaptability.

Accessibility and adaptability highlight the dynamic nature of the person-environment interaction. Barrier-free design solutions should take into account the changing nature of both client and environment. An adaptable environment offers greater flexibility, helping to ensure that the environmental support is appropriate to the needs.

The issue of economic costs underlies all design solutions. The premise that cost is the prohibiting factor in promulgating a barrier-free environment should not be accepted prematurely. The evidence indicates that barrier-free design can be achieved without economic burden to the builder, designer, or architect.

These fundamental issues should provide the framework for developing policies to ensure a barrier-free environment. The next section examines the federal role in this area. It is followed by an assessment of current standards within the context of who benefits, accessibility and adaptability, and finally the costs of design.

3.5 THE FEDERAL ROLE

The role of the federal government in promoting barrier-free environments began in the early 1960s. It has been marked by a gradual evolution of federal strategies to ensure a barrier-free environment. The following provides a synopsis of the federal role, beginning with efforts to educate the public and culminating with the promulgation of federal design standards with sanctions for accessible environments.

The federal government originally maintained an advisory capacity in promoting accessible environments. In 1961 the President's Committee on Employment of the Handicapped in conjunction with two private organizations, the American Standards Association [now the American National Standards Institute (ANSI)] and the National Easter Seals Association, published *Specifications for Making Buildings and Facilities Accessible to and Usable by the Physically Handicapped* (ANSI A117.1-1961). It heralded the beginning of a national education program to promote the adoption of accessibility standards by state and local governments. Within 4 years, 34 states had responded with legislation or the adoption of building codes. The lack of effective sanctions, however, prevented a total national success (Jeffers, 1977).

The first federal legislative effort to address the needs of the handicapped was to occur a few years later with the passage of the Housing and Community Development Act of 1964. In large part, the legislation sought to identify the magnitude of the problem of accessible environments and to develop strategies to motivate communities to develop solutions. Communities requesting federal assistance were required to submit surveys of their housing stock, including an assessment of housing needs of lower-income persons, the elderly, and the handicapped. Projects seeking to remove material and architectural barriers which restricted the mobility and accessibility of the elderly and handicapped became eligible for federal assistance. Finally, the U.S. Department of Housing and Urban Development (HUD) required that 10% of elderly housing units which they sponsored or assisted be made accessible to the physically handicapped.

Notably, such an approach relied heavily on community initiative to implement accessible environments. For example, the legislation specified that the community identify and not necessarily resolve the housing needs of the elderly and handicapped. Further, the legislation did not require communities to engage in projects to remove architectural barriers, nor was there a requirement that any elderly housing be built at all. Further, there was little guidance as to how to create an accessible environment.

As a consequence of these shortcomings, 1965 amendments to the Vocational Rehabilitation Act (Public Law 89-333) established the National Commission on Architectural Barriers and the Rehabilitation of the Handicapped. Its goals were to:

1. Assess the nature and extent of problems of architectural design

2. Develop an agenda for action

The Commission concluded that there was a general lack of awareness in both the public and the private sectors as to the problems of accessibility. It recommended the development of an education program and, more importantly, called for a legislative allocation of responsibilities for ensuring an accessible environment.

Soon after, the Architectural Barriers Act of 1968 (42 USC 4151-5157) was passed. It represented the first federal law to provide explicitly for access. It mandated that any building construction financed, in any part, with federal funds would have to make provisions for accessibility by the handicapped. The General Services Administration (GSA), HUD, the Department of Defense (DoD), and the U.S. Postal Service (USPS) were given the responsibility for setting standards for accessible residential structures. Unfortunately the legislation did not provide for enforcement.

The Rehabilitation Act of 1973 (29 USC 792) marked explicit federal recognition of the scope of rehabilitation and developmental needs of disabled persons. More importantly, it provided for specific sanctions and enforcement procedures to ensure that the rights of the disabled were being met. Thus it provided governmental authority to ban federal funds from anyone who discriminates. It stated (Section 504, Title V, 1973 Rehabilitation Act):

> No otherwise qualified handicapped individual in the United States...shall solely by reason of his handicap be excluded from the participation in, be denied the benefits of, or be subjected to discrimination under any program or activity receiving Federal financial assistance, or under any program or activity conducted by an Executive Agency or by the U.S. Postal Services.

To ensure compliance with earlier federal legislation (most notably the 1968 Architectural Barriers Act), the Architecture and Transportation Barriers Compliance Board (ATBCB) was established. Its mandate was to investigate complaints, hold public hearings, issue compliance orders, and seek enforcement of its order by the courts, if necessary. The Board also was to establish minimum guidelines and requirements for standards issued under the 1968 Architectural Barriers Act. The standards would be designed to (42 USC 4151-4154a):

> ...insure that certain buildings and facilities financed with Federal funds are designed, constructed, or altered so as to be readily accessible to, and usable by physically handicapped persons.

In 1981 the Board adopted the *Minimum Guidelines and Requirements for Standards for Accessibility and Usability by Federal and Federally-Funded Buildings and Facilities by Physically Handicapped Persons* (ATBCB, 1982). The guidelines and requirements relied heavily on ANSI A117.1 (1980). As guidelines, they were to be a basis for the development of design standards required of the GSA, HUD, USPS, and DoD.

Three years later the Uniform Federal Accessibility Standards (UFAS) were published and now constitute the sole accessibility standard referenced by the federal government for compliance with the Architectural Barriers Act of 1968. The UFAS closely follow the provisions of the ATBCB guidelines and the ANSI A117.1 format. Indeed, UFAS text that is different from ANSI is underlined, while tables and illustrations that are different from ANSI are italicized.

1 Uniform Federal Accessibility Standards versus standards of the American National Standards Institute

UFAS and ANSI, therefore, provide accessibility standards to be followed by the public and the private sectors. They differ in three significant areas. In contrast to the ANSI standards, UFAS provide extensive scoping provisions for buildings under their jurisdiction (buildings funded or owned by the federal government). As such, UFAS establish the minimum number of elements and spaces required to comply with standards. ANSI specifications are based on the principle of "reasonable number," that is, in order to ensure a minimum degree of accessibility, ANSI provides for the installation of "at least one" accessible element. Builders are then suggested to provide a "reasonable number" of the elements at issue. The specific number is to be based on a variety of factors including (ANSI, 1980, Sec. 2.2.3):

1. Population to be served
2. Availability to occupants, employers, customers, and visitors
3. Distance and time required to use the accessible elements
4. Provisions of equal opportunity and treatment under the law

For example, ANSI specifications state that "if parking spaces are provided, a reasonable number, but always at least one, of parking spaces and access aisles shall comply" with specifications for "Parking and Passenger Loading Zones." As noted in Table 3.5, UFAS expands on the requirement of "at least one" by providing explicit guidelines to be followed by the builder.

On the other hand, where it was felt that research and field experience did not support federal requirements, UFAS reserve judgment, waiting until sufficient information is obtained. Table 3.6 lists areas where ANSI provides specific guidelines while UFAS have chosen to reserve judgment.

Third, UFAS contain accessibility standards for building types not covered by ANSI, including restaurant and cafeteria, health care, mercantile, library, and postal facilities.

3.6 REVIEW OF GUIDELINES

1 Who Benefits?

Both ANSI specifications and UFAS guidelines are based on "average" adult dimensions and anthropometrics. Consequently they are not appropriate for persons who do not have "average" adult measurements. ANSI A117.1 notes (ANSI, 1980, Sec. 2.2.6):

> ...if buildings, facilities or portions thereof serve children primarily, the administrative authority should adjust dimensions and other provisions to make them available for children.

Unfortunately ANSI does not provide any guidance for the administrative authority interested in adjusting provisions according to the nature of the clientele. The UFAS guidelines do not address this concern at all.

Table 3.5 Accessible parking spaces by size of lot

Total parking in lot	Required minimum number of accessible spaces
1 to 25	1
26 to 50	2
51 to 75	3
76 to 100	4
101 to 150	5
151 to 200	6
201 to 300	7
301 to 400	8
401 to 500	9
501 to 1000	2% of total
Over 1000	20 plus 1 for each 100 over 1000

Source: UFAS, Sec. 4.1.1(5).

Table 3.6 Accessibility elements addressed by ANSI with judgment reserved by UFAS

1. Windows in accessible buildings
2. Warning textures on curb ramps
3. Uncurbed intersections
4. Tactile warnings at stairs
5. Windows
6. Door opening force on exterior hinged doors
7. Tactile warnings on walking surfaces
8. Tactile warnings at hazardous vehicle areas
9. Windows in dwelling units
10. Telephones in dwelling units

A more subtle shortcoming, however, exists. As one might expect, the guidelines and specifications address primarily the needs of those with mobility handicaps. This is not surprising, given that it is the most prevalent type of handicap (see Table 3.1). However, as noted earlier, there are 18.7 million persons who are hearing impaired; among individuals 65 years and older, hearing impairments are the third most prevalent chronic condition. Visual impairments affect almost 9 million individuals (of which 3.4 million are 65 and over). As such, designing for the handicapped must address sensory as well as mobility impairments. A review of both UFAS and ANSI documentation reveals a relatively small number of design criteria which are sensory-specific (or elderly-specific).

For example, in terms of the hearing impaired, design recommendations are limited to audio and visual signals for elevator service, the development of audible emergency signals, volume controls for phones, and audio amplification systems for assembly areas. Most attention focuses on the problems of loss of hearing acuity, while little attention is paid to hearing problems associated with speech discrimination under stressful conditions or other forms of hearing impairment (such as ability to attend to simultaneous stimuli). Thus while public phones are suggested to have volume controls (ANSI, 1980, Sec. 4.31.5; UFAS, 1984, Sec. 4.31.5), nothing is said regarding the placement of public phones to minimize stressful listening conditions (reverberations, for example) which can intensify hearing problems. This problem is not restricted to the hearing impaired. Howell (1980) notes that:

> ...rules to compensate for reduction in visual or auditory acuity are still not well enough specified in the research literature in either sensory psychology and medicine, or of engineering in such ways that translate into performance standards for buildings.

In addition, the problems associated with hearing impairments are not restricted to elevator corridors, alarm systems, and telephones.

The most significant design shortcoming is the lack of specifications or guidelines that reflect a broad or holistic environmental context. The design goal is a barrier-free environment, not a barrier-free door or a barrier-free phone. The role of the architect and designer is to take specific specifications and create an environment which does not compromise the dignity of the individual. Guidance is needed in terms of coordinating the discrete specifications into a comprehensive design statement. As such, there appears to be a gap between the total amount of research available and that which is used for practical design applications (Raschko, 1982)

UFAS and ANSI provide a needed set of guidelines and specifications for those seeking to address the basic problems plaguing the disabled population. A closer review indicates that the beneficiaries will be a highly circumscribed set of disabled individuals—adults with physical disabilities that directly affect physical mobility.

2 Accessibility and Adaptability

Both UFAS and ANSI standards provide specifications regarding an adaptable environment (albeit limited to bathrooms and kitchens). In addition, they both require that consumer information regarding adaptable features be provided for each accessible dwelling unit available for occupancy (ANSI, 1980, Sec. 4.34.4). However, UFAS note that "accessible dwelling units may be designed for either permanent accessibility or adaptability." They therefore explicitly recognize the complementary nature of accessibility and adaptability, and provide the builder with flexibility in the development of design alternatives to meet barrier-free specifications.

3 Costs of Barrier-Free Design

The UFAS address the issue of cost within the context of defining substantial alterations. Specifically, total costs of an alteration include but are not restricted to electrical, mechanical, plumbing, and structural changes over a 12-month period. If the total cost is 50% or more of the full and fair cash value of the building, the alteration is considered substantial. Regardless of the cost, alterations, even if substantial, must comply with the standards, except to the extent where this is structurally impractical. If the costs of at least one accessible route, at least one accessible entrance, and one accessible toilet facility exceed 15% of the total cost of all other alterations, then a schedule may be established to provide the required improvements within a 5-year period [UFAS, 1984, Sec. 4.1.6(3)].

3.7 CONCLUSION

The federal government has played an increasing role in providing a barrier-free environment. The demographics support the contention that the handicapped group represents a significant portion of our population, but as yet a barrier-free environment has not been achieved. The 1982 President's Commission on Housing recognized this problem and saw the needs of the frail elderly and handicapped as yet unfulfilled. It called for special programs and the development of a task force "to address these housing needs in the context of the social and health needs of this group" (President's Commission on Housing, 1982). This chapter provides a framework for approaching these concerns by presenting specific issues associated with barrier-free design.

The distinction to be made between the handicapped and the disabled is critical to understanding the goals of barrier-free design. It clarifies the nature of the interaction between the person and the environment and provides support for the contention that barrier-free design will have a positive effect on the well-being of not only the individual but society as a whole. The distinction between the handicapped and the elderly sensitizes one to the diverse characteristics of the handicapped population. Design must recognize the diversity, as must guidelines and standards.

A review of current guidelines and standards suggests that they do not entirely meet the complex demands of a barrier-free environment. The problems are two-fold. A lack of appropriate information is the first issue. Design statements for the sensory impaired need to be developed. They should reflect the best available empirical data on the causes and effects of specific disabilities, rather than rely on limited personal experience, interviews, or intuition. In this regard researchers should be encouraged to share and develop research findings which can then be linked to appropriate design statements. Such an approach has been used in developing design specifications for the hearing impaired (Chen and Abend, 1985) and could be applied to other impairments.

In addition, the available research should be complemented by further investigation as to how the built environment affects behavior, as well as how behavioral factors should influence building design. Clearly, ambiguity in a barrier-free environment can be counterproductive. However, this does not mean that the architecture has to be sterile, or that building design need be gratuitous with an overindulgence of audio and graphic aids such as to tell residents and visitors where to enter or where to leave (Stephens, 1978). Ironically, such an approach only serves to reinforce societal prejudices regarding the disabled. We must therefore improve the quality and importance of user information used in the design process and provide vehicles for its dissemination.

Finally, efforts made to develop standards for the "average" adult should be matched by efforts to develop standards for the "nonaverage" adult and children. A centralized clearing house, such as the ATBCB, should be charged with the dissemination of the information. All this research will entail a pooling of efforts by a variety of disciplines, including architects, engineers, the social sciences, and the medical sciences. No single discipline should presume to have the solution, since the problems facing the handicapped encompass the entire environment.

The issue of cost is the second concern. Though accessibility and adaptability are recognized in the construction of new buildings, this does not resolve the problems associated with existing structures. The cost of private financing of alterations can be prohibitive. The President's Commission (1982) suggests the use of federal funds, but this will be inadequate. An alternative is to develop financing mechanisms to allow homeowners to use the equity in their homes for alterations without relinquishing occupancy. One model would entail a home alteration loan from a local authority, based on a percentage of the owner's home equity. In contrast to traditional loans, which use the housing asset as collateral, such as second mortgages, the outstanding debt would not be due until the owner moves or passes away and the house is sold. Similar home equity conversion instruments have been used to defer the payment of property taxes and home repairs. This would be particularly advantageous for the elderly disabled. Presumably they have accumulated a substantial sum of home equity, which could be used for such a purpose. Further, in contrast to other general loan programs, this approach ties directly to the housing asset and can be self-supporting, that is, it will not rely on government financial support. In addition, it would give the homeowner control over the nature and extent of the alterations to be made.

For over a quarter of a century the federal government has been actively involved with developing a barrier-free environment. These efforts have evolved from a national education program to the development of guidelines for federal agencies engaged in the construction of buildings, sites, or facilities. Despite these efforts, the goal of a barrier-free environment has not been achieved.

Architects, builders, and designers, among others, must attempt to resolve the problem with inadequate information. The handicapped must face the problem, with financial resources often inadequate to the task at hand. In both cases the solutions are relatively straightforward: better information, more resources.

Society, however, must attempt to resolve the issue of a barrier-free environment, while contending with prejudices which exist regarding the handicapped. In this case the solution is not entirely straightforward. The reluctance of the public to accept the disabled has fostered a barrier-filled environment, and has contributed to the slow adoption of a barrier-free environment. A barrier-free environment is a critical component in reducing public antipathy toward the disabled.

3.8 CONDENSED REFERENCES/BIBLIOGRAPHY

ANSI A117.1 1980, *American National Standard Specifications for Making Buildings and*
ATBC Board 1982, *Minimum Guidelines and Requirements for Standards for Accessibility*
Bednar 1977, *Barrier-Free Environments*
Berkowitz 1974, *Cost Burden of Disabilities and Effects of Federal Program Expenditures*
Bowe 1978, *Handicapping America Barriers to Disabled People*
Brill 1977, *Evaluating Buildings on a Performance Basis*
Byerts 1978, *Elderly Housing: Challenge and Opportunity*
Chen and Abend 1985, *Developing Residential Design Statements for the Hearing-Handi-*
Conway 1977, *Human Response to Tall Buildings*
Council on Tall Buildings Committee 56 1987, *Design for the Handicapped*
Cranz 1977, *The Impact of High-Rise Housing on Older Residents*
De Jong 1983, *Physical Disability and Public Policy*
Feller 1982, *Health Characteristics of Persons with Chronic Activity Limitation*
Howell 1980, *Designing for Aging: Patterns of Use*
Howell 1984, *Elderly Housing: Warping the Design Process*
Jeffers 1977, *Barrier-Free Design: A Legislative Response*
Jones 1980, *Access Today*
Lang 1974, *Designing for Human Behavior: Architecture and the Behavioral Sciences*
Lawton 1968, *The Ecology of Social Relationships in Housing for the Elderly*
Lawton 1973b, *Ecology and the Aging Process*
Lawton 1975, *Planning and Managing Housing for the Elderly*
Miller 1976, *The Magical Number Seven, Plus or Minus Two*
Morgan 1976, *Beyond Disability: A Broader Definition of Architectural Barriers*
Morton 1978, *Bearing Down on Barriers*
Nahemow 1977, *Elderly People in Tall Buildings: A Nationwide Study*
President's Commission on Housing 1982, *The Report of the President's Commission on*
Raschko 1982, *Housing Interiors for the Disabled and Elderly*
Rehab Group, Inc. 1980, *Digest of Data on Persons with Disabilities*
Robert Scharf Associates 1981, *The Cost of Accessibility*
Rubin 1980, *Building for People*
Snyder 1983, *Testimony Before the Subcommittee on Commerce*
Spradlin 1982, *The Building Estimator's Reference Book*
Steinfeld 1980, *Designing Adaptable Housing to Meet Barrier-Free Goals*
Stephens 1978, *Hidden Barriers*
UFAS 1984, Uniform Federal Accessibility Standards Federal Register
U.S. Bureau of the Census 1980, *General Social and Economic Characteristics*

U.S. Bureau of the Census 1980, *Structural Characteristics for the Housing Inventory*
U.S. Department of HUD 1977, *Housing for the Elderly and Handicapped: The Experience*
U.S. Department of HUD 1979, *Management of Housing for Handicapped and Disabled*
U.S. House of Representatives Subcommittee 1983, *Travel Problems of the Handicapped*
U.S. Senate Special Committee on Aging 1980, *Aging America: Trends and Projections*

4

Barrier-Free Design
in Canada

Concern about barrier-free design in Canada is approximately 30 years old. Since 1960 considerable progress has been made on a number of fronts. The development of building standards has paralleled activities in the United States as collaboration between U.S. and Canadian organizations in both research and standards development has been beneficial in the past and should be encouraged in the future.

Human rights legislation in Canada, although quite recent, may have profound impacts on barrier-free design activities by redefining the population for whom we are designing, possibly to include smokers and people with allergies, and by providing increased impetus for the work through easier grievance procedures. The fresh approach provided by examining an environment from the point of view of someone with a disability often highlights environmental characteristics which are unsatisfactory for most of the population. Thus the solutions to design for the disabled are of benefit to all, although more significant for the disabled.

As in most of the chapters on national approaches, the focus here is on public-sector activities. However, some private-sector activity is also noted. In addition, a brief view of the transportation and residential areas is provided. Progress in several technical areas is highlighted, including (1) fire safety, for which there is now considerable legislation; (2) modifications to heritage buildings, for which there are good examples showing that it is not the enormous problem initially envisaged; (3) signage for the visually impaired (complicated because of the use of two languages; and (4) building design for the hearing impaired. Although none of these are specific to tall buildings, all areas have applicability to them, and fire safety and guidance within buildings for visually and hearing impaired become considerably more complicated—and more crucial—as buildings become larger and taller.

4.1 LESSONS AND PROGRESS

Over the last 30 years considerable progress has been achieved in making the built and natural environment of Canada accessible to and usable by disabled

49

people. While missed opportunities for accessibility still do occur and there may be some frustration with what appears, in day-to-day activities, as slow progress, in retrospect it seems that Canada is doing well. There is considerable activity within various levels of government as well as in the private sector. At the federal level it is now government policy that all new and existing facilities are to be made accessible (Treasury Board of Canada, 1985). In the private sector accessible hotels and banks are the norm. A multitude of very active disabled-consumer organizations have been formed, which vary in scope from local to national, in constituency from specific disability types to all-encompassing, and in function from recreational to political lobbying.

This chapter deals primarily with building design and the problems of access, which are, however, reflective of a more fundamental problem of attitude—the attitudes of the general public and the designers. We are still trying to change the image of a building user to include people with a range of abilities. While progress is being made, one difficulty is that the "disabled" are often seen only as people who use wheelchairs. The resulting overemphasis on a limited range of problems—and the resultant solutions—is echoed by every chapter in Part 1 of this Monograph. This enduring problem has not changed dramatically since it was noted in Chapter 3 of *Planning and Environmental Criteria for Tall Buildings* (Council on Tall Buildings, Group PC, 1981). Greater improvement will come as people with disabilities are included as a usual consideration. An example is a local radio review of restaurants, which includes not only comments on the quality of food and service but also on the degree of accessibility. How does barrier-free design fare with respect to other relatively new issues such as energy conservation? Are there some lessons to be learned?

The concern about energy conservation, in the last few years, has resulted in a large reduction of wasted energy. Within a very short time, the problem has been understood and acted upon. Energy conservation has even, in some cases, become an inspiration for design. On the negative side, the implementation of energy-conserving measures in a single-minded fashion, without considering other design requirements, has had some serious implications. Tighter buildings, reduced amounts of fresh air, and lower lighting levels can result in reductions in air quality and in another whole set of problems.

There are at least three lessons to be learned. First, if the client has a strong interest, the designers will soon follow suit. Second, requirements for accessibility need to be integrated with the other requirements that designers juggle. Third, consideration of disabled people needs to be incorporated into the tradition of design as cost estimating or structural analysis is now and, in fact, should be part of cost estimating in regard to accessibility and adaptation.

A number of legislative changes lead in the direction of encouraging client interest in accessibility. In addition, accessibility appears to have been a source of inspiration in some buildings. The court complex in Vancouver, B.C., with its "stramp," is representative of the latter. It is interesting to note that this stramp was the only barrier-free design example used in a *Scientific American* (1983) article on the disabled. One should be careful, however, in using some of these solutions, which have visual impact but are lacking in other respects such as railings.

One area in which there is considerable potential for conflict between accessibility and other requirements concerns historic buildings and their preservation. Fortunately there are now enough examples in Canada of how to solve both problems, so that one can no longer assume that making a historical building accessible will destroy its heritage value. The Parliament buildings in Ottawa provide a good example.

One of the advantages of designers looking at buildings from the point of view of people with different disabilities is that they will gain a fresh perspective. Designers begin to see solutions that they had accepted in the past as requiring improvement. Major problems for the disabled often turn out to be, at the least, nuisances for everyone else.

4.2 WHO ARE THE DISABLED?

From the designer's point of view it is important to try to understand whom we are designing for and what the expectations are in terms of building use. The requirements for a wheelchair user will be different for a person who has strong arms than for one who is a quadriplegic. In general, the model being considered at present in Canadian building codes is a person with good use of his or her arms and of average adult size. Perceptual disabilities are considered to a lesser extent, but are receiving increased attention. Severe allergies could be included in the definition of a physical disability, but are not currently considered by code writers.

The Canadian Human Rights Act (Canadian Human Rights Commission, 1983) defines disability as:

> ... any previous or existing mental or physical disability including disfigurement and previous or existing dependence on alcohol or a drug.

The same act defines *physical* disability as:

> A physical disability, infirmity, malformation or disfigurement that is caused by bodily injury, birth defect or illness and, without limiting the generality of the foregoing, includes epilepsy, any degree of paralysis, amputation, lack of physical coordination, blindness or visual impediment, deafness or hearing impediment, muteness or speech impediment, and physical reliance on a guide dog or on a wheelchair or other remedial appliance or device.

Sometimes politics enters into the definition. In Russia, until very recently, there have been officially no disabled people. In China there are 20,000,000 disabled people, which is almost equivalent to the total population of Canada.

Statistics on the numbers of disabled people are elusive and arbitrary, depending largely on definition, and are not always relevant. Information from a recently completed Canadian survey is given in Tables 4.1 and 4.2 (Statistics Canada, 1985).

4.3 CODES AND STANDARDS IN CANADA

Canadian design standards for barrier-free buildings have been available since the mid-1960s through the National Building Code of Canada (NBC). The first code, called Supplement #7 to the NBC, was largely based on the U.S. code issued by the American National Standards Institute (ANSI) in 1961. It was several years before Supplement #7 began to be adopted by municipalities, who at that time were the authorities having jurisdiction. Even then it was applied only to government buildings. Because the standard was new, the committee writing the document wanted it to be a guide as well as a code. It included "shall" clauses which were mandatory and 'should" clauses which were advisory. This practice led to considerable confusion and was later abandoned.

Code requirements have primarily addressed the problems of people who use wheelchairs; the model was a person who had reasonably good use of his or her arms and who would act independently. The issue of egress in emergencies was not addressed because access was only required to the main floor. The most recent edition of the NBC (National Research Council of Canada, 1985) now includes requirements to allow safe egress. Unfortunately the present requirements for disabled people are not contained in a separate volume, but are integrated with other code requirements in the Use and Occupancy section. Also, they are not necessarily in concert with recent approaches to egress as discussed in Chapters 10 and 12. Unlike in the United States, requirements for areas such as parking and for components such as drinking fountains and signage are considered outside the scope of the code and have been removed.

The NBC acts as a model code, which must be adopted by some authority having jurisdiction before it becomes law. In Canada, the building code authorities are the provincial governments. (See also the discussion of Japanese provincial adoption and modification in Chapter 2.) Currently all the provinces use the NBC as a base, but make some modifications to more closely suit their particular needs. The most progressive code is the one used by the province of British Columbia, in which the section dealing with accessibility is based on the current ANSI code (1980).

Table 4.1   Disabled Canadian population by age

Age	Percentage disabled
All	13
15–34	5
35–54	10
55–64	25
65+	39

Table 4.2   Disabled Canadian population (percent) by nature of disability and age*

Age	Mobility	Agility	Seeing	Hearing	Speaking	Mental	Unknown
All	65	54	14	26	5	3	8
15–34	48	40	9	17	11	10	15
35–54	61	52	9	19	4	3	12
55–64	71	59	9	24	2	2	7
65+	73	60	21	35	4	2	3

*Because of multiple disabilities the percentages do not add up to 100 across an age group.

In addition to its code, the province of British Columbia has published a guide that has the BC code printed in black and explanatory material and diagrams printed in red (Ministry of Municipal Affairs, 1984). This appears to be an excellent solution to the old should/shall problem. Components considered outside the scope of the NBC have been included in the BC code.

The question of life safety for disabled people is beginning to be resolved in Canada and provides an interesting focus on which to compare various codes and standards. Table 4.3 lists the differences by comparing the NBC, the BC code, the Public Works Canada (PWC) standard (1985), and some proposed amendments to the National Fire Protection Association Publication 101 (NFPA, 1983). This whole area has recently been very active in Great Britain and the United States with the Board for the Coordination of Model Building Codes and with the studies undertaken for the Architectural and Transportation Barriers Compliance Board. Public Works Canada (1988 a, b) recently published two documents on life safety and disabled people. More detail on principles of and approaches to life safety can be found in several other chapters, especially Chapter 10.

One of the interesting debates in the building code area centers on the separation of legal and technical requirements. In the United Kingdom, building codes are developed along the lines of performance codes with back-up documents of deemed-to-satisfy solutions. The purpose is clear and the system allows flexibility in solutions. In contrast, in the United States the ANSI code specifies what one should build to make a facility accessible, but not under what conditions one is required to make buildings accessible. This allows more people to use the standards and reduces variability. It is much easier to get agreement on what constitutes an accessible washroom than it is on how many washrooms are needed in a variety of situations. Comparison of the ANSI code to the Uniform Federal Accessibility Standards (UFAS) in Chapter 3 highlights that the U.S. situation is also complex. In some respects the debate pits the ANSI approach against the UFAS one.

Another valuable aspect of performance-based requirements is that they make clear what one is trying to accomplish and for whom. This is often a political decision, but an important one to have clear in everyone's mind.

The committees that write codes and standards provide valuable forums for exchange between disabled consumers, architects, fire officials, and others interested in an environment which does not exclude disabled people. In addition, they can generate research activities which help to provide the required knowledge base.

Variations between one code and another within countries or across national boundaries can be cause for concern. Two examples of interest are elevator design and tactile warnings. In the first case, variations result in special, therefore more expensive, installations. With regard to tactile communication, British Columbia now requires doors leading to exits to have knurled door handles. In the United States the same indication is used for doors leading to hazardous areas.

To provide a consistent technical standard for use across the country, the Canadian Standards Association (CSA) is producing a barrier-free design standard, B651. This standard will be similar to the ANSI A117.1.

Table 4.4 compares ANSI A117.1 with two Canadian codes, namely, the BC code (Ministry of Municipal Affairs, 1984) and CSA B44 (Canadian Standards Association, 1980). There is an additional Canadian standard, treating elevators for the handicapped, which is not described here (Canadian Standards Association, 1981).

Table 4.3   Comparison of life safety considerations in codes

Requirement	BC code (1984)	NBC of Canada (1985)	PWC standard (1985)*	Proposed NFPA 101 Sec. 5-12 (1984)†
Egress measures, scope and application	Applies to new floors added vertically or to extensions of existing stories (in combination with these existing stories or alone) and to each floor area from which more than one exit is required, and to which disabled people are required to be provided with access.	Applies where a barrier-free access is provided above first story in an unsprinklered building.	Applies to all new buildings which are unsprinklered and to each of its floor areas required to have at least two means of egress.	Applies to new buildings with accessible stories except when building is sprinklered (other exceptions exist as well).
Safety measures	Every floor area has a minimum of two separate paths providing different directions of travel to one or more areas of refuge described below.	Every floor area is designed for one of the measures below.	Every floor area has a minimum of two separate paths accessible to wheelchair users and providing different directions of travel to one or more areas of refuge described below.	Each story is divided by a 1-hour fire resistance into at least two smoke compartments, or has ramps to grade, or opens onto grade, or is such a large open space that not all exits can be affected by the same emergency.
Areas of refuge or equivalent measures	1. An exterior exit door to an acceptable open space 2. Horizontal exit 3. Floor areas or parts of floor areas conforming to other code requirements 4. Vestibule or corridor served by a fire fighters' elevator, protected against fire and in buildings over three stories protected against smoke movement	1. Served by fire fighters' elevator, or 2. Divided into two zones so the disabled can be accommodated in each zone, or 3. Have an exterior exit at ground level or a ramp leading to ground level	1. An exterior exit door to an acceptable open space 2. A horizontal exit 3. Every floor area divided into at least two zones conforming to other code requirements, each zone providing an area of refuge so that disabled persons can be accommodated in each zone 4. Vestibule or corridor providing an area of refuge, served by a fire fighters' elevator, protected against fire and in buildings over three stories protected against smoke movement	
Size of refuge area or protected floor zone or smoke compartment	1220 by 1220 mm (48 by 48 in.) for each nonambulatory occupant but not less than two such spaces.	Area on each side of horizontal exit is sufficient to accommodate occupants of both floor areas at a rate of 1.5 m² (16 ft²) per person in a wheelchair.	1220 by 1220 mm (48 by 48 in.) for each nonambulatory occupant but not less than two such spaces.	Minimum 100 ft² (9.3 m²), and when other than the elevator lobby, it has 15 ft² (1.5 m²) per person for 1% of the occupant load for that story.

*Application guidelines for the technical standard are under development by Public Works Canada.
†Submission described here was formulated by the Subcommittee on Means of Egress (proposal #101-676).

Requirement	BC code (1984)	NBC of Canada (1985)	PWC standard (1985)*	Proposed NFPA 101 Sec. 5-12 (1984)†
Identifying areas of refuge	Designated as such on building plans, and identified as such in building.		Identified as a point of assembly during evacuations for disabled persons.	
Fire fighters' elevator or otherwise protected elevator		Fire fighters' type: required only to go from street level to every floor normally served by elevator system that is above grade in the building (means basement may not be served).		Each compartment has an exit or is served by an elevator with a protected power supply.
Exit door identification	Opening hardware on exit doors identified by roughened surface on exit travel side, with exit doors in a contrasting color to wall they are set in, different color from any door in same area.			
Floor identification in exit stairs	Designation mounted on stairway side of wall at latch side of door to exit stairs, in Arabic numerals, minimum 60 mm (2¼ in.) high, raised approximately 0.7 mm (0.027 in.), located 1500 ± 25 mm (59 ± 1 in.) and not more than 300 mm (12 in.) from door, and contrasting in color with background.		Designation mounted on stairway side of wall at latch side of door to exit stairs, in Arabic numerals, minimum 60 mm (2¼ in.) high, raised approximately 0.7 mm (0.027 in.), located 1500±25 mm (59±1 in.) and not more than 300 mm (12 in.) from door, and contrast- ing in color with background.	
Warning system	In certain sleeping-type occupancies at least one sleeping unit has a strobe light (7-W · sec, 80 flash/min output) with translucent or clear lens identified by "Fire" or "Smoke" signs as appropriate, located minimum 2150 mm (84 in.) high, linked to fire or smoke alarm system.	Building (or parts) intended for the hearing impaired have, in addition to audible signal devices, visual signal appliances installed so that at least one is visible throughout the floor area or portion thereof.		

Table 4.4   Comparison of code/standard requirements for elevators

Requirement	ANSI A117.1-1980	BC code (1984)	CSA B44, App. E (1980)
Internal car size dimensions	68 in. (1730 mm) minimum width by 51 in. (1291 mm) minimum depth from return panel or by 54 in. (1370 mm) minimum depth from door; minimum width of 54 in. (1370 mm) allowed for car capacities of less than 2000 lb.	1725 by 1295 mm (68 by 51 in.) minimum.	54 in. wide by minimum 54 in. measured to door, or by minimum 51 in. measured to return panel, and if designed for a wheelchair turning radius allowance, then wall/wall or wall/door minimum clear distance is 54 by 68 in.
Door size	36 in. (915 mm) wide.	915 mm (36 in.) minimum clear width.	32 in. minimum clear width.
Door operation	Open and close automatically.		Automatic horizontal sliding.
Door reopening mechanisms	Mounted at 5 in. (125 mm) and at 29 in. (735 mm), no contact required, effective for minimum of 20 sec.	Mounted at 125 ±25 mm (5 ±1 in.) and at 740 ±25 mm (29 ±1 in.) or other acceptable detector system, no contact required, stops or fully opens the doors.	Mounted at height of 5 in. and 29 ±1 in., no contact required, effective for minimum of 20 sec, stops and reopens the doors to minimum 32 in.
Car/hall leveling tolerances	½ in. (13 mm) under rated loading to zero loading conditions.	± 12 mm (±½ in.)	±½ in.
Sill gap	1½ in. (32 mm) maximum.		
Car floor finishes	Stable, firm, relatively non-slip, and if carpet, then securely attached with firm (or no) under-cushion and maximum pile height of ½ in. (13 mm).	Slip-resistant flooring or low-pile carpet laid without undercushion.	Nonslip surface that permits easy movement of wheelchairs.
Handrails		On rear and side walls with top at 815 ±25 mm (32 ±1 in.), minimum of 40 + 12 mm/ −0 mm (1½ + ½ in./ −0 in.) clear of walls.	Provided on all nonaccess walls with top at 32 ±1 in., minimum of 1½ in. clear of walls.
Lighting	5 footcandles (53.8 lux) minimum at car controls, platform, car threshold, landing sill.		5 footcandles minimum at car controls and landing sill.
Car controls, height	No floor buttons higher than 54 in. (1370 mm).	CL top button maximum 1370 mm (54 in.), CL lowest button minimum 890 mm (35 in.)	CL top button 54 in. maximum, CL lowest button 35 ±1 in.
Car controls, size and type	Raised, flush, or recessed, ¾ in. (19 mm) in smallest dimension.	Raised, flush, or recessed, 19 mm (¾ in.) minimum dimension with 9 mm (⅜ in.) maximum depth for flush/recessed buttons when operated.	Raised, flush, or recessed, ¾ in. minimum with depth of flush/recessed buttons when operated not to exceed ⅜ in.

Requirement	ANSI A117.1-1980	BC code (1984)	CSA B44, App. E (1980)
Car controls, markings	All buttons marked to their left by raised or indented standard alphabet letters, Arabic numerals, or standard symbols contrasting with their background, with main entry floor button indicated by raised or indented star (identification complies with ANSI signage requirements).	Buttons identified to their left by symbols, or by Arabic numerals or sans-serif letters, or both, minimum 16 mm (⅝ in.) high, raised 1 mm (0.039 in.) on a contrasting color background, with main entry floor button indicated by an adjacent star symbol.	Floor buttons identified to their left with symbols or with Arabic numerals on a contrasting color background, with such markings being ⅝ in. high minimum and raised a minimum of 0.030 in.
Car controls, visual operation indicators	Floor button signals provided to indicate when call is registered and when answered.	Indicate when call registered and when answered.	Indicate when each call registered and when answered.
Car controls, location	On front wall for center-opening doors, and on side or front wall next to door for side-opening doors.	On side wall when front return panel is less than 470 mm (18½ in.).	In a position accessible from a wheelchair on entering an elevator.
Car controls, emergency controls	Alarm and stop buttons and other controls are grouped at panel bottom with centerlines at 35 in. (890 mm) minimum.	Below floor control buttons along with "door open/close" controls and other essential identification.	Emergency controls and door operating buttons grouped together at top of control panel.
Visual car position indicators	Located in elevator car above control panel or over door in numerals ½ in. (13 mm) high minimum	16 mm (⅝ in.) high characters on a contrasting color background	Indicates when stopping or passing a floor and is 1 in. high minimum on a contrasting color background.
Audible car position indicators	Verbal announcement or audible signal in car of minimum 20 dBA, with frequency no higher then 1500 Hz.		
Floor designation at hoistway entrances	On both jambs with centerline of indented or raised 2 in. (50 mm) high sans serif characters located at 60 in. (1525 mm) (identification complies with ANSI signage requirements).	Centerline of 38 mm (1½ in.) high sans serif letters and/or Arabic numerals, raised 1 mm (0.039 in.), centered at height of 1524 mm (60 in.) on each jamb.	On both sides of door jambs in Arabic numerals 1½ in. high and raised 0.030 in. minimum to identify every floor.
Arrival signals and door timing	$T = D \div K$, where T = minimum time (sec) from notification of call response to moment doors start to close, D = distance from 60 in. (1525 mm) in front of farthest call button which controls that elevator to the centerline of its door, and $K = 1\frac{1}{2}$ ft/sec (455 mm/sec).		

Table 4.4   Comparison of code/standard requirements for elevators (Continued)

Requirement	ANSI A117.1-1980	BC code (1984)	CSA B44, App. E (1980)
Door delay	Remains fully open for 3 sec minimum in response to car call.	Is fully open for 3 sec minimum in response to hall call.	Minimum period of 3 sec between time doors start to open and doors start to close unless interrupted by door close or car call buttons.
Visual signals for arriving cars	At each hoistway entrance and visible from vicinity of hall call buttons, in-car lanterns acceptable if visible from vicinity of hall call buttons.	Hall or in-car signals with elements designating "up" or "down."	Hall or in-car lanterns.
Visual signals, height	CL at 72 in. (1830 mm) minimum.	1830 mm (72 in.) minimum.	72 in. minimum.
Visual signals, indicator size	2½ in. (64 mm) minimum in smallest dimension.	Each element is 50 mm (2 in.) in smallest dimension.	
Audible signals for arriving cars	Indicator signals once for "up" and twice for "down," verbal annunciator at each hoistway entrance is acceptable.	Indicator of 24 dBA minimum loudness signals once for "up" and twice for "down" in hall; verbal annunciator is acceptable.	Hall or in-car lanterns give audible signal when car stops at a landing.
Lobby call buttons	"Up" button is on top.	Located one above the other.	Mounted one above the other.
Call button, height	Centered at 42 in. (1065 mm).	Centered at 1065 ± 12 mm (42 ±½ in.).	Centerline at 42 ± 1 in.
Call button, size	¾ in. (19 mm) in smallest dimension.		¾ in.
Call button, visual indicators	Indicate when registered and when answered.	Indicate when registered and when answered.	Indicate when registered and answered.
Emergency communication	Two-way communication required.	If provided, then telephone is set in cabinet, or two-way communication system accepted.	Intercommunicating system or telephone required.
Emergency communications, height	54 in. (1370 mm) maximum.	Phone at 1220 mm (48 in.) maximum.	48 in. maximum height.
Emergency communications, markings	Raised or recessed lettering and/or symbols located adjacent to device (identification complies with ANSI signage requirements).	International symbols for telephones 38 mm (1½ in.) minimum height and raised minimum of 1 mm (0.039 in.).	International phone symbols located on cabinet, of 1½ in. minimum height, raised 0.030 in. minimum, and in a contrasting color.
Emergency communications, telephone cord	If handset used, then cord had minimum length of 29 in. (735 mm).	Minimum length 915 mm (36 in.).	Minimum length of 36 in.
Emergency communications, hearing-aid compatible		Equipped with hearing-aid coupler coil.	

4.4 OTHER RELATED CODES

In Canada there are requirements other than building codes, which should be considered in order to provide a more complete picture of the legal forces acting on barrier-free design. Of particular interest are human rights codes.

The Canadian Human Rights Act was amended in July 1983 and states:

> Every individual should have an equal opportunity with other individuals to make for himself or herself the life that he or she is able and wishes to have, consistent with his or her duties and obligations as a member of society, without being hindered in or prevented from doing so by discriminatory practices based on...disability...

In addition to stating that it is a discriminatory practice to refuse to employ an individual because the individual is disabled, the act states:

> It is a discriminatory practice in the provision of goods, services, facilities or accommodation customarily available to the general public:
>
> (*a*) to deny, or deny access to, any such good, service, facility or accommodation to any individual, or
> (*b*) to differentiate adversely in relation to any individual,
>
> on a prohibited ground of discrimination.

There have been very few complaints related to disability made to the federal Human Rights Commission in the last few years. The provinces seem to be more active, with the province of Ontario having received 438 complaints in 1984/1985 (The Ottawa Citizen, 1985).

4.5 FEDERAL GOVERNMENT

Public Works Canada (PWC) is the real-estate arm of the Canadian government and is somewhat similar to the General Services Administration/Public Buildings Service in the United States. Access for disabled people has been part of their policy since the 1970s. They are just now completing a program to make all their new and existing buildings accessible.

The whole area of problems faced by disabled people was clarified by a special House of Commons committee who issued its first report, *Obstacles,* in 1981. There were 130 recommendations on which the committee followed up during subsequent years.

The PWC standard now used by the government is based on the BC code, which is strongly related to the ANSI code. Other activities of PWC have included seminars on *Life Safety and the Disabled* (PWC, 1982) and on *Barrier-Free Historical Buildings.* A series of postoccupancy evaluations has been conducted and an evaluation guide is currently being developed.

Other departments, including Transport Canada, the Institute for Research in Construction (National Research Council of Canada, 1983), and the Canada Mortgage and Housing Corporation (1982) have been active in this area.

4.6 TRANSPORTATION

During the last few years there has been development related to transportation on a number of fronts. One of the key actors has been the Transportation Development Centre, the research arm of Transport Canada. They have developed guidelines for wayfinding by people with visual impairments through the Canadian National Institute for the Blind and are currently working on a similar document through the Canadian Hearing Society. It would be profitable to compare these guidelines to the approaches described in Chapter 12.

Other projects include wheelchair lifts for intercity buses, quick-release hand controls for cars, and a small carrier for alternative transportation (SCAT). While inaccessible urban rapid transit facilities are still appearing, both railways and airlines have been actively pursuing accessibility.

4.7 RESIDENTIAL FACILITIES

Most building codes in Canada do not require residential facilities to be completely accessible. Typically, access to public entrances, shared laundry facilities, and suites, but not the suite itself, is required. Houses are exempt.

The Canada Mortgage and Housing Corporation (CMHC), a federal Crown Corporation dealing with housing and community issues, provides accessible housing through its social housing and renovation programs. About 5% of the 25,000 units provided each year through these programs are accessible.

There are many other residential developments of note across the country. One example is the recently opened Creekview Cooperative in Vancouver. This is a large apartment unit with five bedrooms, serving five severely physically disabled people.

4.8 RESEARCH NEEDS

More research is required to ensure that the funds being spent on retrofitting existing buildings and on solutions proposed for new buildings are reasonable. Anecdotal experiences and the advice of individuals based on their own disability are helpful but of limited use.

Research results originating in other countries can be used, but care must be taken in transposing the results. Different kinds of wheelchairs, rehabilitation techniques, and climates should be considered. In Canada, for example, since there is considerable snow in the winter months, the curb cuts are designed for use by people in wheelchairs *and* for the snowmobiles fitted with a plow used to clear the sidewalks. Many of the curb cuts found in the United States would be too narrow and improperly placed for snow-clearing activities.

Research is not a panacea. It cannot answer political questions and, if improperly conducted, can be misleading. The old requirement allowing a ramp slope of 1 in 7 was based on research. Unfortunately the subjects used in the experiments were athletic university students. Subsequent British and U.S. studies have provided more realistic information.

Two areas recently investigated by PWC are the design of meeting rooms for the hearing impaired and wayfinding in public buildings. In looking at the problem of orientation and wayfinding for visually impaired people it was found that too many people have difficulty finding their way around buildings. The solution of making all signs tactile would, at best, make the visually impaired as lost as everyone else. Clear, consistent signage, simple plan configurations, grouping of like facilities, and locating those offices which receive a large number of visitors close to the entrance are aspects of the solution which will help everyone.

Because Canada is a bilingual country, most of the federal government's conference facilities are equipped for simultaneous interpretation. These systems can be easily adapted for use by people who use hearing aids with T-switches. For the deaf, sign language interpretation (ASL in English, QSL in French) is available to all departments without charge. In the medium-sized meeting rooms without simultaneous interpretation facilities, portable FM systems are recommended. In small meeting rooms, improvements in the acoustic environment, attention to lighting, and the use of appropriate tables, that is, tables that are not long and narrow, for example, are recommended. PWC has just completed an analysis of meeting rooms which showed that the background sound level that typically exists is at a noise control level of about 40 dB when it should be substantially less. Modifications to resolve these problems will result in an improved environment for all users: however, it will be especially noticeable for the hearing impaired.

4.9 SUMMARY

In many areas there is still a lack of understanding of the environmental problems faced by disabled people and the consequences of these problems on their daily activities. Research is required. Consideration of disabled people as part of the normal building population has not as yet been internalized by the design professions. The new human rights legislation should help encourage barrier-free design as a design tradition. With cooperation and help from people in other countries, not only Canada but all nations can improve the quality and rate of implementation of barrier-free environments.

4.10 CONDENSED REFERENCES/BIBLIOGRAPHY

ANSI A117.1 1980, *American National Standard Specifications for Making Buildings and*
Canada Mortgage and Housing Corporation 1982, *Housing Disabled Persons*
Canadian Human Rights Commission 1983, *Office Consolidation of the Canadian Human*
Canadian Standards Association 1980, *Safety Code for Elevators, Dumbwaiters, Escala-*
Canadian Standards Association 1981, *Safety Code for Elevating Devices for the Handi-*
Council on Tall Buildings, Group PC, 1981, *Planning and Environmental Criteria*
House of Commons 1981, *Obstacles*
Ministry of Municipal Affairs 1984, *The Section 3.7 Handbook: Building Requirements for*
National Research Council of Canada 1983, *Evacuation Techniques for Disabled Persons:*
National Research Council of Canada 1985, *National Building Code of Canada*
NFPA 1983, *A Compilation of NFPA Technical Committee Reports for Public Review and*
Public Works Canada 1982, *Life Safety and Disabled People: Seminar Summary*

Public Works Canada 1985, *Barrier-Free Design: Access to and Use of Buildings by Phys-*
Public Works Canada 1988a, *Life Safety for People with Disabilities: Literature Review*
Public Works Canada 1988b, *Life Safety for People with Disabilities: A State-of-the-Art*
Scientific American 1983, *Physical Disability and Public Policy*
Statistics Canada 1985, *Highlights from the Canadian Health and Disability Survey*
The Ottawa Citizen 1985, *Complaints Swamp Ontario Rights Body*
Treasury Board of Canada 1985, *Accessibility Improvement*

5

Building Design
for the Disabled
in the Netherlands

The standards that are appropriate with regard to housing and living for all members of a society change with the position of the various groups within that society. Therefore the present state of legislation and design of buildings and environments in the Netherlands, as in other countries, should be recognized as a step within an ongoing process.

This chapter, then, begins with a conceptual description of the term *disability*, followed by an outline of the historical development of the position of the disabled in Dutch society. The emancipation of the disabled is a theme that runs through history like a thread. By emancipation we mean the freeing of the disabled from a totally separate, totally dependent position to one of community acceptance and involvement. The focus of attention will be on two areas in particular: public facilities and housing.

5.1 DEFINITION OF DISABILITY

To be able to make arrangements for a certain category of people or to make a design, it is necessary to have a precise idea of those people. In the Netherlands, however, there is no official description or definition available. One of the reasons for this is that one wants to consider people as individuals and not as members of a group, especially a group that is in danger of being judged negatively in social interaction. Another reason is that it is difficult to give a uniform description of a very heterogeneous group, as discussed previously. For practical and political purposes, often the description of the World Health Organization is used, which distinguishes between impairment, disability, and handicap. Since the concept of handicap should be understood against the background of the other two, we list all three (World Health Organization, 1980):

Impairment refers to the loss or abnormality of the structure or function of the body.

63

Disability refers to the limitations or lack of ability in performing activities that are considered normal for a particular individual. It is normally a consequence of impairment.

Handicap refers to the impact of impairment and/or disability on the individual and on the wider community involved. When such impact implies problems in relationships, limitation on life opportunities, with consequent disruption of social integration into ordinary community life, then an impaired or disabled person is a handicapped one.

This description does not offer insight into the diversity of occurring disabilities. In medical circles, very detailed classifications exist. For social and political purposes, a rough tripartition is often used: (1) sensory and motor defects, including visual disorders, marked speech and communication difficulties, and physical problems such as endurance; (2) intellectual defects, including limited mental abilities, retardation, and specific educational problems; (3) social and emotional disorders, including insanity, behavioral disorders, acute neuroses and phobias, and certain specific deviations, such as autism (Communautair Actieprogramma, 1982). Together, these definitions help in understanding the disabled population. For designers of public buildings, houses, and accommodations, these descriptions are of course too vague to be a guide in the practice of designing. Nevertheless, they are important. Thus in the description of the concept *disability,* its social aspect is indicated quite clearly. The environment is such a social aspect. The design can in some cases introduce facilities which neutralize "defects." The social aspect, however, goes beyond that. Then one thinks of a normal, social performance. So when designing, one should not only pay attention to the physical aspects but also to the social and emotional ones. Too much use of specialized facilities, for instance, may strongly emphasize a social separation of disabled people and consequently may stand in the way of social functioning. Something similar can be the case when separate entrances are constructed in a public building, such as the backdoor for disabled people.

Likewise the emphasis on diversity is not without importance. All too many designers consider themselves released from making further provisions if they have thought of just one or two aspects. It will be clear that a ramp for wheelchair users must not be an excuse for dispensing with the markings on stairs and glass doors for people with imperfect eyesight or with induction loops for people who are hard of hearing.

5.2 POSITION OF THE DISABLED IN SOCIETY: HISTORY

Phase 0, in preindustrial times, showed the blind, the paralytic, and the cripple in subordinated social roles, mostly as beggars. The disabled person is left to his or her fate, or even exploited. Any assistance that is given is seen as pure charity out of the goodness of the giver's heart.

Phase 1 is characterized by the rise and growth of industry and a mass working class. Private institutions were founded partly to care for the disabled in a more systematic way. The disabled continued to be dependent on charity, but in a more collective and institutional way. This occurred mainly within total institutions, which protected the disabled from the outside world and the outside world from the disabled, who had no means of access. The first interest groups for the disabled—societies for the deaf (1884) and the blind (1885)—were formed during this phase.

Phase 2 can be summed up as rise of the welfare state. The welfare state arose in the 1920s and 1930s as an answer to the challenges of economic crisis and depression. It attempted to guarantee a minimum of care, including health care, some economic security, and social respectability for all its members, especially weaker groups. This was seen not as a favor, but as a *right,* an emancipation from the subservience of charity. The standard of living was raised from a subminimal to a minimal level—emancipation in an economic sense.

Within the welfare state, weak groups were expected to assemble into interest groups that actively sought the support of the government. Some of these groups became relatively strong, such as labor movements, whereas others, including groups of disabled, were among the weaker ones. Thus not until late in the process of this phase could disabled people share in the support of the welfare state. Beginning in 1966, with the General Disability Insurance Act, and continuing with the Extra Medical Expenses Act of 1968 and later extensions of those acts, disabled persons were provided with an economic foundation, the opportunity to work under adapted conditions in special workshops, and insurance against exceptional medical expenses. Aspects of these two sets of regulations and the Enactment for Financial Support for Housing for the Disabled provided for improvements in housing conditions, including subsidies for the adaptations of houses for disabled persons.

Organizations for the disabled were by no means powerful players in the political scene during this time, especially because the category of disabled persons is so diverse and their interests are so varying that they did not form an integrated movement. However, health-care institutions—originating from private initiative—have brought about in the Netherlands a strong, extensive, and differentiated system of institutions for the care of disabled people.

Thus the welfare state has provided advantages for the disabled. On the other hand, it requires that people become dependent on facilities and on an obscure, complex system of regulations. This dependence may go further than necessary—on the one hand because the facilities extend beyond necessity, and on the other because the receiving party is feeling, or pretending to be, more dependent than is strictly necessary. Such processes, analyzed and described by Goffman (1961) among others, have been noticed in the Netherlands (Hout, 1983). This effect of dependent behavior requires a new type of emancipation: emancipation from the welfare state and its facilities.

Phase 3 is the phase in which the disabled begin engaging in more public activity. Medical, paramedical, and technological progress bring about many changes in the living conditions of many disabled people. For example, communication, mobility, and prosthetic technology increase the possibilities for the disabled to enter public life. Also, the above-mentioned urge to emancipate from the welfare state and its institutions and facilities stimulates the disabled to become more visible to the public.

This emancipation is not easy for the disabled. There appear to be physical barriers concerning distance, accessibility, and usefulness of accommodations, buildings, and facilities. Furthermore there are also social and mental barriers which hamper the integration of the disabled into social life. Outside the walls of the institutions many disabled persons turn out to be far behind others.

Emancipation of the disabled in this period focuses on eliminating this gap. The policy which is aimed at this is called *retardment policy.* A few aspects of this policy merit to be mentioned. First of all, policy bodies on the local and regional levels were confronted with disabled people to whom they had not paid attention in the past because, as a rule, disabled people stayed in boarding institutions. Second, these committees often had little practical knowledge of the possibilities of eliminating the retarding effects of institutionalization.

Participation by disabled in policy-making has become necessary. In this regard, major complications present themselves. Completely differing categories of disabled people sometimes turn out to have overlapping interests. On that account, public authorities ask for cooperation of the different categories, but this cooperation is not always realized wholeheartedly.

An extremely sensitive issue presents itself. We allude to the danger that a retardment policy, aimed at eliminating the retardment, forms a paradox with its effect. This functions as follows. The disabled person is considered, implicitly or explicitly, a member of a retarded group. In order to make use of the "extras" society places at this group's disposal, the disabled individual must prove to be up to the standards which are set for these facilities, continually having to prove the nature and seriousness of the disability. One may expect that from this test, which each time is effected by medical examinations and other means, a strongly role-affirming influence emanates. The disability is, so to speak, made more highly explicit and all-encompassing.

Phase 4 is the present period. We emphasize two of its aspects: inclusive policy and crisis in the welfare state. The inclusive policy is a reaction to the negative effect of the retardment policy just mentioned. Inclusive policy means that all planning of facilities takes the disabled into account beforehand by using barrier-free designs. This should be done in such a way that later adjustments will be as small and as inexpensive as possible, and that no extra rules, allowances, or benefits will be necessary for the disabled beneficiary. This inclusive policy is a phase in the emancipation of the disabled which many still consider a dream.

The crisis in the welfare state is what most people experience as the present-day harsh reality for disabled people. As in other countries, such as the United States, although the demand for facilities is growing, the government can no longer meet the expenses (Doorn, 1978). A few strategies, which are intended to prevent disaster, come to the fore. One is denationalization of help, which means that the accent of assistance falls on self-help, relations, neighbors, friends, or volunteers. Another strategy is decentralization, shifting responsibilities and execution from higher to lower authorities and from authorities to private initiatives.

In summary, this historical survey has outlined a number of phases, with some typical characteristics for each phase. However, the phases cannot be sharply demarcated in time. If anything, they overlap. One cannot state that characteristics that are called typical for a phase do not occur in other periods. Even now one is often confronted with rules, laws, habits, attitudes, and, certainly, buildings that date from earlier phases.

5.3 EMANCIPATION IN LEGISLATION AND DESIGN

The continuous thread in the historical survey shows different phases in the growth toward emancipation of the disabled. In this section this thread will be examined in relation to design.

1   Phases Preceding the Concept of Emancipation (Phases 0 and 1)

In preindustrial times there were no facilities for people with handicaps. The disabled person belonged to the "outcasts," brought up the social rear, or at best tolerated within the narrow circle of family, neighborhood, or parish, not infrequently as an eccentric.

The private charity institutions in phase 1, in their outward forms, usually strongly reflected the importance and the ideological background of their founders and boards. Less attention was paid to their functions. Many buildings for the blind, the deaf, the mentally deficient, and the psychiatric patient date from the second half of the last century and the beginning of this century. A large number originated from monasteries. The buildings, such as hospitals, living quarters, and sometimes also schools, were usually constructed in accordance with the style of the monastery (Fig. 5.1).

The location is frequently out of the way. An often heard explanation is that one wants to isolate disabled people from society, for example by hiding them in the woods.

2   Emancipation in a Material Sense (Phases 2 and 3)

As was pointed out, the fact that a person has a right to medical attention is a form of emancipation, because then the person is no longer dependent on charity. Existing institutions expanded and new ones were founded. Many institutions now contain 500 beds or more. It is also of importance that the range of medical treatments was being extended widely to include paramedical care such as physiotherapy, speech training, occupational therapy, and art therapy. This meant an

Fig. 5.1   Monastery-style older building.

exponential increase in staff and working capacity. Next to the often pompous main buildings from the past, functional, rational buildings arose, usually in the multistory hospital style (Fig. 5.2). In 1985 there were 111 approved institutions in the Netherlands for the mentally defective only, of which 51 have more than 250 beds. This development toward large-scale housing and health care produced a reaction. Emancipation during this period meant liberation from the grip of the welfare state and its institutions. Many disabled people do not consider themselves clients of the welfare system, but a condition for its preservation, or even a product of the system. An avant-garde of disabled people is turning to the world outside the institution and holding its own there.

3 Disabled People and Public Buildings

It has already been mentioned that the confrontation with public life has not been easy for the disabled. The moment many disabled enter public life, the public buildings prove to be unsuited for them. Especially the physically disabled find that it is practically impossible to function reasonably in public buildings because of many material obstacles and inconveniences. While there is no legislation in the Netherlands that regulates the layout of public buildings in this respect, unlike regulations that exist in Singapore and Canada and as discussed in other chapters, this does not mean that nothing is happening. Of great importance is the creation of a number of guidelines. These have been set down in a substantial reference book called *Geboden Toegang*. Now in its seventh edition, its purpose is as follows (National Organization of the Handicapped, 1983, p. 10):

Fig. 5.2 Multistory hospital-style building.

An indication of the possibilities to create a society which is accessible to everyone. Developing the necessary criteria which relate to the adaptation of both existing facilities and those that have yet to be built. These criteria should be included integrally in the compilation of building instructions, standard specifications, builders' estimates, conditions for subsidies, and so on. Giving information to all those connected with the realization of these goals.

In addition to this standard work, some other books, reports, and brochures deserve to be mentioned, such as a publication of Veilig Verkeer Nederland (Safe Traffic Netherlands, 1982) and special booklets on office buildings, catering establishments, educational and training institutions, and swimming pools (Provinciale Stichting Limburg, 1985). It is impossible to review the detailed information available in these and other sources, but some general guidelines are given here.

Three central notions keep occurring in literature and practice: distance, accessibility, and usefulness.

Distance, Accessibility, and Usefulness.   An object is within reach when no special problems are experienced in reaching the entrance. A space is accessible and traversable when both the entrance itself and all spaces within, which are open to visitors and employees, can be reached without encountering any obstacles. We speak of usefulness when people are able to function optimally within a given space.

In defining distance, accessibility, and usefulness, one starts from the functioning of people and the measures, materials, and appliances belonging to them. One must distinguish among wheelchair users, people with imperfect hand and arm functions, short people, and visually, hearing, and organically disabled people.

To illustrate, two figures are presented; Fig. 5.3 shows the reach of the average male and female wheelchair users, and Fig. 5.4 analyzes some actions. These concepts apply specifically to such tasks as laying out a built-up area or bridging level differences, to usable space, and to general architectural provisions for houses, apartment buildings, public buildings, general purposes, and recreation.

Building Layout.   In laying out the built-up environment, a number of issues crop up regularly. One element is paying attention to sufficiently spacious passages, both in width and in height, such as on pavements. For the visually disabled, tactile guidance systems have been developed, such as guidance lines, sometimes in the form of ridgy tiles which indicate the walking direction, and use of rubber tiles which alert the disabled to an obstacle or street crossing. A controlled street crossing is illustrated in Fig. 5.5. Street furnishings should include sufficient resting places, located at intervals of 100 to 200 (325 to 650 ft), preferably sheltered from sun and rain.

The avoidance or bridging of level differences is a topic that is receiving much attention in the literature, specifically, ramps, staircases, stairlifts, cage lifts, and lifting platforms in swimming pools.

Usable Space.   The notion of usable space is important; *Geboden Toegang* devotes an entire chapter to it (National Organization of the Handicapped, 1983). Kinetic studies of wheelchair users are being made. The total spatial requirements in a given space such as a foyer include the usable spaces of the elements in combination as well as maneuvering space, that is, a "driving" lane between the elements and a turning circle in every space. Using experiments based on this principle, indications can be given about the layout of all kinds of spaces, such as showers, toilets, kitchens. living rooms, work rooms, and rooms in public build-ings.

Architectural Provisions.   General architectural provisions are concerned with the various aspects of a building that can be of importance to a disabled per-son, such as doors and passages; windows; fastening and closing gear; walls, floors, and ceilings; control of the indoor climate; measures in relation to sound, light, and colors; hot-water supply; and fire safety, evacuation, and alarm sys-tems. For public buildings and facilities, guidelines are available with regard to toilets, showers, fitting rooms, counters, checkout desks, telephones, slot ma-chines, sound amplification, induction loops, acoustics, color contrasts, safety, and signposting.

In *Geboden Toegang,* special attention is paid to recreation. Examples include providing seats for wheelchair users in theaters and at sports events, and facilities for gardening (such as raised plantboxes) and access to fishing (Figs 5.6 and 5.7).

Implementation.   An important question is whether or not these guidelines are being realized. This is only partly the case. For buildings yet to be constructed a number of these guidelines and facilities can be enforced. In order to build, a

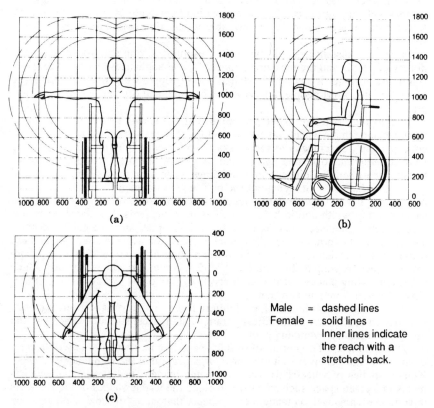

Male   = dashed lines
Female = solid lines
         Inner lines indicate
         the reach with a
         stretched back.

Fig. 5.3   Arm span of wheelchair user. (*a*) **Front view.** (*b*) **Side view.** (*c*) **Top view.** (*National Organization of the Handicapped, 1984, p. 27.*)

building permit must be obtained, and in order to get that permit, the building must fulfill the conditions laid down in a building bylaw that has been drawn up by the municipality. Most municipalities work with a standard building bylaw in which a number of regulations are included regarding distance, accessibility, and usefulness as well as other aspects. The problem, however, is that monitoring the observance of the local building laws often leaves much to be desired.

For existing buildings the possibilities to enforce facilities are fewer. Surely, under the Housing Act the owner of a building can be summoned by the munic-

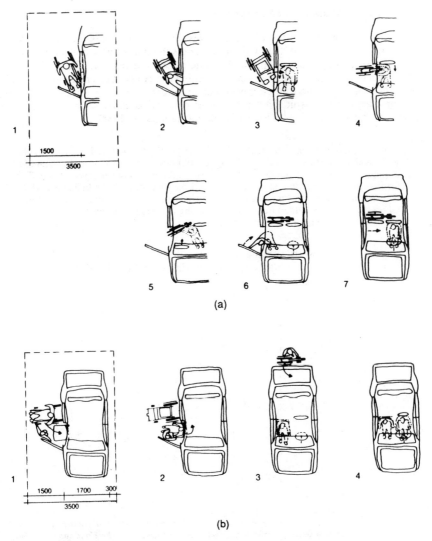

Fig. 5.4   Getting into a car. (*a*) Self-driving wheelchair user. (*b*) Wheelchair user as a passenger. (*National Organization of the Handicapped, 1984, p. 32.*)

ipality to adapt the building—if it is intended for the public—with regard to distance, accessibility, and usefulness. But in practice this can only take place if subsidies are available for the projected adjustments. This is not always the case.

An investigation with regard to the distance, accessibility, and usefulness of public buildings, for which instructions have been issued (Provinciale Stichting Gelderland, 1982) does not always produce favorable results. Thus an investigation into Dutch railway stations (Guffens, 1983) showed that only 25% met the standards of accessibility and usefulness.

4 Disabled Persons and Housing

The view on housing for the disabled follows in broad outlines the phases in the historical development of the position of the disabled in society described earlier. It is not surprising that housing and emancipation are related. The boarding institutions in the development phases preceding the concept of emancipation have already been mentioned. In a report on an architects' investigation into the housing of chronically hospitalized patients in general psychiatric institutions, this phase is characterized as follows (Blonk and Hoekstra, 1984):

> ...Up to (and including) the 1950s, the idea of psychiatry was...dominated by the traditional psychiatric hospitals. Their out-of-the-way location on often beautiful grounds reflects society's averse attitude toward the mentally defective person. The hospital function determined the exterior and the interior of these buildings, which made it clear that the hospitalized people were considered patients. Also, the internal organization was tuned to prolonged nursing and medical attendance, to a maximum of control and a minimum of risk.

A small step toward emancipation is the advent of large-scale housing projects. This form of living is meant especially for the physically disabled. It

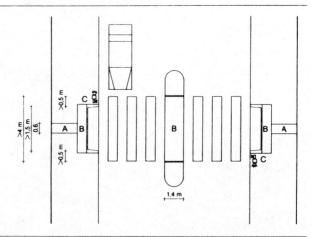

Fig. 5.5 Controlled street crossing: A = ridgy tiles, 0.6 m; B = studded rubber tiles, 0.6 m; C = rattle/tick device, traffic light. (*National Organization of the Handicapped, 1984, p. 38.*)

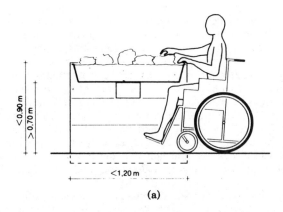

(a)

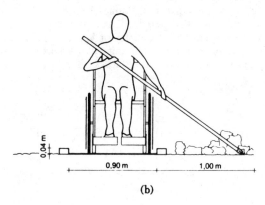

(b)

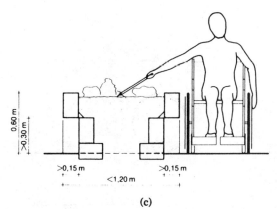

(c)

Fig. 5.6   Gardening. (a) Raised plant boxes with room for wheelchair underneath. (b) Low borders
with narrow lane. (c) Raised plant boxes reachable from sides. (National Organization of
the Handicapped, 1984, p. 193.)

originated from the physical rehabilitation centers, which have long been medical in character. In their function as assistance-giving institutions, they may exert negative influence on the development of the disabled person.

In the 1960s the idea to turn the centers into village communities presented itself (Gennep, 1985), as this was to provide greater independence and mutual assistance. A well-known large-scale project is actually called *Het Dorp* (the village; see Fig 5.8). Such a project, of which the Netherlands have four, offers housing to physically disabled people over 18 years of age. It is a collective form of living, but consists of 40 separate living units. These are meant to guarantee a certain degree of independence. The realization of Het Dorp in Arnhem has, for that matter, not (or not only) been brought about because of actions or pressures from disabled inhabitants. The process has certainly been guided by the authorities. Criticism was directed at the fact that the inhabitants were regarded as members or specimens of a category and consequently took on a tainted social identity.

Partly as a result of this criticism, the small-scale housing project arose; a similar framework, but having fewer than 40 units. This small-scale project comes under the category of family-substituting units (Fig. 5.9). "This facility arose from the attempt to offer disabled people, if possible, a place in society, in as normal a pattern of life as possible" (Ministry of Welfare, 1984). Such a home is situated within the working and living community of a village or residential district. In principle, the residents have to be absent during the day, that is, they

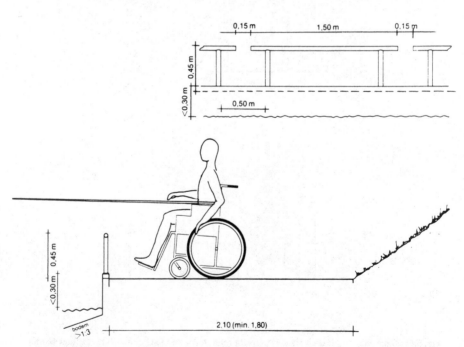

Fig. 5.7   Fishing facilities with interrupted safety rail. (*National Organization of the Handicapped, 1984, p. 198.*)

Fig. 5.8   "The Village," separate living units for physically disabled over 18 years of age.

Fig. 5.9   View inside a family-substituting unit.

must stay in a center which has been set up especially for disabled people, where they can participate in various activities, work in a sheltered workshop, go to a special school, or have other regular occupations. One of the conditions for subsidies is the existence of proper supervision in order to get the intended connection with society. Family-substituting units exist for mentally deficient people as well.

Although this form of living is in fact a further step toward emancipation, it should be stated that medical and other professional staff, by way of their changed insights, perhaps constituted the most important force toward change. With regard to the care of mentally deficient people, Gennep (1985) mentions two theories—the development theory and the normalization principle.

The first theory shows that being institution-oriented has a negative influence on the development of the inmates. Large institutions are institution-oriented; smaller facilities are more person-oriented. The second approach has a positive influence on the development of the residents. The normalization principle states that other people's living conditions and ways of living should be made accessible to mentally deficient people. This fits with the principle: *as normal as possible, as specialized as necessary.*

The architectural layout of such a family-substituting unit contains, in principle, a single bed-sitting room for each resident, as well as sufficient space for the following activities:

Community life and collective meals

The pursuit of hobbies

Meetings of head and staff

Reception of visitors

Staff on night duty

Administration and closed files

Preparation of meals and domestic activities

Medical examination

Sufficient sanitary facilities and storage capacity

A further development toward small-scale housing is the annex to a family-substituting unit, similar to the idea of halfway houses for prisoners. The residents are being trained to lead completely independent lives afterward. These annexes are intended for mentally deficient people.

In psychiatric housing and housing for persons with mental deficiency, developments occur as well, although initially these take place within the institution. The architects' investigation arrives at a tripartition in housing facilities:

1. *Renovated or unrenovated pavilions in the old style* These are evaluated negatively. Among the numerous negative aspects, having little privacy and the anonymity of the furnishings stand out clearly.

2. *New-style pavilions* These are recently built, usually low-rise units on the grounds of the institution, linked by traffic spaces (Fig. 5.10). Sometimes the living quarters are internally connected by a nursing post or another general facility. Residents have their own front doors, sometimes fitted with nameplates and door bells. The living quarters consist of a living room, a kitchen, private sanitary equipment, several bedrooms for one or more persons, and

sometimes a small garden. These pavilions are judged more positively, but criticisms include too little family atmosphere, too small bedrooms compared to the common living room, no bed-sitting rooms, and not all units can be reached directly from the outside; in summary, an unclear blending of pavilion and living unit.

3. *Socio-houses*   These houses are bought or rented by the institution. They include facilities of various types, often old mansions or villas which have been fitted for housing. The rooms in the socio-houses are usually more homelike. Comparatively fewer people sleep together in one room. There is a more direct connection with the outside world. Yet even socio-houses, especially when larger buildings have been converted, still smack strongly of the institution.

5 Housing for the Physically Disabled

For the physically disabled these developments include adapted housing, cluster houses with facilities for general daily needs (GDN), and buildings executed in an adaptable and visitable way.

Adapted Housing.   Disabled people who live in a normal house and encounter difficulties can get a subsidy intended for technical adjustments in relation to their physical defects according to the standards and guidelines established in *Geboden Toegang* (National Organization of the Handicapped, 1984). The subsidy has a lower and an upper limit. In order to qualify for a subsidy, approval must be obtained from a medical authority, the Communal Medical Service, which looks into adjustment plan in detail. With this arrangement many can be

Fig. 5.10   New-style pavilions with private living quarters for patients.

helped, especially people who can easily manage their daily activities. If they cannot, their housemates are burdened heavily. Important disadvantages are the complexity of all the actions that have to be taken before the adjustment has been realized, the fact that all this has to be paid beforehand, and the long time it takes before everything is completed, which may result in unnecessarily prolonged stays in a rehabilitation center. However, independent housing, which now becomes a possibility, is an important step in the emancipation process.

The GDN Cluster.   This facility is intended for disabled persons who want to live independently in a house which is as normal as possible, but who are dependent on help from others for certain actions (Fig. 5.11). These are the general daily needs, such as getting in and out of bed, washing and shaving, going to the toilet, and the like. For this category of disabled people clusters of 12 to 15 houses are built, which are scattered among other houses in a residential district or housing estate. Each cluster includes a unit in which, but particularly from which, GDN assistance is given. This is done on call, 24 hours a day, 7 days a week. This housing facility closely approaches the ideal of the emancipation of disabled people.

A foundation called FOCUS has imported this idea from Sweden. It has the characteristics of a social movement which tries to effect reforms from the bottom upward by social agitation. In the movement toward emancipation, three values come to the fore: autonomy, individuality, and coequality.

Autonomy means the right to make one's own decisions, such as on the necessary assistance one needs, the way to spend one's day, how to spend one's income, and the like. These aspirations seem self-evident, but are no empty formula, considering other existing ways of housing for the disabled. Most facilities have a fixed order of the day. Health care is tied to working hours and work schedules, and often the assistance interferes with various other aspects of the

Fig. 5.11   GDN cluster for the physically disabled.

life of a disabled person. The conditions to reach autonomy in the GDN cluster
are:

1. Assistance on call, so that the inhabitant takes the initiative and determines
the time since assistance is available 24 hours a day.
2. Payment to the GDN assistants under the General Disability Insurance Act.
This act does not stipulate conditions for personal assistance. Assistance
should be purely instrumental, without additional medical, nursing, pedagog-
ical, or psychological aspects.
3. Having a private income. The residents have their own income or allowance,
which is paid directly to them. Often the money comes from an allowance to
which they are entitled under the General Disability Insurance Act.

Individuality is the right to be accepted and treated as an individual instead of
going through life with a tainted identity. This danger exists in institutions as well
as in large-scale housing projects like Het Dorp and in small-scale projects such
as family-substituting units. A condition for individuality is that the exteriors of
the houses do not differ from others and that the houses—though they must not
be too far from the central-aid unit—be scattered among houses of nondisabled
people.

Coequality is the right to be accepted as equal by the other members of society
and the right to act accordingly. An important condition here is the already mentioned private income, but also having one's own house, of which one can dis-
pose under circumstances similar to those of others. This is realized by not
grouping the houses under a particular institution or foundation, but renting them
from a normal housing association, which is customary in the Netherlands, or
from a municipality, which takes care of building socialized housing. This initiative has led to permission from the government for the construction of 35
projects, a large number of which have already been completed. A positive evaluation may lead to a larger number (Prinsen, 1984). The projects hardly resemble
each other in design. They occur as single-family two-story houses and as apartment buildings. It should be mentioned that the GDN cluster housing as it has
been set up by the FOCUS foundation is no longer the only initiative in this field.
At present experiments are being carried out to provide around-the-clock care
and home care along different lines.

Adaptable and Visitable Ways of Building. With GDN cluster housing an optimum
situation has not yet been reached, for the use of a special facility is still necessary. Also, there are waiting lists, the need for permission, and the existence of
restrictions in the choice of residence and the location of the house. Moreover,
maintaining contacts can be limited because while people can receive visitors,
due to the inaccessibility of the other houses, they often cannot return the visits.
In recent years a new development has been started, namely, adaptable and visitable ways of building.

These concepts are applicable to houses under construction. Visitable building
means that a disabled person can pay a visit in a house without encountering architectural obstacles. *Geboden Toegang* describes such facilities. The most important criteria are widening of the hall, enlarging the toilet, and installing wider
doors.

Adaptable building means building houses in such a way that they can be
adapted for occupation by disabled persons. Adaptable houses meet all the requirements for visitable houses plus several additional conditions. The most far-

reaching of the 12 conditions listed in *Geboden Toegang* are a combined bath, shower, and toilet of sufficient size (about 4 m² [43 ft²]) with strong brick walls, and in houses where there is a second floor, the possibility for the installation of a lift. It is recommended to build all houses in a visitable way and all houses for the aged as well as a number of all types of new houses in an adaptable way.

The advantages of visitable and adaptable housing partly cancel the disadvantages mentioned under adapted housing and the GDN clusters. The fact that aging persons can, in case of infirmity, keep on living in their houses for a longer time is also mentioned as an important experiment. Some of the objections being raised against adaptable building are that it is too expensive and would result in too much nonfunctional space for nondisabled persons, and that the technical execution would be too difficult. In response to these objections a number of architects were invited in 1984 to present their designs at a symposium (Gelderse Council, 1984). Some of the conclusions were that adaptable and visitable housing is possible, technically as well as financially, in most houses, with little or no extra expense. In cooperation with the National Housing Board an attempt will be made to have 25 housing associations throughout the country realize 20 adaptable houses each. Figure 5.12 shows the floor plan for an adaptable single-family house which was included in the exhibition (Veen, 1984).

Adaptable building can be seen as a phase in the emancipation of disabled people. Just as was the case with GDN cluster housing, it serves the autonomy, the individuality, and coequality of disabled people. Adaptable building even goes beyond that, because the policy of separation or special treatment gives way to an inclusive policy. As indicated, inclusive policy means that under all public reg-

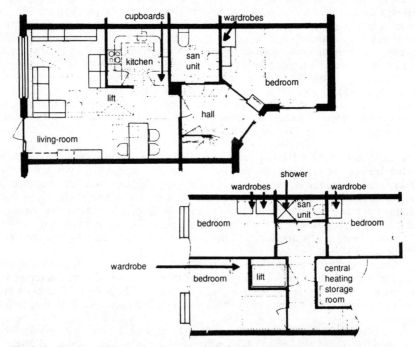

Fig. 5.12 Veen's and Kruynes's Adaptable single-family house. (*Veen and Kruyne, 1984.*)

ulations the facilities must be usable by all—including disabled people—to the same degree. This forestalls sometimes difficult and more expensive adaptations during construction, which moreover would harm the social position of the people concerned.

5.4 CONCLUSION

At first sight it may seem that with adaptable building and inclusive policy thinking, an ideal situation has been reached in the emancipation process of disabled people with regard to housing. This is not the case, however.

First, adaptable building applies only to housing that has yet to be built and to a negligible part of recently built houses. It does not offer a solution to the problem, except perhaps in the long run. Thus adaptation of houses will remain necessary. Besides, adaptable building is far from being common knowledge among public authorities, principals, and designers. Adaptable building is a technical, economic, organizational, and perhaps, even a mental concern of the participants in the building process. Adaptable building, on its own, does not solve the problem of housing for mentally and emotionally deficient people. However, there is more. Up until now housing for disabled people has not been looked at against the background of what we called phase 4 in our historical survey, the crisis in the welfare state. What has been accomplished in the past is now being threatened. The following concepts dominate the present era: economizing, deregulation, and decentralization.

1 Economizing

Government subsidies, benefits, and contributions are getting smaller, both in number and in amount. An example is the Enactment for Financial Support for Housing for the Disabled. Under this enactment a maximum amount has been established beyond which no further compensation is possible; then a personal contribution is required from the applicant. In view of the history of the welfare state, this is quite understandable. During the good times all kinds of facilities came about gradually, all of which are being reduced now. The disabled person can find himself or herself in a position where this economizing has a cumulatively negative effect on his or her financial position.

Another tendency in the economization is that a more careful check will be kept on the conditions that have to be fulfilled in order to obtain state support. This includes the need for better planning prior to starting new facilities, both for separate facilities and for the total package. Some facilities in the housing sector, such as GDN cluster housing, also experience delays because further inquiries into expenses and efficiency are deemed necessary.

2 Deregulation

Deregulation is the second concept that receives much attention. The term means a reduction in government instructions. In the field of housing, and subsidized housing in particular, these instructions are very detailed. In general this tendency is to be applauded because designers have been hampered severely in their creativity, and the process of obtaining building permits is time-consuming and therefore expensive and frustrating. When building for the disabled, the new tendency can be advantageous, but an important instrument is in danger of getting lost, namely, the possibility of establishing mandatory requirements with regard to distance, accessibility, and usefulness.

3 Decentralization

Decentralization is based on the thought that funds for social housing are transferred to the municipalities under less detailed conditions than before. At first sight this seems to offer opportunities for the disabled. This expectation will, however, not always come true. On the local level, the interest group of disabled people is rather small and the persons who can dedicate themselves to this are few. In addition, local expertise is often very limited. Among the disabled the future is viewed with concern. Therefore there is a search on for ways to make strategic use of the available expertise by way of regional, provincial, or even national cooperation.

From a general point of view, two tendencies can be discerned. One is a further emancipation, the other a regression to phase 0. The latter is dreaded by many. In conclusion, it is worth mentioning that the move toward the emancipation of disabled people in the design of public spaces, houses, and public buildings is a very general one. The tendency toward small-scale projects is rather evident. It emerges also from large institutions in the form of out-pavilions, annexes, socio-houses, and the like.

Thus the decentralization of central facilities such as kitchens, wash rooms, and maintenance is a likely development. The location of the projects is certainly important and is preferred near built-up areas rather than in the country. The location of adapted houses, socio-houses, and FOCUS projects near general and special facilities is an important subject. The grouping together of disabled people in a way that resembles hospitals and treatment centers should be avoided. Naturally, all housing and institutions should be accessible and usable by the disabled. Thus far this goal has seldom been achieved and is unlikely to be met in the present political climate.

5.5 CONDENSED REFERENCES/BIBLIOGRAPHY

Blonk 1984, *At Home in an Institution?*

Doorn 1978, *The Welfare State in Practice*

Diutemeyer 1981, *Encyclopedia of Social Work*

Gelderse Council 1984, *Symposium for Adapted Living and Adaptable Buildings*

Gennep 1985, *Remedial Education on Housing*

Goffman 1961, *Asylums*

Goffmans 1985, *Total Institutions*

Gouldner 1971, *The Coming Crisis of Western Sociology*

Guffens 1983, *Accessibility and Usability of Netherlands Railway Stations for Handi-*

Guffens 1985, *Evaluation of the District Project for Handicapped People in the Nether-*

Guffens 1988, *You Tend to Take It for Granted, Experiences of Handicapped People in*
Heek 1972, *Welfare State and Sociology*
Hout 1983, *Discharged Psychiatric Patients*
Ministry of Welfare 1984, *May I Come In...? Functional Model for Living for Physically*
National Organization of the Handicapped 1983, *Requirements for Access: Manual for*
Nolte 1983, *Suggestions for Saving Housing for the Handicapped*
Oranje 1984, *Overview of Adaptable Construction*
Prinsen 1984, *Evaluation of FOKUS Clusters*
Provinciale Stichting Gelderland 1982, *Guidelines for Research on Accessibility*
Provinciale Stichting Gelderland 1984, *Requirements for Accessibility, Entrance, and Use-*
Provinciale Stichting Limburg 1985, *Guidelines for Adaptable Housing*
Safe Traffic Netherlands 1982, *Accessibility, Entrance, and Usability*
Veen 1984, *The Adaptable One-Family House*
Voordt 1983, *Building for Everyone Including the Disabled*
World Health Organization 1980, *Classification of Impairments, Disabilities and Handi-*

6

Housing for the Elderly and the Disabled in Israel

Israel defies easy classification as a traditional, developing, or developed society. By virtue of the geographic region in which it lies and the particular composition of its population (comprising indigenous Jewish and Arab populations augmented by mass immigration from 104 countries following the establishment of the state in 1948), it contains components of all three.

It is a small country (21,500 km^2) with 4,467,700 inhabitants (end of 1988), 82% of them Jewish (Central Bureau of Statistics, 1988). It is largely an urban society with 90% of the population living in urban localities and having many characteristics of industrialized societies with regard to problems of health, disability, and aging. However, it also embodies many characteristics and values of traditional societies, and along reasonably well-developed health and welfare systems there are also kinship and family solidarity values (United Nations, 1982).

Mortality and morbidity rates show patterns prevalent in the Western world. Fertility (3.06) is higher than in all Western countries, except Ireland. Since the establishment of the state, infant mortality has decreased to 12 per 1000; life expectancy has risen and is now 74 years for Jewish men and 77 for Jewish women. (For non-Jews it is 72 for men and 74 for women.) At age 65 life expectancy averages 16 years for both ethnic groups. As a consequence of these trends, Israel has a younger age structure than most Western countries and a persistent increase in the population over 65, at present nearly 9% of the total population (Barnea, 1990; Kop and Factor, 1985).

The health-care system is based on voluntary health insurance, which covers 94% of the population, 83% of the insured subscribing to the General Sick Fund (GSF) of the General Federation of Labour and the rest to smaller sick funds. These funds provide all primary and most secondary ambulatory care. Hospital beds are owned and operated by the government (Ministry of Health), the GSF, and some voluntary health organizations. All hospitals (including psychiatric, geriatric, and nursing-care facilities) have defined catchment areas, irrespective of their ownership.

The government National Insurance Institute (NII) supports elderly and disabled through Social Security benefits and income supplements and, lately, through the long-term care insurance law for the elderly. The Ministry of Defense provides support for disabled veterans.

6.1 THE ELDERLY

1 Demographic Trends

The proportion of the over 65 population has risen very rapidly since the establishment of the state in 1948, from 3.5% of the total population to almost 9% in 1988 (10% for the Jewish and 3% for the non-Jewish population). This population comprises at present some 395,000 people, 369,000 Jews and 25,100 non-Jews. The rise in those over 75 has been even more dramatic, from 58,000 in 1970 to 130,000 in 1988, and is projected to reach 193,000 by 1995 (with those aged 80 and more to nearly double their numbers) (Central Bureau of Statistics, 1988). Women comprise a higher proportion of the elderly because of their longer life expectancy.

Two-thirds of the aged are married (81% of men and 41% of women). As age increases, this proportion decreases, and at age 75 only 75% of men and 33% of women are still married; in the above 80 age group 58% and 11%, respectively. There are more widows than widowers due mainly to the age gap between marriage partners. The proportion of those who never married or who divorced is very small (United Nations, 1982; Brookdale Institute of Gerontology, 1982).

2 Cultural Background and Socioeconomic Conditions

The educational status of the elderly still reflects the phenomenon of immigration: a high proportion is without any formal education (15% of men and 25% of women did not attend school). Particularly disadvantaged are those who came from Near Eastern or North African countries, who comprise 28% of the elderly population. Only 58% of Jews over 75 speak Hebrew. However, 70% of the literate aged are daily newspaper readers, 50% read at least one book monthly, and 80% regularly listen to radio and/or watch television (United Nations, 1982). The proportion of those with more functional literacy and with high-school diplomas among the aged is increasing as new cohorts are moving into this population.

Retirement is regulated by law (in the case of the Civil Service) or by collective labor agreements. The retirement age is set at 65 for men and 60 for women, with some deviations in hazardous occupations or for health reasons. In most cases it is mandatory and flexibility is limited, except for women who may stay until 65. Labor force participation for the aged is 16% (Brookdale Institute of Gerontology, 1982).

Work-related pensions and old-age pensions of the NII are the two fundamental components of economic maintenance of the elderly. Many of today's elderly are not eligible for work-related pensions as they have not had sufficient years of employment to earn pension rights, and among those who have had enough time, a considerable percentage have only minimum seniority, providing the lowest pension. For many elderly an NII old-age pension is the only, or major, source of income, and 40% of the recipients also receive supplementary benefits, an indication of the economic vulnerability of the elderly. Indeed, some data suggest that only 25 to 30% of the elderly are in an economically comfortable position.

The aged are primarily an urban presence, 92% of them living in urban localities. Of the urban aged, 70% are concentrated in the country's three largest cities—Tel-Aviv, Jerusalem, and Haifa—in which the proportion of older persons exceeds the national average (United Nations, 1982), probably not only due to the availability of services most commonly used by elderly, but also due to the migration of families with small children to the suburbs.

In 41% of aged households, elderly live with their spouses, 40% are one-person households, and 19% live with others, mainly their children; 29% of the elderly live alone in single-person households. Life on one's own is preferred by most of the elderly of Western background, whereas in other cultural groups old age spent in a household of a son or daughter is regarded part of normative expectation.

Generally, the aged live in uncrowded conditions, 80% in households with a density of two persons per room and 8% in densities of three persons per room. Approximately 70% own their apartments, 25% live in rented apartments, and 5% in housing owned by their children. However, much of the housing of the elderly is in inner cities, in old buildings.

3 Health

The main causes of death in elderly are ischemic heart disease, cerebrovascular disease, and neoplasms; the first two have decreased in both sexes, in the young old and the old old, during the last 15 years. Two-thirds of the elderly in the community are chronically ill, and of those, 45% have hypertension, 25% ischemic heart disease, 19% diabetes, 15% arthritis, and nearly 7% had a stroke; 25% have two of these conditions and 16% three or more. In addition, 25% have difficulty hearing, nearly 50% in seeing (Barnea, 1990).

The utilization of health-care services by the elderly as a group exceeds the national average: they constitute 9% of the population and consume 33% of the annual hospitalization days (with an average stay of 9.0 days, compared to 5.7 days for the younger population). They have contact with physicians 22 times a year (compared to 9 to 12 times among the total population) (Kop and Factor, 1985). All elderly have access to health services, either through their sick fund or through NII. Long-term institutional care is not included in the health insurance and is the concern of government agencies.

More than 95% of the elderly live in the community and only 4.5% in institutions. Of those living in the community, 9% are disabled in activities of daily living and 30% need some help in their household. There is an increase in dependency with age, but even at 85 only 17.6% of men and 11.1% of women are completely dependent on someone else (Kop and Factor, 1985).

During the last decade a comprehensive network of services in the community has been developed and at present more than 50 local authorities operate day-care centers for physically or mentally disabled elderly.

To assist elderly in staying in their own households as long as possible, the long-term care insurance law has been implemented since 1988. It provides long-term benefits (mainly services in kind) and is targeted toward elderly needing significant assistance in their daily personal care or supervision.

6.2 THE DISABLED

As in most countries surveyed in this volume, there are no accurate disability prevalence data, but from fragmentary information available it may be assumed that 10% of the general population (446,000 individuals) is disabled to some extent, and that 100,000 of these have severe or very severe disabilities, half of them predominantly physical and the other half with sensory or psychological impairments or mental retardation.

This is a heterogeneous population in all respects, such as sex, ethnic origin, and educational level. It is also heterogeneous in respect to the nature of the disability. Among the 50,000 physically disabled there are 13,000 with congenital defects (mainly cerebral palsy and spina bifida), 12,000 arthritics, 8000 stroke survivors, more than 2000 lower-leg amputees (mainly due to peripheral vascular disease), 3000 persons disabled because of heart disease, 2000 because of chronic respiratory conditions, 1500 sufferers from Parkinson's disease, and 1500 multiple sclerosis patients. Further to congenital, chronic, and geriatric conditions, two additional groups are prominent: 2500 severely disabled veterans and 7500 victims of road accidents, a major cause of death and disability. These two groups are composed of spinal-cord injured, amputees, and brain-damaged.

Medical services to the disabled are provided in the context of the country's pluralistic health-care system, mainly by the government, sick funds, and voluntary organizations.

The NII financially supports the chronically ill, the blind, the retarded, and the disabled from birth and work accidents (including housewives). At present it is paying disability benefits to 73,000 recipients (43,000 males, 30,000 females). The recipients are individuals who as the result of a physical, mental, or psychological limitation (from birth, illness, or accident) have a medical disability exceeding 70% and are unable to support themselves through work or occupation and do not earn a sum equivalent to 25% of the average wage, or their capacity to earn a living from work or occupation has been reduced by 50% or more. A housewife is entitled to a benefit if she has lost the ability to function in her household or her ability to function has been reduced by 50% or more.

6.3 HOUSING, GENERAL

The demand for adequate environment and housing has become one of the important issues of modern society. Environmental influences are of importance to all, particularly to disabled and elderly for whom their dwelling becomes the significant environmental area because of the limitation in their mobility. For them, their homes are more than shelter, and the adequacy of their housing environment is an essential ingredient of their overall health and life satisfaction. Improving the living and housing standards contributes significantly to the reduction of problems concerning the independence of the disabled and elderly, to an increased satisfaction with life, and to their ability to cope with daily tasks.

Israel is a country of immigration and soon after its establishment, it has been overwhelmed by waves of new immigrants who increased its population fivefold over a period of three decades. It was imperative to house the newcomers, and programs for mass housing were developed to cope with the growing demand. Priority has been given to the provision of shelter to newcomers and to rationalizing housing into economic and viable terms. It is not surprising, therefore, that the need to meet the special requirements of the elderly and disabled has emerged comparatively recently.

6.4   HOUSING FOR THE ELDERLY

As already mentioned, 4.5% of the elderly in Israel live in institutions, a rate similar to that of the United States. These include nursing and psychogeriatric long-term wards in geriatric facilities or hospitals for those elderly requiring constant medical surveillance and care, and nursing homes for those needing permanent assistance and care with only occasional medical intervention (including frail elderly). These two types of institutions are part of the medical establishment. There are also elderly who do not need constant care but are unable,or unwilling, to run an independent household, and are housed in homes for the aged, residential homes, or pensioners' homes of various types, where they are fully provided for and nursed when temporarily ill (Beer and Factor, 1989). These institutional settings are not discussed in this chapter.

The majority of the elderly are interested in and capable of living in a household of their own and do so in regular apartments, sometimes with minor adjustments or the need for some help provided by community services. Others are accommodated in a group of self-contained apartments, laid out and equipped with a specific view to the needs of elderly people, enabling them to continue their own households as long as possible. These arrangements are similar to those called hostels (see Chapter 7) in Singapore and in other countries. They are also somewhat akin to "housing for the elderly" in the United States. In Israel they are named "sheltered housing" or "assisted independent living group housing." This type of housing is the focus of this chapter.

1   Development of Sheltered Housing

At the end of 1986 there were 66 sheltered housing schemes for the elderly with 6020 apartments. Almost 60% of the units belonged to voluntary nonprofit organizations, 10% to the private for-profit sector, and the remaining 30% to the government-supported public housing agencies (referred to as the public sector) with the various organizational auspices serving different target populations (Shtarkshall, 1985).

Voluntary nonprofit organizations were the forerunners in the development of special housing programs for the elderly. They began their programs in the mid-1950s, many of them initially meant for homeless senior immigrants to the country, mainly Holocaust survivors without families. The emphasis, thus, was on shelter as such. These projects served selective groups, mainly according to country of origin or union affiliation.

Eshel (Association for Planning and Developing Services for the Elderly in Israel), supported jointly by the American Jewish Joint Distribution Committee and the Israeli government, participated in the initial planning as well as operation of almost all new projects supported by the government during the last decade. Eshel's initiative introduced new approaches in physical planning as well as in coordination between public housing agencies and social services, as in Lod, Gilo (Jerusalem), Kiryat Gat, and Acre (Shtarkshall, 1987).

The early and middle 1980s saw an expansion in the supply of sheltered housing units primarily by the government sector, accounting for more than half of the growth. There was also an emergence of the private for-profit sector. Its share is relatively small, but it may become the fastest growing sector in the 1990s, serving the most affluent part of the elderly population. The voluntary sector, on the other hand, has been reduced from almost 85% in the late 1970s to almost half in the late 1980s; it is at present reexamining its policy and future customers.

At the same time, and in addition to the development of new sheltered housing, an improvement of the physical standards of old apartments inhabited by the elderly, as well as an upgrading of supportive services, has taken place. This was a response to aging in place and the rising standard of living of the general population; in some multistory buildings, erected in the late 1950s or 1960s without elevators, the latter have since been installed, and in almost all buildings emergency call systems and other services were introduced on site or on a visiting basis. This explosion of retrofitting activity parallels developments in Singapore. All new constructions built in the 1980s are oriented toward the future needs of aging in place. Government-supported projects are required to comply with new design guidelines (developed in cooperation with Eshel), specifying adaptations of all apartments and public spaces to wheelchairs, emergency call systems, safety measures, and provisions for clubs and social activities (including communal kitchens), as well as office and apartment on site for the house mother.

It is worth mentioning that between 1981 and 1987, while the ratio of sheltered housing units per 1000 elderly increased from 12 to 16.7, the ratio of beds in old-age homes and similar residential institutions dropped from 20.7 to 19.6, possibly implying a clear preference in those elderly interested in company and security to look for housing arrangements rather than for institutional settings, as they had a decade earlier (Beer and Factor, 1989).

2 Variations in Sheltered Housing Schemes

There ia a wide variety in the availability and amount of services, mode of delivery, and physical design among various schemes of sheltered housing. In all, residents are encouraged to use their own furniture, utensils, and other personal belongings, to arrange them according to their own tastes (with due attention to safety and security), and to run their own households.

Regular housing projects in Israel lack the function of an on-the-premises manager or concierge. This function, called house mother, is essential for the definition of a housing project as a sheltered one and exists in all schemes. The house mother (or the warden in British terminology) plays a key role: she serves as a "friendly neighbor," monitoring residents' needs and their overall well-being. In most cases the house mother lives on site. An emergency call system and coordination of support in case of need are, together with the house mother, part of the minimum service provided. Other services may be available on an optional basis, either on site or visiting from the community, and include a social activities center, hot meals option (for those in need or for all residents), cleaning, maintenance, assistance in personal care, shopping, and nurse or physician attendance.

Staff operating within the scheme may consist of a director, a house mother (living on the premises), a nurse, and maintenance personnel, but could also be minimal (house mother only) and rely on community visiting services.

The size varies from small projects (20 to 40 units) to the largest one (800 units). In general, government projects are usually smaller (up to 100) and private ones larger (150 to 350 units). The voluntary sector operates on smaller scales (30 to 120 units) except Mishan, which runs large-size projects.

Financial Arrangement. Payment is generally not related to the level of services offered by the various schemes. There is usually a basic rent that covers a service package, with additional services financed through separate payments. An entrance fee is required in most schemes, not refundable if the resident spends more than 4 years with the housing project. Some schemes also offer a shared ownership option. Thus payments may vary from only a subsidized rent of Israeli $20 monthly to $180,000 for the purchase of a lease (in addition to a monthly rent). In government-sponsored programs, all payments are based on eligibility criteria, with a monthly rent and no entrance fee.

Care and Criteria for Admission. Most sheltered housing projects practice age segregation; only in later years have some schemes attempted integration with other age groups (see Gilo and Kiryat Gat in the following section).

Most projects are free-standing, the larger ones usually high-rise construction. Only 15% (usually the larger projects, of more than 180 units, including also almost all new private projects) are located adjacent to a nursing unit or include one next to the housing scheme. Projects unconnected to a nursing unit ensure an institutional option—when needed—under the auspices of the same agency but on another site, or may assist the family in locating a suitable institution. In these cases it is, however, the responsibility of the family or the resident to take care of the arrangements. In government projects continuous care is not guaranteed, but community social services identify and assist to provide suitable institutional placement when required, but sometimes after some waiting.

Admission priority criteria exist in all programs since demand for sheltered housing usually exceeds supply. Voluntary organizations have admission criteria according to country of origin, language, trade union membership, or date of immigration (for newcomers). Government-sponsored programs give preference to needy elderly. In the private market the rate of payment defines the target population.

All schemes address, at the entrance point, independent elderly.

3 Innovative Housing Schemes of the 1980s

In the 1980s the government sector was the most expansive and innovative, and four of its schemes will be described to illustrate the new trends (Lod, Gilo, Kiryat Gat, and Acre). The voluntary sector established recently a unique and interesting project (Nofim), which will also be described, as well as an elegant project of the private sector (Mediterranean Towers) apt to become a milestone.

Lod—Public Sheltered Housing. This is a project typical of those built in the 1980s by the government according to new guidelines developed in conjunction with Eshel, which emphasizes coordination of housing with services. It is a newly constructed, eight-story building with 48 apartments of two small rooms each (40 m² [130 ft²]), all designed for wheelchair-bound elderly who are able to walk a few steps. All public areas are barrier-free environments. The target population is low-income and needy elderly. A house mother lives on the premises and a 24-hr emergency call system is in operation. A social and recreational club on the ground floor caters to all residents and also admits 100 elderly from the community. Homemaking, personal care, hot meals, and counseling are available when need is recognized. They are provided by community visiting services, coordinated by a community social worker who also acts as supervisor of the project. A board of directors includes representatives of the agencies that cooperate in the project (government housing agency, community social services, local elderly association, Eshel), establishing a coordinated mode of operation as developed by Eshel.

Gilo—Age-Integrated Sheltered Housing.   This innovative, intergenerational demonstration project (Fig. 6.1) is aimed at studying new options for housing the elderly and evaluating whether age integration is an effective and viable alternative. It is a joint venture of Eshel and the Brookdale Foundation J.D.C. within a government housing construction in Gilo, a new neighborhood in Jerusalem.

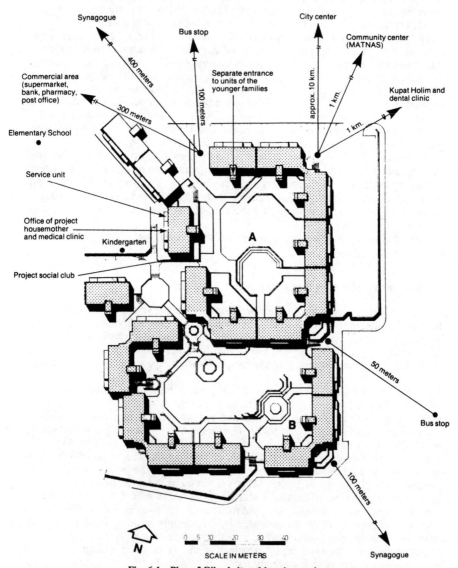

Fig. 6.1   Plan of Gilo sheltered housing project.

In the 1960s attempts in Israel to integrate special housing for the elderly in regular public apartment buildings had not been successful. A similar experience in the United States was described as "a lethal mix of problem young people and vulnerable elderly" (Teaff and Lawton, 1987). Following these experiences, the Gilo project was planned and implemented meticulously.

The project consists of 51 apartments designed for the elderly, which are incorporated in the ground-floor level of several regular four-story buildings arranged around two large, open courtyards. It includes a house mother on site, an emergency call and supportive services system, and a club, similar to the organization and services described in Lod, with the addition of a visiting physician and nurse twice a week because of the distance from the community primary clinic.

The project has succeeded beyond expectations (Bendel and King, 1985). Its benefits outweigh some negative aspects (such as occasional noise) and contribute favorably to the quality of life of the elderly involved, in the views of both the elderly and the young residents of the buildings. Factors thought to have contributed to the success include the physical design and planning, integration of the elderly with socioeconomically stable younger persons (apartment owners), services offered, and devotion of the staff. All these cause the project to be so different from the experiences in the 1960s.

Kiryat Gat—Regular Public Housing Adapted for the Elderly. In regular public housing the phenomenon of aging in place occurs. Buildings constructed in the 1950s and early 1960s to cope with mass immigration and the establishment of new towns have small apartments and are not attractive for large, young families. Thus the combination of low housing mobility and aging in place creates naturally occurring clusters of communities of elderly with special needs. Public housing agencies, Eshel, and other organizations joined to help the elderly remain in their natural environment, physically upgrade the buildings, and create a new stock of sheltered apartments for other elderly.

Kiryat Gat was one of the first models of such a venture. The project includes four public housing buildings located next to several shops, clinics, and public transportation. The buildings contain 120 apartments, in which 60% of the dwellers are elderly with low incomes and other needs requiring support. These buildings were adapted into sheltered housing, a process which entailed:

Improving the physical environment: upgrading apartments, staircases, entrances, and outdoor spaces

Introducing a supportive system of services: house mother, emergency call system, and social and recreational club to cater to residents as well as elderly from the community (see Lod)

Replacement policy: to ensure future stock for the elderly, all apartments on the first two floors were reserved for elderly, the top floors to be inhabited by screened nonelderly

This project, as well as similar others, were developed and implemented based on the positive experience gained in the Gilo project, following the principle of controlled age group integration. One of the versions of such a project, in Nazareth, includes a care unit for eight elderly, meant as respite or holiday admission for their families.

Acre—Sheltered Housing Adjacent to a Regional Home for the Aged.   In 1975 a typical Eshel home for the aged was built in Acre to serve all elderly in the northwestern part of the country. The institution is operated by a voluntary nonprofit organization (regional Eshel association) and is public-oriented. It is a continuous-care institution of 150 beds, consisting of 36 beds for the well aged, 26 beds for frail and infirm elderly, 68 beds for the nursing unit, and 20 beds for the mentally infirm. It contains all necessary medical, social, and recreational facilities (including medical and dental services, occupational and physiotherapy, auditorium, library, and synagogue) and a day center which serves also those elderly who continue living in their homes but utilize the facilities of the institution.

Four years ago a new high-rise sheltered housing building of 84 apartments was erected adjacent to the old-age home, similar in sponsorship and operation to the Lod model.

Nofim (Jerusalem)—Sheltered Housing.   Established by a voluntary nonprofit cooperative, it consists of 153 elegant apartments of one-and-a-half to three-and-a-half rooms, luxurious community facilities with spacious activity room and auditorium, restaurant and snack bar, health clinic, occupational and physical therapy, and more. It also contains a 15-bed nursing unit.

The project is advertised as "for those who have reached retirement age but are not ready to retire from community activity and social life and desire to continue and independent life style."

The innovative aspect of this project is not only the high physical standards and richness of services, but rather the self-government by the residents. The project was initiated by a group of senior citizens with the sponsorship of the Association of Americans and Canadians in Israel. The ownership structure is also unique: mandatory redeemable investment in the amount related to the relative share of the construction cost of the apartment—in other words, "buying in."

Mediterranean Towers—Private Sheltered Housing.   This is the most luxurious project in the country (Fig. 6.2). It is located on the coast in Bat Yam and consists, in its first stage, of a high-rise building of 177 apartments. The second stage is now under construction and will have 150 additional apartments and a nursing wing of 50 beds. All apartments are equipped for a full, independent household with kitchen and bathroom. Lavish public grounds, swimming pool, health center, clinic, bank, and supermarket are part of the development. There are a nurse, security services, as well as a variety of optional services such as personal care, household help, and restaurant.

The project is conceived for continuous care. Entrance is either by refundable leasing or, for half that price, a nonrefundable entrance fee. It was established by Mishkenot Clal Investment Group, one of the larger private companies in the country. Similar projects are being developed in other parts of the country, in a variety of sizes and costing, all of them having as target population the higher-income affluent elderly.

6.5   HOUSING FOR THE DISABLED

The ultimate goal of rehabilitation of younger disabled is resettlement in the community and integration into working life similar to the retardment policy of the Netherlands (Chapter 5) and deinstitutionalization policies in the United States and elsewhere. Adequate and easily accessible housing plays an important role in the achievement of these goals. This section does not report on institutional settings and opportunities for the disabled, but rather focuses on appropriate housing for those disabled who are capable and willing to resume a productive and at least partly independent life in the community.

For these disabled, their dwelling is not their only essential significant environment. Stairs or unsuitable elevators, absence of ramps, inadequate and inaccessible parking, and other physical obstacles do not allow the disabled to function either independently or with minimal help in leaving the accommodation or in coming back to it. The disabled are thus hindered in pursuing an active life outside it except where, thanks to statutory regulations, many and varied provisions at least in public places have been made to provide the disabled better and easier accessibility. Dependence on assistance from family members while functioning within an unadapted residence is also considerable, and creates physical an emotional stress for both the disabled and their family members. Thus there is certainly a need to provide housing in which the disabled person would be able to control, intellectually and physically, his or her destiny (Eldar and Solzi, 1986).

Unfortunately there is no agency or organization—government-sponsored, voluntary, or private—which plans and initiates housing projects for the disabled, an activity that does exist in the case of the elderly. This is probably due to the fact that the population of physically disabled in need of special housing is not as large as the population of the elderly, nor projected to increase at such a pace. In addition, the heterogeneity of this population may create difficulties in planning a project which would address the differing requirements of all subpopulations. Furthermore, experience has shown that disabled persons do not like to live clustered with other handicapped individuals and prefer to reside dispersed, in loca-

Fig. 6.2 Mediterranean Tower at Bat Yam.

tions in which they can find suitable employment, their spouses interesting occupations or other activities, and their children adequate schooling. Thus the solution of the housing problems for the disabled is, in general, left to the party responsible for the social rehabilitation of the individual disabled, which will depend on the cause and circumstances of the illness or injury that resulted in the disability.

The Ministry of Defense is responsible for disabled veterans. In the past it has purchased or rented apartments and houses, adapted them individually to the needs of the veterans, and rented them to the veterans at very low rates. The disadvantage of this arrangement was that the veteran had to reside in a location in which the ministry happened to have available accommodation, and not where he or she wanted to live and could find a suitable occupation. Furthermore, this arrangement sometimes resulted in several disabled veterans living in one block or neighborhood, with a demoralizing effect. Since the late 1970s, therefore, the ministry asks the disabled veterans and families to look for possible suitable accommodation in locations of their preference, and assists them financially—with a grant and a loan—to purchase or rent it and perform all adaptations needed. This enables disabled veterans to live where they want and to decide what their homes should look like. If needed, the ministry provides services to severely disabled who live in their own housing (such as escort, transport, personal help) and assists them in studies, vocational rehabilitation, and job placement.

For those disabled in road accidents, the insurance company usually takes care of the financial arrangements of exchanging the housing in which the disabled resided prior to disability, or purchasing or renting accommodations and adapting them to the needs and functional ability of their disabled clients. The NII is similarly responsible for work accident victims and those civilians disabled by inimical action, usually acts of terrorism.

Others, disabled from birth or following an illness, are less generously provided for. Physically disabled, limited by at least 80% in their mobility, are entitled to an adapted apartment by the Ministry of Housing, rented through one of its daughter organizations which either build designed apartments within their housing projects or adapt them according to requirements of the individual disabled. The most active of these organizations is the Jerusalem-based Prazot, the municipal housing agency which during the last 15 years has adapted 150 apartments for the disabled.

Persons who were disabled following a stroke or an amputation (mostly elderly) obtain grants from the Ministry of Health to perform adaptations in their apartments.

Mentally retarded are cared for by a voluntary association (Akim) subsidized by the government, usually in sheltered housing with housekeeper, teachers, and other staff. Psychologically disabled in need of a therapeutic community for resocialization live in dwellings (usually shared apartments), provided and staffed by the Richmond Fellowship, an international organization with a branch in Israel, or by some psychiatric hospitals following their patients' discharge.

6.6   THE RURAL ENVIRONMENT

As mentioned, the aged are primarily an urban phenomenon and this chapter focused on those living in urban localities. As an addendum, though, it is appropriate to mention elderly who live in rural areas (10% of the aged population) where a mixture of traditional villages exists along with planned modern communities of two types unique to Israel, the moshav and the kibbutz.

1 The Rural Arab Elderly

The non-Jewish population of elderly consists of only some 25,000 individuals who live in towns (Nazareth, Shfaram, and Acre) or in traditional villages. Of the village elderly, 28% are over 80 (versus 22% of the total non-Jewish elderly and 15% of the Jewish elderly), and 82% receive NII income supplements (since, being ex-farmers, they are not entitled to work-related pensions).

A study of a representative sample of villages showed that 60% of the elderly live with their children in multigenerational households, only 18% of these with a married child and most of them with single children, a high proportion of the latter with unmarried daughters aged 28 and over (Weihl et al., 1986). The majority of dwellings of these multigenerational households are modern stone or concrete structures in adequate physical condition with toilets, showers, kitchens, electricity, and running water. There are, however, no special adaptations to specific requirements of elderly (or disabled) except in a few cases, individually designed and implemented.

Of rural elderly, 40% live in monogenerational households (21% alone, 19% with their spouses) in older buildings with deficiencies inherent to this type of dwelling. However, many of these elderly make use of the facilities or services available in adjacent or nearby children's homes.

Thus it would seem that in spite of the socioeconomic changes of the past decade from a traditional to a modern type of society, family ties in the Arab rural society remain extensive and strong and that the changes have not affected unfavorably the degree of attention paid to the needs of elderly, compensating for some deficiencies in their housing.

2 The Moshav

The moshav is a cooperative village in which the purchase of agricultural equipment and the marketing of produce are shared, but most of the production and consumption are private. Aged settlers in the moshav are more dependent economically on others, mainly the family group, because the moshav does not provide substitute light employment for the heavy agricultural work which the aged performed in the past.

Most households are multigenerational, and dwellings are modern and contain the necessary facilities. Adaptations, if at all, were designed and implemented only according to individual needs.

Being small, the moshavim (plural) were unable to establish services of their own, but lately a network of services for elderly began to develop, based on the moshav itself and on regional health, day care, and occupational centers.

3 The Kibbutz

The kibbutz is a voluntary collective in which production as well as consumption are shared, all members participate in decisions, and life is based on social egalitarianism and mutual responsibility.

Aging in the kibbutzim (plural) is a relatively new phenomenon, but its rate is even greater than in the general population. The percentage of aged over 65 increased from 2.5% in 1961 to 10% in 1988 (Yehudai, 1985). The kibbutz now faces the aging of a whole generation of its founders. It has developed several ways and means of caring for its elderly, such as gradual retirement and a flexible work policy, enabling the elderly to move toward a less demanding role and a progressive reduction in work hours, sheltered workshops (with option for individual schedules even at night), and a well-coordinated supportive network of services. In the sphere of special housing, three levels of living arrangements were defined.

Adjusted apartments, designed to meet special needs of the elderly. They are located near to the center of the kibbutz where all communal facilities are (central dining hall, library, social and cultural clubs), enabling even the disabled to continue living in their own households. These apartments have improved accessibility and some internal adaptations.

Sheltered apartments, for those needing some assistance in activities of daily living. These apartments are barrier-free, fully adapted, and appropriately equipped and are located within a "nursing home complex" (in kibbutz terminology, the care center), enabling their residents to be supported by the services of the care center but within their own apartments. There are usually two such apartments for every 40 kibbutz members over the age of 65.

Nursing homes, for those in need of continuous nursing and medical care, in addition to assistance. These are situated in the care centers, adjacent to the clinic and treatment facilities, and serve also for the care of young kibbutz members when temporarily ill and in need of bed rest. Two beds are planned for 40 members over the age of 65 and an additional two beds for young members.

However, in some kibbutzim the increasing aging with the growing need for nursing care, as well as economic constraints, have created a situation in which the nursing complex of the care center is expanding and no new additional sheltered apartments are being built. These kibbutzim focus on adapting regular housing to the needs of elderly, providing their inhabitants with emergency call systems and special means for transportation.

6.7 CONDENSED REFERENCES/BIBLIOGRAPHY

Barnea 1990, *Aging and Development of Health Services for the Elderly in Israel*

Beer 1989, *Long-Term Care Institutions and Sheltered Housing: The Situation in 1987*

Bendel 1985, *A Model of Community, Age Integrated Living for the Elderly*

Brookdale Institute of Gerontology 1982, *Aging in Israel*

Central Bureau of Statistics 1988, *Statistical Abstract of Israel*

Eldar 1986, *From Dependent to Independent Living*

Habib 1987, *The Needs of Disabled Elderly in the Community at Present and in Coming*

Kop 1985, *Changing Characteristics of the Israeli Population and the Utilization*

Shtarkshall 1985, *Sheltered Housing for the Economically Disadvantaged Elderly*

Shtarkshall 1987, *Sheltered Housing for the Elderly in Israel—Development over the Past*

Teaff 1978, *Impact of Age Integration on the Well-Being of Elderly Tenants in Public*

United Nations 1982, *Aging in Israel*
Weihl 1986, *Living Conditions and Family Life in the Rural Arab Elderly in Israel*
Yehudai 1985, *Needs of the Elderly Population in the Kibbutz*

7

Design
for the Disabled
and the Elderly
in Singapore

Singapore is currently entering a phase where diverse issues relevant to its future development have been raised and discussed nationwide. These have subsequently been compiled into an "agenda for action," which the government plans to implement as part of the nation's building program over the next decade and beyond. Among the items included in the agenda is concern for the needs of the disabled population in Singapore.

7.1 BACKGROUND

As the country grows in maturity, there has been a gradual change in the attitudes toward disability. The underlying philosophy which Singapore adopts is that the disabled should be treated as equal members of society. As such, they ought to be accorded equal opportunities for developing and expressing their physical, mental, social, and economic capabilities to the fullest.

In the past the community's response to the disabled population was either to institutionalize or to put the onus for care on the disabled person's family. However, a wider sense of responsibility is becoming more discernible. Agencies such as the Community Chest of Singapore, which implements the SHARE program for charity cooperation, promulgate awareness, empathy training, and the integration of the disabled into the community, while professional bodies work toward effective provisions of facilities.

As yet, the disabled of Singapore are not particularly vocal as a group nor very conspicuous individually, since mobility is still quite limited and habitual reliance on family support has tended to discourage independence.

It is a commonly held belief that disabled persons in Asia do not wish to go out very often; but the situation is liable to change as increased opportunities and awareness through communication generate an increase in expectation. An aging but relatively established generation will expect to enjoy continued mobility and lifestyle as before despite increasing physical impairment (Harrison, 1988). It is also recognized that the physical and attitudinal environment largely determines how effectively a disabled person can cope with his or her impairment.

7.2 DEMOGRAPHIC DATA

Based on the United Nations estimate, one in 10 persons throughout the world suffers from some kind of disability. However, the definition used is wide and includes even alcoholics and drug addicts. This may not be an entirely appropriate basis for estimating the size of the disabled population in Singapore.

So far, there has been no comprehensive survey on the number of disabled persons in Singapore. The Ministry of Community Development maintains the computerized Central Registry of Disabled People (CRDP). It records the personal particulars and status of the disabled, such as mobility and the ability to perform certain activities of daily living. Only persons with permanent disabilities are registered with the ministry. The total number of registered disabled persons in Singapore and the distribution according to categories of disability are given in Table 7.1. When these figures are compared to those of Japan, the United States, or Canada, statistics indicate that the percentage of disabled persons in Singapore is very small indeed. It must, however, be noted again that classification criteria do vary internationally. Furthermore, since there have not been any strong incentives for registration, the figures may not be representative of the actual status. It was suggested that a more realistic estimate might be 67,000 people who could benefit from improvements in the built environment (Singapore Institute of Architects, 1979/80). In addition, the number of elderly persons aged 60 and above is approximately 200,000 and is projected to reach 332,390, or 11% of the total population, by the year 2000.

7.3 DEFINITION OF THE DISABLED

The generally accepted definition of disability in Singapore is as follows (Ministry of Social Affairs, 1983):

> People with disability are those whose prospects of securing, retaining places and advancing in educational and training institutions, employment and recreation as equal members of the community are substantially reduced as a result of physical or mental impairment.

This definition encompasses the World Health Organization's interpretation of disability.

To those who are more concerned with the aspects pertaining to the built environment, the *Design Guidelines on Accessibility for the Disabled in Buildings* published by the Development and Building Control Branch, Singapore Public Works Department (Ministry of National Development, 1985), states that:

The disabled are those people who, as a consequence of physical disability or impairment, may be restricted or inconvenienced in their use of buildings because of:

(i) The presence of physical barriers, such as steps or doors which are too narrow for wheelchairs

(ii) The lack of suitable facilities such as ramps, elevators, staircases, and handrails

(iii) The absence of suitable facilities such a toilets, telephones, and suitable furniture

In relation to the physical environment, disabled people may be divided into:

1. Ambulant disabled
2. Wheelchair-bound
3. Sensory disabled
4. Temporary disabled

Ambulatory disabled are those who are able, either with or without personal assistance, to walk on level ground and negotiate suitable graded steps provided that convenient handrails are available.

Wheelchair-bound are those people who are unable to walk, either with or

Table 7.1   Distribution of disabled people by age group, sex, and nature of disability as of July 11, 1988

Age, years	Intellectual			Hearing			Skelemusculo		
	Persons	M	F	Persons	M	F	Persons	M	F
0–2	25	11	14	4	3	1	2	1	1
3–5	117	73	44	53	29	24	1	0	1
6–12	1153	695	458	257	125	132	1	1	0
13–17	847	492	355	211	111	100	4	1	3
18–21	564	339	225	256	144	112	13	8	5
22–24	567	330	237	370	201	169	31	23	8
25–29	676	393	283	297	176	121	207	130	77
30–34	421	248	173	368	216	152	296	200	96
35–39	180	110	70	252	140	112	277	196	81
40–44	58	36	22	157	92	65	229	151	78
45–49	29	15	14	121	72	49	119	94	25
50–54	18	14	4	82	48	34	85	69	16
55–59	14	10	4	88	59	29	68	54	14
60–64	6	5	1	104	65	39	46	40	6
65–69	2	2	0	78	47	31	22	18	4
70–74	1	1	0	92	51	41	20	19	1
75–79	0	0	0	84	54	30	10	9	1
80+	0	0	0	105	56	49	12	10	2
Total	4678	2774	1904	2979	1689	1290	1443	1024	419
Percent		37.5			23.9			11.6	

without assistance, and who, except when using mechanized transport, depend on a wheelchair for mobility.

Sensory-disabled people are those who, as a consequence of partially or totally impaired sight or hearing, may be restricted or inconvenienced in their use of buildings because of lack of suitable facilities.

Contrary to the practice in some other countries, manipulatory disabilities are not a special category and would probably be counted as ambulatory disabled in Singapore. It is important to note that these categorizations are not mutually exclusive. Many, especially the elderly, may be sensory disabled as well as wheelchair-bound.

Temporary disabled people include those who are sick or victims of an accident. Expectant mothers can be included in this category.

Finally, there are those whose disabilities are so profound that they are in need of constant attention and perhaps fully institutionalized care. The design needs of such cases are very specialized and therefore lie beyond the scope of this chapter and, in fact, this volume.

Table 7.1 Distribution of disabled people by age group, sex, and nature of disability as of July 1, 1988 (*Continued*)

Age, years	Visual			Psychiatric			Neuromuscular		
	Persons	M	F	Persons	M	F	Persons	M	F
0-2	5	1	4	0	0	0	3	3	0
3–5	9	3	6	0	0	0	13	7	6
6–12	59	33	26	0	0	0	129	80	49
13–17	49	23	26	0	0	0	152	81	71
18–21	64	33	31	3	2	1	106	63	43
22–24	31	23	8	2	2	0	81	48	33
25–29	89	55	34	45	31	14	132	79	53
30–34	65	34	31	94	74	20	116	73	43
35–39	95	63	32	148	110	38	83	54	29
40–44	77	57	20	136	100	36	34	26	8
45–49	76	52	24	115	81	34	13	12	1
50–54	76	53	23	119	78	41	12	8	4
55–59	79	44	35	105	62	43	15	11	4
60–64	80	54	26	74	44	30	3	1	2
65–69	99	63	36	20	17	3	7	5	2
70–74	108	60	48	14	11	3	4	2	2
75–79	63	34	29	15	11	4	1	1	0
80+	85	37	48	9	6	3	1	0	1
Total	1209	722	487	899	629	270	905	554	351
Percent		9.7			7.2			7.3	

7.4 ADMINISTRATIVE STRUCTURE

The Ministry of Community Development in Singapore is the main body responsible for administering the formulation and implementation of policies and provisions related to the disabled. The objective is to create, with the support of other concerned ministries, an environment imbued with supportive facilities which is conducive for disabled people to develop their physical, mental, and social capabilities to the fullest extent. To achieve this objective, the Advisory Council on the Disabled was established in April 1988 under the purview of the Ministry of Community Development. The general terms of reference of the Advisory Council are:

1. To identify and examine the problems and needs of the disabled people

Age, years	Multiple disabilties			Others			Total		
	Persons	M	F	Persons	M	F	Persons	M	F
0–2	2	1	1	0	0	0	41 0.3%	20	21
3–5	37	22	15	2	0	2	232 1.9%	134	98
6–12	63	31	32	0	0	0	1662 13.3%	965	697
13–17	31	23	8	0	0	0	1294 10.4%	731	563
18–21	15	9	6	0	0	0	1021 8.2%	598	423
22–24	16	12	4	1	1	0	1099 8.8%	640	459
25–29	36	27	9	0	0	0	1482 11.9%	891	591
30–34	33	21	12	1	1	0	1394 11.2%	867	527
35–39	30	17	13	1	1	0	1066 8.6%	691	375
40–44	14	9	5	1	1	0	706 5.7%	472	234
45–49	14	10	4	1	1	0	488 3.9%	337	151
50–54	15	7	8	1	1	0	408 3.3%	278	130
55–59	13	6	7	1	1	0	383 3.1%	247	136
60–64	7	7	0	1	1	0	321 2.6%	217	104
65–69	2	1	1	1	1	0	231 1.8%	154	77
70–74	1	1	0	0	0	0	240 1.9%	145	95
75–79	2	2	0	0	0	0	175 1.4%	111	64
80+	3	3	0	0	0	0	215 1.7%	112	103
Total Percent	334	209 2.7	125	11	9 0.1	2	12458	7610 0.0	4848

2. To review the existing policies, programs, and services for the disabled

3. To recommend policies and a plan of action that will enable their greater participation and integration into society.

Three committees were subsequently formed under the Advisory Council to study specific areas of concern:

1. Education and training
2. Employment, accessibility, and transportation
3. Community involvement and residential care

Of these, accessibility and transportation merit the attention of architects and others involved in facilitating the integration of disabled people into the built environment by offering greater independence to those who have so far found barriers that prevent them from achieving this. In fact, the committee responsible for these aspects has just completed a report on the employment, accessibility, and transportation for disabled people (Advisory Council on the Disabled, 1988).

It is noteworthy, however, that much effort has been expended previously in the development of educational programs for the disabled. The ministry has been working closely with the Council of Social Services and its affiliates with the view to upgrading educational, training, and employment opportunities for disabled people.

The Singapore Council of Social Services is the national coordinating body for voluntary social services provided by some 168 of its affiliates. Its main objectives are to:

1. Give consultation to affiliates
2. Make recommendations to the government
3. Identify service gaps and pioneer programs to fill these gaps
4. Promote volunteerism through the Voluntary Action and Development Centre

The Council pioneered two new programs for the disabled in 1987, the Margaret Drive Special School for multiple-handicapped children and the Hostel for the Disabled. It has also set up a job placement center to help the disabled find employment in the open market. The centre also runs a production workshop.

The government is of the view that such specialized education should be provided for by voluntary welfare organizations with assistance from the Ministry of Education in terms of specialized teachers' training and the offer of financial grants, which currently amounts to S$2000.00 per pupil enrolled. Seven voluntary organizations currently provide education programs for the disabled, but only four have come under the grant scheme. These are:

1. *Under the grant scheme:* The Spastic Children's Association, the Canossian School for the Hearing Impaired, the Margaret Drive Special School, and the Movement for the Intellectually Disabled of Singapore (MINDS)

2. *Not under the grant scheme:* The Singapore Association for the Deaf, the Singapore Association of the Visually Handicapped, and the Association for the Educationally Subnormal Children.

7.5 PLANNING CONCEPT OF ACCESSIBILITY AND MOBILITY

Accessibility and mobility are two inseparable aspects related to designing for the disabled. Since these concepts have been discussed in more detail in other chapters, we shall focus attention here on specific local approaches that vary from those of other countries considered in this Monograph.

A truly barrier-free environment should consist of three distinct but interrelated components, namely, the private domain (the home and its immediate surroundings), the public domain (recreational, social, and commercial activities), and the linkage between them (Fig. 7.1). Within the realm of the private domain development, the Housing and Development Board (HDB) in Singapore, a statutory body under the auspices of the Ministry of National Development, plays a vital role and probably has the widest impact on current and future progress in providing barrier-free access for the disabled population. This unique local situation warrants further detailed discussion.

7.6 MASS HOUSING DEVELOPMENT IN SINGAPORE

Singapore is a small island nation with a total area of only 614 km^2 (380 mi^2). Land is therefore always at a premium for any building development, and this has strongly influenced the initial decision to develop high-rise, high-density housing. Its success is indeed an achievement unparalleled in any other country in the world. This has been widely acclaimed and is well documented (Lam, 1988).

The HDB is the sole national authority responsible for physical planning and implementing public housing development in Singapore. Today over 85% of the total population of 2.5 million lives in housing produced by the HDB, of which some 78% of the units has been purchased by the occupiers. One important fact, which can be attributed to the success of high-rise, high-density living, is that the development is conceived as an integral part of an established master plan for New Town development. This point is most relevant to any discussion on the provision of barrier-free access for the disabled within a community.

The physical planning of each New Town is based on a concept as illustrated in Fig. 7.2. All the necessary amenities and facilities are provided for to enable each New Town to sustain a defined level of socioeconomic self-sufficiency. The

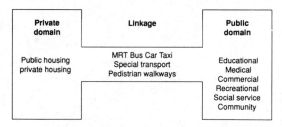

Fig. 7.1 Linkage between private domain and public domain.

layout reflects the main criterion of ensuring convenience for the residents to get access to the essential facilities for daily living, such as the market, shops, schools, and recreational centers. This existing planning framework, with its inherent objectives which cater to all the basic as well as social needs, provides a good rational basis for extending the design consideration to include disabled residents.

In 1977 HDB initiated a study on barrier-free design to facilitate accessibility for the physically disabled within the New Town. Guidelines for design were introduced in 1978 and subsequently revised in 1985 (Table 7.2). Where physical conditions permit and within cost justification, barrier-free features, such as ramps which lead from footpaths and parking lots to the elevator lobby of a residential floor, and wheelchair access to elevators with lower height of control buttons, are the typical features provided for. These features will also benefit the aged. Ang Mo Kio Town Centre is the first town center to have such barrier-free features incorporated in the design (Fig. 7.3).

Since 1980, accessibility features were implemented in all new HDB housing estates and as of 1987, elevator landings were provided at every floor in a new block of apartments. Whenever possible, the HDB will also provide additional accessibility facilities in its routine maintenance and upgrading program to housing completed before 1978. Furthermore, requests from individuals or organizations with special needs will be considered sympathetically. A scheme is already in existence to replace steps with ramps outside a disabled person's apartment and to provide season ticket parking at designated reserved lots.

The HDB administrative policies are tailored to grant priorities to families with disabled members or to individual applicants themselves to select apartments on the ground floor or on a floor with an elevator landing.

At Kampong Ubi Housing Estate the lower two floors of five units of shophouses were converted to form a hostel for a group of handicapped people, including wheelchair-bound and ambulant disabled (Fig. 7.4). This venture is un-

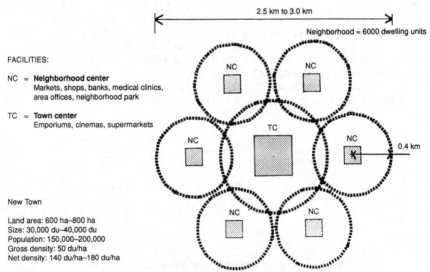

Fig. 7.2   Conceptual diagram of New Town development.

Table 7.2 Summary of Housing and Development Board revised guidelines for designing for the disabled (Ministry of National Development, 1985)

Areas of provision	Revised guideline	
	Existing provision	Additional provision
(I) Residential buildings		
(A) Circulation along upper floor access corridor	Allow for two wheelchairs to pass by	
(B) Vertical circulation	Lift accessible by wheelchair	Lift landing at every floor (80% of apartments are accessible directly from lift)
(C) Access to external environment	(i) Lift lobby to apron (ii) Apron to car park (iii) Apron to access road/car park entrance (iv) Apron to precinct center/playground, landscaping, etc	(i) Paved car parking lot (ii) Apron to lift lobby of nearest block with car parking facilities (if car park is away from building)
(D) Pedestrian crossing to other side of road	—	Provide ramp and kerb for wheelchair movement
(E) Other facilities	—	(i) Toilet at RC center also can be utilized by handicapped person (ii) Sign of access displayed at location where toilet facilities are provided
(II) Commercial complex, public buildings, neighborhood, and town center		
(A) Access to building/center	(i) From car park to adjacent part of building/center (ii) From access road/ car park entrance to walkway to building/center	(i) Paved car parking lot —
(B) From any part of building/center	(i) To and within entire building/center on ground floor	(i) Pedestrian crossing on access road to other part of build-ing/center
(C) For public spaces in neighborhood and town center, and public building (market, hawker center, emporium, community center, swimming complex, etc)	(i) Staircase for locomotory disability if lift is not provided (ii) Public toilets—at least one to each male/female toilet can be utilized by handicapped person	(i) Entrance doorway accessible by wheel-chair users (ii) Sign of access dis-played at location where facilities are provided

dertaken in collaboration with the Council of Social Services. The hostel serves as a "halfway home," offering training and opportunities for disabled persons to lead an independent life. Necessary modifications to the building included the widening of doorways to 1.0 m (3.0 ft), ramps for access, special sanitary provisions, public telephone mounted at a lower level, and handrails on both sides of staircases.

7.7 ACCESSIBILITY IN THE PUBLIC DOMAIN

The Ministry of National Development administers the implementation of policies relating to the built environment in the public domain mainly through the Urban Redevelopment Authority (URA) and the Public Works Department (PWD). These correspond quite closely to agencies in other countries, such as Public Works Canada. The URA has introduced accessibility facilities in some of its projects. The Hill Street Centre and South Bridge Centre (Figs. 7.5 and 7.6) are notable examples of public buildings that are completely accessible to the disabled.

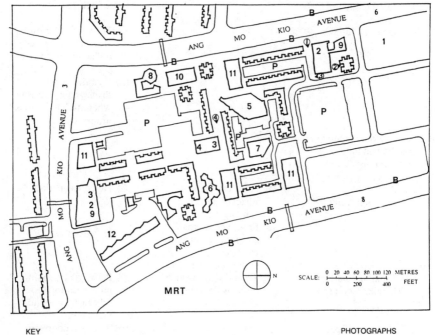

KEY

1 Library	7 Polyclinic	P = Car park
2 Supermarket	8 Mosque	MRT = Mass rapid transport station
3 Emporium	9 Restaurant	B = Bus stop
4 Offices	10 Area/Post office	
5 Market	11 Cinemas	
6 Food Center	12 Bus interchange	

PHOTOGRAPHS

1 = View 1
2 = View 2
3 = View 3
4 = View 4

Fig. 7.3 Ang Mo Kio New Town. (a) Map.

Fig. 7.3   Ang Mo Kio New Town. (*Continued*) (*b*) **Walkways.**

Fig. 7.3   Ang Mo Kio New Town. (*Continued*) (*b*) Walkways.

The PWD has undertaken similar measures in many of its projects, such as the Changi International Airport. In 1983 the department established and published its own design guidelines on the accessibility for the disabled in buildings (1983). Since 1970 the PWD has adopted a standard practice of providing curb-cut ramps at all public footpaths and at pedestrian crossings whenever space is available. Ramps have also been incorporated into the construction of some recent overhead pedestrian bridges across expressways.

In April 1988, the PWD made a survey of Orchard Road, a major shopping, hotel, and commercial area in Singapore, to assess the extent of accessibility of walkways and approaches to buildings. They noted the difficulties imposed by curbs and steep ramps, by inaccessible public telephones, automated teller machines, and bank counters as well as insufficient signage for disabled persons (Fig. 7.7). This lack of a concerted approach to the provision of amenities may be a real discouragement to the use of these buildings by people with a range of disabilities.

While some building owners have provided ramps and toilet facilities for wheelchair users, there have been comments that these are underused, possibly resulting in an unwillingness to make similar provisions in future development. In fact this underuse might be attributed to a lack of continuity between the building and its outside pavement, where steps or curbs preclude access by the wheelchair user. This again highlights the delicate interplay going into full access, noted in other chapters.

However, it should be noted that Singapore experiences heavy tropical rainfall, which makes deep storm drains and high curbs or coamings necessary to prevent storm water from entering buildings. These ubiquitous features give rise to problems of changing levels for both ambulant disabled and wheelchair users alike. At present the PWD is studying the reconciliation of pavement design for both access and water control. Given an increase in the level of cooperation between private owners and public agencies, the prospect of a barrier-free environ-

Fig. 7.3   Ang Mo Kio New Town. (*Continued*) (*b*) Walkways.

ment could become a reality in the near future. The accommodation to the country's special circumstances mirrors Canada's concern with the level of snow and the intensity of cold weather discussed in Chapter 4.

Another aspect of the problem of underutilization is the lack of publicized information on the location of suitable facilities for disabled access. The publication of *Access Singapore* by the Singapore Council of Social Services in 1981 went some way toward rectifying this situation (Fig. 7.8). This information is now

Fig. 7.4 Kampong Ubi hostel. (*a*) General view. (*b*) Ramp access and call box at reduced height.

rather outdated and the council is currently embarking on a survey of the many new buildings not included previously in order to compile a comprehensive guide and also, perhaps, to help identify buildings which are not contributing toward a barrier-free environment.

Fig. 7.4   Kampong Ubi hostel. (*Continued*) (*c*) **Handrails to both sides of staircase.** (*d*) **Ramp access to bus stop.**

Fig. 7.5   Ramp access at Hill Street Centre.

Fig. 7.6   Elevator control panel at low level. Pidemco Centre (formerly South Bridge Centre).

Fig. 7.7　Automatic teller machines, Ang Mo Kio Town Centre.

AGENCY	SELECTED ENTRANCE	LOCATION OF
Disablement Resettlement Unit (DRU) Ministry of Labour Prince Edward Road Singapore 0207 Tel: 2217222	Front. 3 steps. (12.6 cm or 5 ins)	DRU. On ground floor. Left hand side of the building.
Rehabilitative Services Section (RSS) Social Welfare Department Ministry of Social Affairs Pearl's Hill Singapore 0316 Tel: 914111	Side entrance at right side of the building. Ramp provided. Symbol of Access Sign displayed at this entrance.	RSS. On ground floor. Left hand side of the building. Front entrance of building has 2 steps (12.6 cm and 5 cm). Wheelchair available at information desk. Look out for Symbol of Access Sign for directions to the toilet.
Singapore Council of Social Service (SCSS) 11 Penang Lane, 1st Floor Singapore 0923 Tel: 3361544	Front: Levelled ground leading to entrance of lift which serves every floor.	SCSS. On 1st floor. Toilets on every floor at the corridor end of the building.
Singapore Tourist Promotion Board (STPB) 131, Tudor Court Tanglin Road Singapore 1024 Tel: 2356611	From Ellis Road. Ramp approach to Tudor Court. One step (1¼ cm or ½ ins) to entrance of the Information Office.	Information Office on the ground floor.

Fig. 7.8　Extract from *Access Singapore*, indicating type of information provided.

In Singapore there are many atrium-type shopping and commercial complexes. An outstanding problem is to provide emergency exits in case of fire. Elevators are generally deemed unsatisfactory for this purpose. At the moment, the implications of these are being considered with respect to the redrafting of existing fire codes.

7.8   TRANSPORTATION AS LINKAGE

Transportation systems serve as important linkages between the private domain and the public domain for all people (see Fig. 7.1). The Committee on Accessibility and Transportation particularly surveyed the transport facilities for the disabled in Singapore. It concluded that the present provisions are inadequate, but some encouraging directions for improvements were proposed. It should be mentioned that there are certain difficulties in projecting the likely demand for specialized provisions, although it can be argued that appropriate improvements to the transportation system would encourage more disabled people to travel, as well as benefiting the elderly, pregnant women, and mothers with toddlers, among others.

Singapore has a very efficient bus service, a new Mass Rapid Transit (MRT) system, and good road networks with parking adjacent to or integral with nearly all public buildings. It also has an extensive and reliable taxi service. Private cars are expensive, both to buy and to run, on account of high import duties and road taxes. Although some financial concessions are made to disabled people wishing to own a vehicle, there are relatively few purpose-made or converted vehicles on the road. Instruction for disabled drivers is available and the committee's report recommended that imported vehicles for disabled people be exempt from duties. Reserved parking places and season ticket schemes are already in existence and could be extended if more users needed them.

The greatest problem is that the majority of disabled people who are potential drivers tend to be relatively low wage earners and would need strong incentives to invest a major part of their income in owning a vehicle. Ironically the problem of transport is one which appears to keep a number of disabled people from securing employment at a distance from their own home.

Bus and MRT fares are cheap, yet these systems do not specifically address the needs of the disabled. During the design of the MRT, cost and safety considerations did not justify the provision of elevator access and emergency evacuation routes for severely disabled persons. Furthermore, it was also anticipated that potential delays which may be caused by this category of users will jeopardize the efficiency of the transportation system. It can be argued that alternative transport methods, such as taxis, are more suitable. Taxis, although more expensive than the MRT, are seen to be one of the best solutions. To this end, the committee recommends the establishment of a voucher system, similar to the Swedish system, to take some of the financial burdens off the disabled passenger. In order to help finance this proposal, it is suggested that an annual sum of S$500,000.00 be levied on the existing bus companies and the Mass Rapid Transit Corporation (MRTC), since they would not then be required to make provision for severely handicapped users.

Some other recommendations do cover bus and MRT services for the less severely handicapped such as the ambulatory disabled or those with hearing and visual impairments. They include improved signage, concessionary fares for registered disabled passengers, and audible announcements for those MRT users with limited visual faculties.

As in the United States and other countries, voluntary welfare associations operate special buses. Although these are supported financially through the SHARE scheme, they are generally expensive to run (about S$1300.00 per person in 1986). The committee suggested a centralized coordination system to poll the services and to establish radio links between the buses and a central office. Such a scheme would benefit the more severely disabled, as many of these buses have hydraulic lifts to take wheelchairs. They currently perform services which bring people from home to day-care centers, but their usefulness could be further extended.

7.9 LEGISLATION AND COST IMPLICATIONS

The committee's report also emphasized the need for coordination to achieve a barrier-free environment and to set a common standard between public and commercial buildings. It concluded that legislation is the only way to ensure that accessibility becomes a norm in Singapore.

Unlike ANSI codes in the United States and related codes in other countries, there is currently no formal legislation or a code of practice on access to buildings for the disabled in Singapore. The Research and Documentation Committee of the Singapore Institute of Architects published the paper entitled *Barrier-Free Design for the Physically Handicapped in Singapore* in 1979/80. The purpose was to draw the attention of architects and developers to the marginal cost of providing accessibility features at the design stage. This seemed to have limited impact. It is maintained that for new construction works, the increased cost of meeting reasonable legislative requirements for the provision of these facilities does not normally exceed 1% of the total construction cost.

On the question of relative cost implication for commercial buildings, the URA undertook a controlled costing exercise using the Cuppage Centre as a model and concluded that the inclusion of such features as ramps, wider doors, and toilet accommodation for wheelchair users would have added only 0.11% to the original cost at 1980 prices. Based on this result, legislation, therefore, should not adversely affect new developments in financial terms, and greater benefits may yet be realized when the buildings are made accessible to a larger number of people.

In Singapore, broad national goals have been achieved with great success, and it is easy to see now with hindsight that more attention could have been accorded to the disabled population, which at that time was perhaps undiscernible. Initially government policy has resisted legislation that might deter or slow down the building program. Nevertheless, various individual agencies have in fact drawn up their own design guidelines and codes and aimed for higher standards, almost in advance of demand. In the private sector, voluntary codes have only attained limited impact, which consequently resulted in a rather disjointed scenario in terms of the provision for access and mobility for disabled people.

Changes that will bring recommendations much closer to becoming enacted are imminent. In late 1990 new policies and recommendations have been issued. These will no doubt have a major impact on future developments in the areas of concern of this volume. Judging by Singapore's previous track record, the removal of barriers in the built environment and the opening up of more independent personal living for the disabled population cannot be far away.

7.10 POSTSCRIPT

Since 1988 Singapore has taken major steps to facilitate access to buildings by disabled people. In fact, things have moved so quickly that it is often difficult to appreciate the full implications of the relevant measures. Most significantly the Building Control Act 1989, brought in on April 14, 1989, now states in its regulations (Division 2 para 36) that:

> Where a proposed building is one to which disabled persons have or may be reasonably expected to have access, that building shall be designed to the satisfaction of the Building Authority in such a manner as will facilitate access to and use of that building and its facilities by disabled persons.

The regulation then defines types of buildings and the specified areas within a building where accessibility is required (generally "areas intended for public access") and, more particularly, the requirement that the design be in accordance with the *Code on Barrier-Free Accessibility in Buildings* (Public Works Department, 1990).

This last document is largely based on the earlier SIA publication, *Barrier-Free Design for the Physically Handicapped in Singapore.* The main thrust is to facilitate the use of wheelchairs, and requirements include accessible parking spaces, circulation areas (both internal and external), including widths of doorways, dimensions of ramps, handrails, elevators, staircases for the ambulant disabled user, and so on; a sanitary provision is also included to accommodate both the ambulant disabled and wheelchair users. The code also requires the display of the international symbol of access for the disabled on all buildings that make such provisions. Figure 7.9 shows the scope of the requirements of the Code on Accessibility. The code further stipulates minimum provision of facilities in certain types of buildings; for instance, hotels must provide one guestroom for disabled users for every 200 rooms (or part thereof), banks must provide at least one appropriately designed service counter, and so on.

In addition to requiring new or retrofitted buildings to be accessible, the Singapore government, through its Ministry of Finance, also introduced a scheme to encourage owners of existing buildings to modify their premises so that access for disabled workers is facilitated; any expenditure on such work is tax-deductible (up to a maximum of $100,000). The scheme was introduced in December 1989, but the tax advantage can be claimed retroactively for work in progress from January 1989. In order to help owners to avail themselves of this benefit, the Singapore Institute of Architects and the Singapore Council of Social Services simultaneously launched a scheme called the Accessibility Advisory Service to provide advice to anyone contemplating modifying their building. A team of volunteer architects provides this initial consultation free of charge.

In December 1989 the Singapore Council of Social Services also published an updated edition of *Access Singapore,* a guide to accessible buildings in the city, which tabulates major publicly accessible buildings and the facilities which they offer, including parking links, circulation, and other amenities such as telephones or bank automated teller machines at low level. This useful booklet helps to highlight some of the recurring problems in access to public buildings, the most common one being the presence of steps between the external walkway and the building's entrance.

Although there is still much to be done, major upgrading of the infrastructure of the city, particularly in the provision of footways, road crossings, and entry points to buildings, is currently under way. It comes at a time of major invest-

	Facility	Signage	Size	Height	Width	No step	Nonslip	Notes: additional provision
1	Car parking	•			•	•		Close to entrance; "RESERVED" sign; room for wheelchair alongside car
2	Pathway links				•	•	•	Barrier-free; no kerbs or gratings
3	Ramps				•		•	Easy gradient, short length/landing
	Steps			•			•	Easy rise, no projecting nosing
	Handrails		•	•				Shape of grab rail important
4	Entrances				•	•		
	Door handles			•				Type of handle important
	Automatic doors					•		Speed of closure important
5	Lift (elevator)	•			•	•		Door closure speed important
	Control panels			•				Audible/Braille signals (optional)
6	Stairway			•			•	Easy rise; no projecting nosings
7	Counters, etc.			•				Clearance underneath
8	Toilet cubicle		•				•	Adequate provision (M or F)
	Door	•				•		Outward opening/sliding/folding
	WC			•				
	Grab bars			•				Essential at both sides of WC
	Washbasin			•				Taps easy to operate
	Bath or shower	•					•	(Optional); grab rails essential

Fig. 7.9   Provision required in code on accessibility.

ment in refurbishment of existing building stock, and with this and the changes wrought by the legislation for new buildings, Singapore will have achieved much to the benefit of the physically disabled.

7.11 CONDENSED REFERENCES/BIBLIOGRAPHY

Advisory Council on the Disabled 1988, *Employment, Accessibility and Transportation for*
Harrison 1988, *Designing for the Disabled in Singapore*
Lam 1988, *High-Rise Public Housing Developments in Singapore*
Ministry of National Development 1985, *Design Guidelines on Accessibility for the Dis-*
Ministry of Social Affairs 1983, *Towards a Better Profile of the Disabled in Singapore*
Public Works Department 1983, *Design Guidelines on Accessibility of the Disabled in*
Public Works Department 1990, *Code on Barrier-Free Accessibility in Buildings*
Singapore Council of Social Services 1981, *Access Singapore: A Guidebook of Accessible*
Singapore Institute of Architects 1979/80, *Barrier-Free Design for the Physically Handi-*
Singapore Institute of Architects 1982, *Designing for the Handicapped*
United Nations 1983, *Designing with Care*
Wong 1985, *Housing a Nation: 25 Years of Public Housing in Singapore*

Part 2 – Topics and Technology

8

The Growing Needs of Elderly Persons Aging in Place in Subsidized Housing

The chapters of this Monograph present many of the latest design and safety features used to improve living conditions in multifamily housing and public spaces for the elderly and handicapped. In this chapter the focus is directed specifically to characteristics of subsidized housing for the elderly and its role in meeting the challenges of increasingly aged populations. It complements related discussions, especially Chapter 9. It also provides more specific, management-oriented information.

Before presenting detailed design features, guidelines, and technological breakthroughs, it is important to describe the broader picture of the aging process in purposely built facilities for the elderly, many of which consist of tall buildings, and the emerging needs these facilities face as their residents age in place.

8.1 BACKGROUND RESEARCH

A primary reason to conduct the research reported on in this Monograph was to keep elderly and handicapped persons in assisted independent living environments and out of long-term dependent care institutions. With the proper environmental, administrative, and support-service changes to independent living environments this can be done. This discussion will show that transfers from independent to dependent living environments are common and growing, while keeping frail but well persons in properly converted independent housing produces significant cost savings to the public and increased quality of life for the residents.

The continuous growth of specially designed facilities to house the independent elderly in the United States and abroad has produced numerous management and staffing problems and increased costs as the residents age. Since 1982 one of the most influential services to U.S. housing management has been the monthly newsletter *Housing the Elderly Report.* In a recent nationwide survey of its readers, the newsletter found that aging in place and the transfer and retention decisions necessary are now the most persistent and troublesome problems managers face (CD Publications, 1988). Holshouser (1986) estimated that in the United States each year 9000 elderly move to nursing homes from public housing alone. Neno et al. (1986) estimated that 24% of the elderly households in federally assisted housing (165,000 households) were vulnerable and at risk of being moved to more dependent care facilities.

Whenever a person is transferred from independent housing to dependent care, the costs increase substantially. There is a growing concern by many observers that housing managers are incapable of accurately monitoring resident independence and correctly initiating transfer proceedings (Bernstein, 1982; CD Publications, 1987; Sheehan, 1986; Suggs et al., 1986). Finally, two different literature reviews produced in recent years present multiple findings indicating 12 to 60% of the elderly who have been institutionalized could live more independently if appropriate assisted independent living facilities were provided in the community (Heumann and Boldy, 1982; Hendricks and Hendricks, 1986). The following shows the substantial cost savings that will materialize when residents are retained in conventional housing units for independent living that have been converted to assisted independent living with housekeeping and congregate dining—congregate housing—rather than being transferred to dependent care institutions.

In a recent study, Heumann (1985) selected seven congregate housing and seven long-term care facilities representative of these facility types in the midwestern United States. The study sites were chosen from a careful stratification of existing facilities, using characteristics critical to a fair cost comparison analysis. Costs were collected from the congregate housing sites first. Then, with the levels of support dependencies in congregate housing known, costs for housing and support of elderly with *comparable support dependencies* were collected at the long-term care facilities.

When comparing the costs incurred by the actual mix of private-pay and public-aid residents in the long-term care facilities studied to the actual rents and service fees paid by comparable residents of congregate housing, congregate housing produced a yearly cost savings of $1320 per person, or $195,000 for the average-size congregate facility per year.

These savings were conservative, however, because the congregate facilities tended to be built after 1980 and the long-term care facilities before 1970. This resulted in higher capital costs and debt services to congregate housing. Normalizing capital costs and debt services to 1985 for all facilities resulted in a fairer comparison and simulated a cost for facilities being built and occupied in 1985. With normalized capital costs and debt services, congregate housing produced cost savings of $4233 per person per year and $630,000 for the average facility. Remember, these were costs for elderly persons receiving the *same* support services in both types of facility. Since 1985 costs have tended to rise faster in long-term care institutions due to the presence of higher-paid on-site professional staff (nurses, therapists, dieticians, and social workers) not present in congregate housing.

These figures represent only the quantifiable cost savings. In addition, the study found numerous quality-of-life factors which favor congregate housing but cannot be quantified when comparing assisted independent living with dependent care. For the costs incurred, the average congregate housing resident is receiving 37 to 46 m^2 (400 to 500 ft^2) of private apartment compared to 9 to 14 m^2 (100 to 150 ft^2) of semiprivate space around a bed in a nursing institution. Unlike most long-term care facility residents, congregate housing residents retain control of their money, their personal affairs, their daily routine, and the freedom to come and go as they please. Congregate housing promotes self-sufficiency, encourages cost-saving interdependence with friends and neighbors in the community, offsets social isolation, and introduces costly professional support services only at the margin of individual need.

The rapid growth of the oldest and most frail segment of the elderly population is under way in the most industrialized locations of the world today. (This is clearly demonstrated here with the statistics on Illinois, the study universe for the data presented in the body of this chapter, and, of course, in the data presented in the chapters about other countries.) The high numbers of elderly being moved from independent housing facilities to dependent care each year are only going to increase if we cannot adapt existing independent living environments appropriately. Finally, the cost of dependent care when compared to assisted independent living, in terms of both societal resources and personal dignity of the resident, are significantly higher and growing constantly. In light of these combined costs and demographic trends, modifications of existing environments that help residents age in place should produce higher quality of life at lower costs. While the majority of Part 2 of this Monograph deals with useful modifications in living conditions and building design for both comfort and safe movement within a building, this chapter examines the numerous elderly who are already at risk of premature transfer to dependent care due to lack of such modifications, or of inappropriate retention in housing designed for totally independent living.

The data presented in the body of this chapter deal with the subset of the elderly population most likely to live in relatively tall structures. Few elderly persons live in multistory tower blocks; the single largest concentration is in purposely built 5- to 12-story facilities for the independent elderly, and most of this population live in government-subsidized facilities common in most countries of Western society. While a large proportion of elderly persons is living in single-family housing (in the United States approximately 75% as of 1980), about 20% live in multifamily housing, and slightly under half of these live in purposely built facilities for the independent elderly (Lawton, 1985a; Turner and Mangum, 1982; U.S. Department of Housing and Urban Development, 1979; Zais et al., 1982). The remaining 5% are institutionalized. Although these facilities for the elderly are not tall buildings by conventional standards, they are often the tallest buildings within residential neighborhoods of large cities, and they are often the tallest structures in smaller cities, suburbs, and rural towns.

8.2 SURVEY

The data presented in this chapter are from a 1986 survey of on-site managers of subsidized housing for the elderly conducted in the State of Illinois (Heumann, 1987). Illinois is one of only seven states with one million or more persons over the age of 65 (1,259,296 in 1980). On other statistics, Illinois is representative of the rapid growth in housing, support service, and skilled-care costs for the frail elderly in the most urbanized areas of Western society. The percentage of elderly population in Illinois is right at the national average of 11%. From 1980 until the year 2000, the elderly population in Illinois over age 62 is expected to grow by 13%; this is dwarfed by the growth of the population of over age 75, a group that will increase by 52%. Demand for long-term support services as residents age and require assistance with independent living will increase dramatically.

Illinois had an estimated 73,400 subsidized apartments for the elderly and handicapped as of 1983/1984. This represents approximately 7% of the elderly population, which is about the national average for the more urbanized states. This study focuses on the 23 urban counties where 62% of these subsidized housing units (304 facilities) are located. Seventy-six of these facilities (25%) were randomly selected and questionnaires were mailed to the on-site managers. A total of 64 managers responded (84.2%). We have a high level of confidence that the survey is representative of the housing managers of subsidized housing facilities for the independent elderly.

In addition to the site managers, every resident of each site was surveyed as to functional ability and support needs using a questionnaire distributed by the manager, but returned in a sealed envelope to the analysts. Finally a control group of 6% of the Medicaid recipients in Illinois was surveyed using a questionnaire similar to that given subsidized housing residents. Responses from 54% of the subsidized housing residents (n = 5672) and 43% of the Medicaid population (n = 2046) will be used in this analysis to give the reader some comparative responses to the managers' estimates of residents at risk of undercaring if retained, or of overcaring if transferred. Because there is a higher probability of nonresponse among the more frail and disabled residents or Medicaid recipients due to physical or mental disability, the responses from these samples are likely to produce very conservative estimates of elderly persons at risk of inappropriate retention or transfer. As the data will show, the managers' estimates of at-risk residents are consistently higher than the estimates of responding residents. The responding Medicaid population is so much poorer and dependent than the subsidized housing population that the total "at risk" is considerably higher, even though the full support needs of the Medicaid community are probably underrepresented.

The 64 subsidized housing facilities reported on in this chapter were divided into three groups: those built under the federal public housing program; those with Section 8 rent-subsidized apartments and built under the Section 8, Section 202, and Section 236 federally funded housing construction programs; and housing subsidized by the Illinois Housing Development Authority (IHDA).

The primary policy focus of the survey instrument was to determine how many elderly residents are already beyond the definition of independent living, how their dependence is monitored and their support needs are met, when and how they are transferred or evicted, and what changes in the physical design and management operations of these facilities are necessary if the residents are to be housed in the most efficient and appropriate environment for their support needs.

8.3 SUBSIDIZED ELDERLY RISK LOSING INDEPENDENCE

The managers of subsidized housing predict that 12.4% of their residents will have to move to a more dependent environment within a year. This is an increase from the average 11.1% of actual moves to more dependent care plus deaths in the previous year (Heumann, 1987).

Numerous measures were included in the survey to estimate the number of subsidized housing residents at risk of losing their independent housing. The primary definitions chosen for future planning purposes were based on the managers' estimates of residents who "frequently or always have difficulty" completing independent activities of daily living, and managers' estimates of residents who "frequently or always have difficulty and *receive no help."* Receiving no help implies a very serious and *immediate risk* of losing an independent apartment or being inappropriately retained in an apartment. Managers' estimates of these measures were collected for 11 different living activities. Three activities, housekeeping, personal care, and preparing hot meals, were chosen to represent progressively more difficult tasks of independent living. The responses yielded the estimates shown in Table 8.1.

The percentages for problems with cooking hot meals (10.3 and 2.5%) were chosen as the best indicators of risk, because being able to cook is vital to daily nutrition and health, and the physical and mental activities involved are basic to independent living. Inability to complete this activity is a significant indicator of advanced frailty, and retaining a person with this level of daily support is beyond the capacity of most independent living facilities, even with assistance from visiting service providers.

The measure of those experiencing frequent or constant difficulty, and receiving no help, for a very vital task of daily living such as cooking hot meals, yields very stringent and conservative estimates of vulnerability. The 10.3 and 2.5% estimates are considerably lower than estimates provided by other studies using more liberal measures. The purpose of choosing such stringent measures was that there would be no question that the numbers these percentages generate represent people with genuine vulnerability and support needs.

The percentages generated by the 5627 responding residents of subsidized housing were considerably below those of the managers and were not used to represent total resident vulnerability. These residents represent only 54% of the total, and nonrespondents are likely to be more functionally and mentally dependent.

The responding Medicaid recipients were just as likely to underrepresent the total Medicaid population at risk of losing their functional independence. Only 43% responded from this sample. However, no alternative comprehensive estimate is available for this group. Table 8.2 presents a comparison of the Medicaid and subsidized housing results. These percentages show that the responding Medicaid recipients are more vulnerable than subsidized housing residents. One explanation is that they have significantly lower incomes than do the residents of subsidized housing, and have had a history of sporadic employment due to lack of education, poor health, or disabilities. While two-thirds of the Medicaid respondents receive some Social Security (compared to 92% for subsidized housing respondents), 70% require and receive Supplemental Security Income (compared to only 13% for subsidized housing respondents).

Table 8.1   Managers' estimates of resident living-activity skills

	Housekeeping	Personal care	Cooking
Frequently or always have difficulty	18.2%	9.7%	10.3%
Frequently or always have difficulty and receive *no* assistance	6.1%	2.5%	2.5%

1 Significant Subgroup Characteristics

Many cross tabulations were conducted to determine the vulnerability and support needs within subgroups of the primary samples and are all presented in the main report (Heumann, 1987). Three cross tabulations with planning and policy implications are presented here, dealing with (1) the old old, (2) the manager type, and (3) the sponsor type.

Increasing Vulnerability of the Old Old.   The data show that as residents age, they lose significant functional independence and resources. The statistics shown in Table 8.3 for respondents of age 85 and older are not expected to be the norm for a development, because older residents who die or are transferred will be replaced by younger tenants. However, all indications are that managers are finding it difficult to transfer frail tenants successfully and are therefore retaining them. This fact, plus a rapidly aging general elderly population, and therefore an aging waiting list for subsidized housing, means that some facilities will take on these proportions of vulnerability.

The old old Medicaid respondents report much higher percentages of having difficulty with independent living activities when compared to the subsidized housing respondents. This is because the Medicaid respondents are a poorer and more disabled population. Despite the higher percentage of Medicaid respondents having difficulty with activities, relatively fewer of them receive no help

Table 8.2 Comparison of Medicaid and subsidized housing results

	Responding Medicaid recipients	Responding residents
Frequently or always have difficulty cooking hot meals	20.4%	6.1%
Frequently or always have difficulty and receive *no* help with cooking hot meals	2.3%	0.6%

Table 8.3 Living-activity skills for persons aged 85+

	Subsidized housing		Medicaid recipients	
	Having difficulty	Having difficulty and receiving *no* help	Having difficulty	Having difficulty and receiving *no* help
Housekeeping, laundry	36.4%	4.4%	61.5%	3.1%
Personal care, bathing, dressing	20.6%	4.7%	52.1%	3.1%
Cooking, getting in and out of bed	15.5%	3.7%	44.8%	4.2%

when compared with subsidized housing respondents. This is explained by the fact that the average Medicaid respondent (both over age 85 and younger) lives with another adult who can provide assistance (2.1 persons per household), while the average subsidized housing resident lives alone.

Management Types and Resident Support Services. Managers were grouped into types based on their answers to three groups of management activities: (1) activities related to managing the physical plant, (2) basic tenant-oriented activities, and (3) social and support services for the tenants. Seven management types were identified, ranging from traditional physical-plant orientation (17%) to social/support orientation (19%). The most common (44%) were managers involved in a balanced approach of all three activity types.

Retention or Transfer Patterns by Sponsor Type. There was a tendency for managers to have similar patterns of transfer or retention of frail residents by sponsor type, but this was *not* consistent enough to suggest a sponsor policy on retention or eviction. Rather, it seemed to reflect the type of managers sponsors hire and variations in the financial resources of the tenants. Public housing and non-IHDA Section 8 facilities are represented by more managers who profess an "accommodating" management model—an environment that allows more frail residents to remain in the facility. The IHDA facilities are represented by more managers who profess a "constant" model—attempting through stricter transfer policy to retain the original independent population profile.

2 Inappropriate Retention or Transfer

An actual case-by-case evaluation of frail elderly is necessary to determine whether they are being retained in subsidized housing with insufficient support or being transferred to long-term care institutions when they could remain in independent housing with appropriate assistance. Because this methodology was cost-prohibitive, surrogate measures were used. Three findings combine to suggest that both inappropriate transfers and inappropriate retentions are common.

The managers were presented with a situation that past research had shown would require transfer or a permanent increase in the on-site support staff and services to assure that all frail tenants receive proper assistance. The scenario specified that 20% of the residents were facility-bound—unable to shop, cook, or complete personal care activities vital to independent living. The managers were then asked what actions would be taken and who would be responsible. Only 25% of the managers said that they would seek to transfer residents at this point. In the case of public housing, 44% of the managers would attempt to retain tenants with visiting homemaker services only. Other managers would rely on multiple visiting services. None relied on the family at this level of dependence and only 2% relied on elderly neighbors and 7% on on-site staff.

This managerial effort to retain very frail residents may be understandable if there are no viable transfer options, but there is strong evidence that most managers are not prepared to determine adequately what difficulties and support needs their tenants have, nor are they able to retain them with adequate support. Fully 66% of the managers were unable even to estimate the number of their tenants who had the functional limitations and support needs that made them facility-bound.

Inappropriate transfers are also very likely. First, of all the resident moves to more dependent care in the previous year, managers report that 24% were to relatives and friends, 15% to private residences, 3% to congregate housing, and 58% to nursing homes. Again, the fact that 66% of the managers did not know the functional disabilities of their residents brings into question their ability to conduct accurate assessments for transfer. More importantly, only 5% of the managers had a formal professional assessment committee in place to handle transfers. Finally, there is strong evidence that there are few appropriate places to transfer subsidized housing residents.

8.4 CHARACTERISTICS THAT INHIBIT AGING IN PLACE

The typical manager did not have a long career in managing housing for the elderly. She was female, in her mid-40s, with 2 to 3 years of college. She had made a midcareer change, being a housing manager for only 4.7 years. She had been at her facility for a shorter time than the average resident, 3.6 years compared to 5.4 years. Most of the managers managed just one facility, but one-fifth worked 20 hours per week or less at the sampled site.

Some of the facilities displayed a number of characteristics that would prohibit the retention of frail and even slightly dependent residents. The typical site staff consists of four people: the manager, two maintenance staff, and a fourth position divided between additional office staff, maintenance staff, and a social organizer, in that order of priority (Table 8.4). There are just 0.78 staff hours per resident per week, mostly in maintenance staff, which means that there is no on-site staff to assist frail residents.

The average building is 13 years old. Of the buildings, 22% lack a barrier-free

Table 8.4 Selected facility characteristics reported by housing managers from three sponsor types

Facility	Public housing	Non-IHDA Section 8	IHDA	Total
FTE staff	2.9	3.7	4.6	4.0
Average staff hours	87.7	105.6	139.1	109.1
Average staff hours per resident	0.59	0.91	0.84	0.78
Year constructed	1971	1974	1979	1974
Stories in building	9.9	7.9	8.6	8.8
Percent wheelchair-accessible apartments*	58.6	20.2	41.8	35.6
Percent barrier-free	64.0	92.0	84.6	79.4
Percent with no security system	16.0	7.7	0.0	7.8
Percent with no alarm system*	36.0	0.0	0.0	21.9
Staff on site 24 hr	64.0	76.9	69.2	70.3
Communal dining space	68.0	80.8	66.7	73.0

*Significant to 0.01.

design and have no alarm system, both features that are necessary to maintain and ensure the safety of more frail residents. Thirty percent of the buildings lack 24-hr staff, and 27% lack space for congregate dining, additional features that are useful when retaining frail residents. Public housing facilities are the least able to accommodate frail residents. They are the oldest on average (16 years), have the lowest staff per resident ratio (0.59), and are more likely to lack barrier-free design (36%), alarm systems (36%), 24-hr staff (36%), and space for congregate dining (32%).

8.5   PROPOSED SOLUTIONS

Three policy or program alternatives are explored: (1) a laissez-faire approach, (2) development of an explicit sponsor policy on transfer or retention, and the provision of staff training and visiting service coordination necessary to achieve the policy, and (3) conversion of some or all facilities to subsidized congregate housing to allow residents to age in place or construction of new subsidized congregate housing.

1   Laissez-Faire Approach

Because of general welfare cutbacks in recent years in the United States, some gerontologists now see residence in subsidized housing as far more advantageous than residence in conventional housing, even for frail elderly. Some argue that we must prioritize the limited public resources available to frail elderly who have no site manager, maintenance staff, security system, or elderly neighbors who can work with them to cope with increasing frailty.

This approach makes several incorrect assumptions about subsidized housing environments. A laissez-faire approach can seriously affect the well-being of *all* residents, not just the most frail. Building staff assistance in subsidized housing is minimal because the small staff is confronted with so much support need that they must say no to everyone. This study found that Medicaid respondents living in conventional housing receive more staff assistance (from the custodian) than do subsidized housing respondents. Other studies, specifically focused on help from the neighbors in subsidized housing, reinforce what is reported in this study, that is, as persons become more frail, support from neighbors *declines* (Lawton et al., 1985b).

In effect there is far less support found in subsidized housing than is commonly assumed. Allowing the population in subsidized housing to age in place without *doing anything* can actually increase the stress on all care givers (family, neighbors, and staff) and can negatively affect the morale of the entire population. A growing mismatch between environment capacity and tenant competence can reduce tenant abilities to care for themselves, thus increasing the size of the population at risk.

2   Sponsor Policy, Site-Staff Training, and Support Service

At a very minimum, subsidized housing sponsors must develop a clear policy on what disabilities their facility can accommodate, on termination criteria and procedures to monitor resident independence, and on staff responsibilities. If necessary, site managers may have to be retrained or replaced to develop a staff capable of performing the activities involved in managing an aging population.

When clear policy is in place, the entire support network, including residents, family, staff, and visiting community agencies, must be evaluated and coordinated to provide the most unobtrusive, efficient, appropriate, and comprehensive service possible within each provider's limitations. These limitations must be clearly understood so that *realistic* policies are established. A key to support care is minimizing stress and confusion, allowing the independent life-style of the residents to prevail, and eliminating both overcaring and undercaring.

3 Conversion to Congregate Housing to Fully Accommodate an Aging Population

Congregate housing can be defined as *assisted* independent living with a minimum of five hot meals per week and housekeeping services. It can include more communal meals and personal care aid, but it includes no skilled care. The congregate model has been called the most appropriate environment for most elderly, even it they do not partake of all the services, because it allows all residents to live functionally independent lives without stressful, debilitating, and potentially inappropriate transfers. Fully 69% of the subsidized housing respondents preferred this model over moves to family or friends (17%), nursing homes (9%), or other settings (6%) if advancing disabilities forced them to move. Three of the 64 facilities sampled have already been converted to congregate housing and two others have partial conversions (8%).

Most of the facilities in the sample (70 to 80%) have the physical amenities necessary to convert to congregate housing with minimal capital expenses. In these cases the primary costs are for congregate housing services: dining room furniture, food serving equipment, the cost of catering the meals, and the cost of housekeeping staff. Currently there is both a congressional inquiry and a national lobbying effort to develop a 50/50 state/federal formula to fund a congregate housing services program (CHSP). At least seven states already have a congregate housing program or are preparing legislation for a program.

Conversion could be incremental, using an accommodation model and adding staff as needed to meet new resident support needs after an initial threshold of residents requiring congregate services was identified. Another strategy is to designate a number of facilities for congregate housing and fully convert them to serve a regional need. The second scheme has the disadvantage of requiring transfers, but is likely to make the conversion process more cost-efficient. Neither alternative addresses the growing need for new congregate housing within the larger community. Many Medicaid respondents also require assisted independent living environments.

8.6 DEMAND FOR CONGREGATE HOUSING FACILITIES

Of the three policy alternatives, a laissez-faire approach will only exacerbate the problems caused by aging populations living in subsidized housing for the elderly.

Development of a clear and consistent retention/transfer policy and the accompanying support services is one appropriate policy response. However, any policy, no matter how clear and consistent, that attempts to maintain an independent population using strict transfer criteria will not prevent the pressure on site staff to retain frail tenants. This is because there are not enough appropriate transfer points for frail and low-income elderly. Only a policy that extends independent subsidized housing to allow frail tenants to age in place can assure appropriate retention and postpone transfer to a time when dependent care is truly needed. Conversion to congregate housing is the most logical extension of independent group living that allows tenants to age in place.

8.7 CONDENSED REFERENCES/BIBLIOGRAPHY

Bernstein 1982, *Who Leaves—Who Stays: Residency Policy in Housing for the Elderly*
CD Publications 1987, *Housing the Elderly Report*
CD Publications 1988, *Housing the Elderly Report*
Hendricks 1986, *Aging in Mass Society—Myths and Realities*
Heumann 1982, *Housing for the Elderly: Planning and Policy Formulation in Western*
Heumann 1985, *A Cost Comparison of Congregate Housing and Long-Term Care Facilities*
Heumann 1987, *The Retention and Transfer of Frail Elderly Living in Independent Housing*
Holshouser 1986, *Aging in Place: The Demographics and Service Needs of Elders in Urban*
Lawton 1985a, *Housing and Living Arrangements of Older People*
Lawton 1985b, *The Changing Service Needs of Older Tenants in Planned Housing*
Neno 1986, *Support Services for Frail Elderly or Handicapped Persons Living in Govern-*
Sheehan 1986, *Aging of Tenants: Termination Policy in Public Senior Housing*
Suggs 1986, *Coming, Going, Remaining in Public Housing: How Do Elderly Fare?*
Turner 1982, *Housing Choices of Older Americans*
U.S. Department of HUD 1979, *How Well Are We Housed?: The Elderly*
Zais 1982, *Housing Assistance for Older Americans*

9

Response to Living in Buildings Designed for Handicapped and Elderly Persons

The National Center for Health Statistics estimates that there are about 32,000,000 handicapped persons in the United States and that the number increases daily. The same is occurring worldwide. Medical improvements since World War II and the Vietnam War, besides advances in medical research, have saved the lives of many who formerly would have died, albeit with handicaps. The vast increase in life span in the United States, also due to medical advances as well as to reduced birth rates, has resulted in a great increase in the number of aged, and therefore of certain handicaps associated with age. This has still further increased the number of, and focus on, the handicapped and the elderly.

Many infants are still born with congenital diseases, and accidents and wars cause other handicaps. Some learning disabled are mentally alert but cannot coordinate limbs or fine muscular movements. At one time such persons were either looked after by the family or locked away in an institution. The modern way, in the United States and in many others countries, is to try to mainstream such persons into living, working, and traveling like other members of society to the extent possible.

One very important method of achieving this is to design and build apartment (and other) buildings especially for specific groups of people, such as the handicapped residents of Inwood House or the aged or elderly at Revitz House, paying special attention to the physical needs of these groups and trying to make the buildings as barrier-free as possible. Almost no one asks the occupants what *they* think of the buildings they live in, either before they are to be constructed or during residency. One of the objects of the studies of Inwood House and Revitz House was to find out what the occupants thought of the buildings designed especially for them, and if they had any suggestions for improvement which might be of use to future designers.

9.1 INWOOD HOUSE AND REVITZ HOUSE

Inwood House was built in the 1970s, facilitated by the U.S. Department of Housing and Urban Development (HUD), which provided a low-interest loan and subsidized rent for handicapped housing. It is a four-story building with 150 one- or two-bedroom apartment units housing 180 people. There are small grounds outside the complex, with bench seating and a set of bars and swings, and a small parking lot. It is about two blocks from a bus stop (which requires residents to cross a road) and about half a mile from a small shopping center, about two miles from a larger shopping center.

Criteria for admission to Inwood House are: (1) the head of household must be disabled or elderly (62 or over) according to HUD regulations, and (2) the applicant must have a low income as defined by HUD. The tenant pays 30% of his or her total income; the remainder is subsidized by HUD.

Revitz House is a Hebrew Home for the Aged, built for the aged who can function within a building designed especially for their needs (Figs. 9.1 to 9.2). There are a number of interesting parallels and contrasts between the responses and needs of Inwood House for the handicapped person and Revitz House for the able elderly. The comparison shows where handicapped and elderly needs overlap, and where they are distinctly different, in building design and construction.

Other factors outside the building, such as streets, traffic lights, buses, trains, shops, and working sites, must also be taken into consideration in barrier-free design. Making the living quarters barrier-free is only the first step in achieving autonomy for the handicapped or aged person.

Fig. 9.1   Revitz House, front view.

In both Inwood House and Revitz House written questionnaires were used as the most economical way of collecting the data and provided mainly standardized answers.

9.2 PROFILE OF INWOOD HOUSE RESIDENTS

1 Demographics

Ages ranged from young children to the elderly. Although many respondents were in their twenties and thirties, the average age was 40. Inwood House reportedly had more young handicapped than any other known living accommodation for the handicapped.

Most residents were single. There were 15 couples, 10 of which had one or more children. The fact that residents have so many different types of handicaps, as well as different family sizes and a range of different ages, religions, and races makes Inwood House a very unusual kind of facility for the handicapped. Revitz House, on the other hand, was composed only of the elderly, mainly Jewish, with a larger number of couples and no known children.

Residents at Inwood House were 68% White, 27% Black, 2% Hispanic, and 3% Oriental. Many came from low-income families, but some from high-income families had chosen to leave home and live more independently at Inwood.

The range of disabilities was wide, such as cerebral palsy, muscular dystrophy, epilepsy, heart problems, stroke, impaired hearing or vision, limb amputation, learning disabilities, and mental retardation.

Fig. 9.2   Revitz House, entrance and landscaped grounds.

2 Reasons for Coming to Inwood House

Prior to coming to Inwood House, many residents had lived with their parents or had shared an apartment with a friend. They had moved, they said, either because a parent had died or a roommate had left and they did not want to (or perhaps could not) live alone, or because they wanted their independence like most other people in their twenties. There was also a great deal of social life in the building, which is a great advantage for the handicapped or elderly single. The taller the building, the more possible companionship the residents may have, while at the same time having the benefits of the privacy of their own apartments. Asked on the questionnaire whether they were lonely sometimes, often, or never, almost all said they were rarely or never lonely, and that they could have privacy whenever they wanted.

3 Activities

Of the residents at Inwood House, 50% worked either part- or full-time. Of the other 50%, 20% would like to work and were looking for jobs, 20% were elderly and retired, and only about 10% were not interested in working at all. In the evening when people come home from work, there is a great deal of socializing in the lobby on the entrance level and between apartments, and on the balconies overlooking the lobby on each floor, until people retire to make their dinner or go to the communal dining hall.

The same was true for Revitz House, on a quieter level, and more spread out over the day since fewer people worked. However, in both places, and particularly at Revitz House, there were meeting or playrooms which were also frequent sites of get togethers for unplanned or planned activities.

At Inwood House, as at Revitz, the residents ran a coffee shop themselves, organized by volunteer residents. There were also many planned activities for residents run by Montgomery County, which provides recreation for the handicapped and elderly. Classes are offered in ceramics, aerobic exercises, woodwork, weaving, sewing, crafts, writing, dramatics; some residents sell their handicrafts, some publish their poetry. There are movies, social and business meetings, and theatricals put on by residents of both places. Residents are also taken to the theater and on weekend camping trips.

Residents therefore enjoy a highly active and social life, and this is partly due to the nature of the building designed for them, and to the fact that these are relatively tall buildings. This affords many neighbors, and public places in which to meet them. The same people living alone or with a family or in an institution could be lonely, feel too different from everyone else, and be in buildings not designed for barrier-free access and egress.

9.3 RESIDENT RESPONSE TO THE BUILT ENVIRONMENT

In spite of the great satisfaction in general, expressed by residents of Inwood House and Revitz House about the buildings themselves, there were some suggestions as to how the buildings, the grounds, and the surrounding streets, shopping areas, and transportation facilities could be further improved. Attention to these factors needs to be taken into account when planning the design and location of a building.

Regarding the location, one also has to take into consideration the surrounding neighbors, and whether they are going to object to a building for the handicapped. Initially there were neighborhood objections to Inwood House, but these were overcome with constructive suggestions such as high shrubbery around the building, assurances that the building would be well maintained, and some good public relations.

Before building any apartment house for the elderly or handicapped, it is also advisable to note street conditions, access to transportation, proximity of shopping areas, and whether there are major obstacles between the apartment house and the shopping location.

1 Grounds

There is some shrubbery around Inwood House, although some residents, particularly those who like to sit outside on the benches, said they wished there were more greenery immediately around the house. Residents who like gardening have been permitted vegetable or flower gardens on the grounds, and for those who are in wheelchairs, garden beds are elevated so they can reach them. On the grounds immediately outside the front of the building there is also an exercise course composed of low-set bars like those in a jungle gym, for adults, particularly those in wheelchairs, to exercise on. Doubtless the children play on these, too. The ground below the bars is bricked, however, so that the wheelchair resident can wheel under the bars, then reach up to them from a sitting position. Exercising on the bars is important in developing and maintaining the upper body strength necessary for wheeling the wheelchair, as well as maneuvering oneself from one seat to another place, such as another seat, a bed, toilet, or car seat.

There is parking on the grounds for about 100 cars for residents, staff, and visitors. Some residents have cars specially adapted for the physically handicapped person, and a number of mildly retarded persons have cars and drive.

Inwood House has a small open area around the apartment house immediately outside the glass entrance doors. This is composed of two benches covered by a roof. Both at Inwood House and at Revitz House residents like to sit outside on sunny days (Fig. 9.3). At the latter place, since there is no formal outside seating area, some bring chairs from inside to sit on.

Many residents at Inwood House said they would like more outdoor seating available, and that such seating should be in the shade. Apparently the roof over the seating does not provide enough protection from the sun. Given that many residents at both houses cannot walk or ride far to get outside, or cannot do so without help, such immediate sources of contact with the outside world and the people who pass by are welcome to them and might be included in the plans of designers.

2 The Building

The Lobby.   The glassed-in lobby is just inside the front door and directly off the parking lot and street. There are several potted plants and sofas, which give it sightly the air of a hotel. The security office is at the end of the lobby, farthest away from the front door, so that those on duty can see who is coming in and going out. Visitors are supposed to call the code number of the person they are visiting before entering the lobby, but often they just walk in through the open glass doors of the lobby. The lobby is usually alive with residents and visitors, particularly after work.

Some residents though, particularly those living on the ground floor, which is the same as that of the lobby, complained about noise coming from the lobby. Ground-floor apartments are frequently given to those with the most severe disabilities so that they can get in and out of the building with minimum difficulty. Perhaps they should be informed of the noise factor, or perhaps living space should not be built where there is a lobby, but rather the space used for storage and other facilities if this is feasible. This still remains a conflict and, certainly, in some way, the lobby and the apartments for the severely handicapped or for those needing a quiet apartment can be separated. Soundproofing some noisy areas might also be possible. This is a common practice among musicians living in residential buildings.

Elevators. In almost every study on user response to the built environment carried out by Haber (1977a, b; 1986a, b, c) there were complaints about elevators. Elevators are a necessary component in our increasing use of tall buildings, yet they have many problems. The only people who did not complain about elevators were those in the higher income brackets in one study (Haber, 1977b). A frequent complaint at Inwood and all other buildings except high rental buildings was of elevator breakdown, which is especially hard on those with ambulatory handicaps.

The two elevators at Inwood House were larger [1.8 m by 2.4 m (6 by 8 ft)] than most apartment-house elevators to accommodate two or more persons in

Fig. 9.3   Residents socializing outside Revitz House for the elderly.

wheelchairs besides other residents. There is often a fear among the elderly or newly handicapped that the doors are going to close before they have been able to enter or exit from the elevator. Since the elderly and the handicapped are usually slower than other people, they are especially concerned with being given enough time to get into and out of an elevator. Two sensors on the bottom sides of the elevator at Inwood House are designed to prevent the doors from closing as long as someone is at the opening. They are especially placed near the bottom so as to register the entry or exit of persons in wheelchairs.

Despite this, some residents felt that the door closes too quickly on them, but administration said that once inside the elevator, residents can push a button that closes the door. Residents do not seem to realize that they have control of the door closing. It is true that one person inside the elevator could push the close button before another person, who is trying to get in, can do so. Should the light sensors fail to counteract this, another backup system could doubtlessly solve this problem.

Also, either a light could flash (especially for the hard of hearing) or a bell could sound immediately before the door is to close. This would alert the visually impaired as well as others and warn them of the closing or, for that matter, the opening. A "ping" often precedes the stop of an elevator at a floor in regular high-rise buildings, and could here, too. In Jerusalem, Israel, near the railway station, a bell rings before a traffic light changes to "Walk" for the visually impaired (Haber, unpublished). This simple device could be used in many situations, including elevator stops and door openings and closings, in addition to flashing lights for the hearing impaired.

There are areas where the needs of the younger handicapped and the elderly are similar, and areas where they are different. Both need more time to enter and exit elevators. The elderly, however, have a special problem in having to face death more often. Revitz residents wanted the deceased removed without having to ride down in the elevator with them. Alternative times or perhaps a special elevator should be used in buildings for the elderly to remove the deceased out of sight of the residents.

Other tall buildings for the elderly and the handicapped may have other solutions, but designers should keep in mind the "conflicts" mentioned, whereby a barrier-free design useful to persons with one type of handicap may conflict with the needs of those with a different handicap. Although in this chapter we are discussing the handicapped and the elderly in two different buildings, some problems arise when the handicapped and the elderly live together in a greater mix. There are certainly social problems, for instance, where teenagers and the elderly live together or in close proximity, according to Newman (1973). This brings to light the fact that conflicts may arise between any two or more different categories of persons, particularly if the built environment is altered for one of them.

Hallways and Carpeting.   Hallways at Inwood are especially wide so that two wheelchairs can pass each other comfortably. This facilitated noisy "wheelchair races" along hallways outside the apartments, and consequent complaints that such races rip the hallway carpeting. Possibly wheelchair races could be formalized outside at regular periods, and designers might even build in a recreation area that includes a place for wheelchair races.

The wheelchair persons said that the hallway and apartment carpeting was too soft, however, and the wheelchair slid over it so easily that their arm muscles were not being developed as was necessary. On the other hand, some ambulatory residents said the carpeting was too hard on their feet and should be softer.

Doors. There are heavy doors on all apartments at Inwood House. These are good protection for occupants against fire (see Chapter 11 and Haber, 1980); however, some handicapped and elderly residents found them too heavy to operate due to reduced strength or dexterity in their hands and arms. At Inwood House some respondents in wheelchairs whose legs are elevated in front of them on a foot rest also found it hard to get close to the door keyhole from the front.

A similar problem existed in entering stores equipped with doors that have handles on them. Many of the people surveyed suggested automatic doors on all stores, not just the major ones. There are, in fact, buttons for the handicapped to open doors automatically in a number of buildings, such as in the local public library and the nearby Metrorail station. However, as far as is known, this method of opening doors is not standardized across the country or possibly even across the county. Many nonhandicapped people use the automatic buttons also because many doors are very heavy. Whether this extra weight is due to the doors being primarily designed to open automatically, or whether they would be that heavy even if they were not automatic is not known, but it is a factor designers can consider. How does one design for one type of handicap without inconveniencing a person with another kind of handicap or a person who has no handicap at all?

For the handicapped with difficulty in fine motor movement with the hands, fitting a key into a keyhole is sometimes difficult. Here one might consider alternative methods, such as the plastic security card slid into a slot currently used in many hotels. Doubtless several other alternatives could be designed for those with manual handicaps.

All doors had a peephole, that is, a small hole in the door at the height of about 1.5 m (5 ft) through which a resident on the inside can look at the person calling. This was set too high for people in wheelchairs. One might suggest two peepholes in apartments for the handicapped, one at the usual level and another at the height of a person in a wheelchair, unless certain apartments were designated for wheelchair occupants only.

In an apartment house for the elderly it should also be kept in mind that the elderly may lose height with age. Designers should then find the average height for a peephole for the doors of those living in apartments for the elderly. While this may seem like a great deal of trouble to go through to establish the "right" height of a peephole in a door for the handicapped or elderly, it is certainly a security factor. The handicapped and the elderly are more vulnerable than others and need adequate protection. While both houses (Inwood and Revitz) have good security systems, there are always possibilities of someone unauthorized slipping into the buildings.

Because of the difficulties of getting to the door to open it for callers, some residents at Inwood leave their doors unlocked or even ajar all the time. While Inwood House appears friendly, there should be design considerations that would allow handicapped residents easy access and egress, which would then facilitate the security of closed doors and screening callers through the peepholes.

3 The Apartment

The Kitchen. One wheelchair resident suggested that the entrance to the kitchen be made wider because it was a close fit to get the wheelchair into the kitchen without scraping the sides of its entrance. This would prevent wear and tear on the walls of the kitchen or any other room where the entry was too small for a wheelchair. Wheelchair widths and the arm space over the wheel need to be taken into account in constructing inside as well as outside entrances.

The kitchens were large enough for the ambulatory, but again, some wheelchair persons found it difficult or impossible to make a full turn inside the kitchen and had to back out in order to turn around. Some suggestions for customizing the kitchen for wheelchair handicapped included counters or cabinets that could be lowered by levers, a space under the sink to enable the person to get under and close to it, and knobs on the front rather than the back or middle of the stove. Refrigerators, as well, should have the freezer either at the bottom or on the side, opening down the center. However, there will still be some higher storage areas which a wheelchair person cannot reach unless some solution is found.

The Bathroom. A second essential room for anyone, particularly the handicapped and the elderly, is the bathroom. Most home accidents, even for non-handicapped people, happen in the kitchen and the bathroom, so these areas must be particularly well designed. The bathroom has the danger for all of having a wet and slippery floor. In regular apartments or houses there is a small threshold before the entrance to the bathroom, and a step up necessary to get into the shower and, even more so, into a bath.

Residents at Inwood had a choice, where available, of an apartment having a bathroom with a roll-in shower or a bathtub. First of all, the marble bar which usually is placed outside the bathroom was not installed, making for a barrier-free entrance to the bathroom. There was no step before the shower, either. Residents with a roll-in shower wheeled (or walked) themselves directly into the shower area inside which there was a chair with holes in it, allowing water to drain, and transferred themselves from wheelchair to shower chair. Similar showers for multiple paraplegics in buildings designed for them were found in Cairo, Egypt (Haber, unpublished).

Some residents in wheelchairs with good upper body strength preferred a bathtub. In this case a seat was provided in the bathtub. In all cases there were bars on the walls next to both the bath and the toilet and behind the toilet. The same was true of Revitz House and, as has been observed earlier, rails next to baths have been adopted by a number of hotels.

Emergency Communication. In the kitchen and bathrooms at Inwood House there were emergency cords that residents could pull should they need immediate help. Residents said staff response to such calls was excellent. This same system was used for emergency calls at Revitz House. Some residents at Inwood, especially those in wheelchairs, suggested that the cords be longer so they could reach them more easily. But should someone, either handicapped or elderly, have fallen on the floor and be unable to get up, would they be able to reach such a cord even if longer? One might consider a button on the lower part of a wall as an alternative way of obtaining help. Some Inwood residents also asked to have an emergency cord in the living room in case they were there and unable to reach the kitchen or bathroom during an emergency. Inwood residents could also reach the office directly by telephone from the living room or bedroom.

Where handicapped or elderly individuals live alone, devices have been designed for them to wear around the neck, which carry a button that, if pressed, will connect them immediately to the local police or hospital. These are provided free under the National Health system (paid for by taxes) in England to those handicapped or elderly living alone who may need emergency help. In the United States a number of private entrepreneurs have developed and advertise such devices for sale.

Light Switches.   Light switches at Inwood House were on the wall rather than on lamps. Residents said they liked having the switch on the wall as this was easier both to reach and to turn on and off for those in wheelchairs or with manual handicaps. It is also often difficult for the elderly, due to arthritis, to manipulate small objects such as lamp switches.

Designers of new buildings could keep in mind that some people in the building may be in wheelchairs, so that light switches are set low enough for them to reach. The height should not be set by guesswork, but by measuring the average height of arm reach of a person in a wheelchair.

Windows and the View.   Residents at Inwood and, particularly, at Revitz House were very pleased with the view from the windows (Fig. 9.4), which were placed strategically at an appropriate height. It was thoughtful of the designers to set the buildings in as pleasant surroundings as possible, particularly since many handicapped and elderly cannot get out often.

It must be emphasized that over 85% of residents at Inwood House and Revitz House were satisfied or very satisfied with their building. These comments were only suggestions as to how the building and grounds could be even further improved.

Fig. 9.4   The windows of Revitz House provide residents with a pleasant view, as many elderly do not often get out.

4 Streets

The handicapped and the elderly want to get around like other people—and this means having to negotiate not only the building, but also streets, traffic, shopping areas, and transportation. Thus when buildings are designed for the handicapped or the elderly, it is crucial to consider that the surrounding areas be as barrier-free as possible.

At Inwood House, a ramp of concrete led directly from the building to the sidewalk and into the street so that those in wheelchairs or carts could drive straight out of the building and into the public domain. However, some residents complained that the sidewalk which they could use to get to the nearby shopping center, had some problems. Although all the breaks between sidewalk and street had been flattened to allow wheelchairs to cross streets, the sidewalks were so narrow that there was barely enough room for a wheelchair. It seems to have been assumed in the suburbs, by those who built the roads and sidewalks, that there would be few pedestrians. This was doubtlessly true in the 1960s or earlier, when money in the United States was more plentiful and many people owned cars, and when attention to the handicapped and the elderly was still in its infancy. It was also before walking became so highly recommended by health specialists, so that sidewalks are now also used by joggers. For all of these reasons, sidewalks should be widened, sidewalk joints and cracks should be smoothed and level, and other obstructions such as telephone poles and signs should be carefully placed.

A similar concern with regard to sidewalks was raised by residents of Revitz House. Designers felt residents would enjoy grassy walks outside the building. However, elderly residents were afraid of the uneven surface of grass and of slipping, especially when the grass was wet, and suggested that concrete walks outside the building would be safer for them to walk on than grass, no matter how nice grass looked. Similarly, designers deliberately placed the mail box outside the building because residents "ought" to go out. However, when there was ice on the ground, elderly residents were afraid to go out to the mail box for fear of slipping and requested that the mail box be moved inside.

Both wheelchair users and elderly handicapped persons may have a common need for hard, even street surfaces. However, they differ as far as ramps are concerned, which often are essential for those in wheelchairs but may cause difficulties for some elderly who are ambulatory. Designers need to weigh the pros and cons of designing for different types of residents, as it may not be possible to aid everyone equally. We are aware that effort in design has been concentrated on the needs of those in wheelchairs, and on the elderly perhaps to a lesser extent, and that there are many other handicaps which have received scant awareness or attention in building and street design.

5 Shopping Area

The ability to shop for themselves gives the handicapped and the elderly the chance "to be like other people," a wish many at Inwood House expressed. Residents who were ambulatory and those in wheelchairs could, in spite of the problems of the sidewalks discussed, still get themselves to the nearby shopping center, either on their own or by bus.

As mentioned, some residents wished that all doors on shops, not just those on major stores, opened automatically as they were often too heavy for the handicapped or those in wheelchairs to manage. The latter are often impeded from door access by their own footrests extending beyond their hands, which makes it difficult if not impossible for them to open or close some doors. In the supermarket, special carts which fit over the top of the wheelchair enabled wheelchair shoppers to push the cart along in front of the wheelchair.

At Revitz House, although a major shopping center was within a few blocks, it was separated from them by a six-lane highway. Since most did not own cars, there was no way that with their slower walk they could cross that highway on foot in time before the traffic lights changed. This oversight in not linking an apartment house to a shopping center in such a way that residents could get there themselves without help, was a big problem for the residents, and one which planners could take into account. It is not enough to design a barrier-free building for the handicapped and elderly; one must also provide barrier-free streets and shopping areas within the immediate vicinity if the residents are to be as self-sufficient as they would like and could be. (See also Blank, 1982, for similar findings in Kansas City, Kans.)

Some form of safe crossing, such as a bridge (here there is the problem of steps or ramps) over the highway or an elevator up to a walkway which crosses the highway and another to go down on the other side, are all possibilities by which people could get from one side of the road to the other. These types of crossings, as well as underground crossings connecting one side of a major highway to the other, have been observed in London, Jerusalem, and many other places.

9.4 TRANSPORTATION

In discussing transportation, which is normal and easy for those *not* handicapped or elderly, several components must be kept in mind. One can assume that few handicapped or elderly living in such a special housing situation are able to drive or have their own cars, because of their handicaps or age, or even for economic reasons, since the handicapped and the elderly in the United States often have low socioeconomic status. (The handicapped usually cannot get jobs, or if they can, they sometimes cannot get to them. The aged often live on low fixed incomes which do not increase much with inflation, if at all. Thus even if they can drive, they cannot afford a car.) This means that both groups must rely either on public transportation or, if available, on relatives or friends.

Public transportation as described by Inwood and Revitz House residents is full of barriers, even though there has been considerable improvement in the last 5 years. There is a bus stop two blocks away from Inwood House. However, even among those who could get to it, several difficulties were expressed.

1 Traffic Lights

The bus needed was on the other side of the road from Inwood House. There was a traffic light enabling people to cross, but it changed too fast for physically handicapped and elderly to get across the road in time. The same observation was made by residents of Revitz House, who had a six-lane highway to cross before reaching the shopping center.

2 Bus and Subway Access

There was a high step at the entrance of the bus. This high step becomes difficult for both physically handicapped and elderly in getting on and off. The subway did have an entrance with a ramp into it for those in wheelchairs. However, one of the nearest subway entrances for those not in wheelchairs has so many steps down that it is very difficult for some middle-aged ambulatory persons to go from the street level to the subway, particularly when carrying packages or luggage. Designers of transportation need to keep these factors in mind when considering barrier-free access to public transportation.

Where elevators are available to take the handicapped from the street to an elevated train, the elevator is not always working. In this case the wheelchair person has made the perhaps arduous trip to the subway for nothing if there is only an elevator and no ramp. If the steps are too much for an ambulatory but handicapped person, the same problem applies.

Some partial solutions have been found. Some public buses were designed with a lift on them. Also, a person needing such a bus could call the downtown Metro to send a bus with a lift and it would come to the route of the caller. The lift is behind the door of the bus and is lowered by the driver for the handicapped passenger.

The county also authorized licenses for 20 special taxis which are built wide and high enough for a person in a wheelchair to fit in, wheeling in directly from the outside. A ramp is placed from the ground to the entrance of the taxi, which itself is very wide. However, residents report that this ramp is so steep that the driver always has to push the wheelchair up; its occupant cannot do so alone.

It is necessary to reserve such special taxis 3 hours ahead of the time needed unless the intended user is waiting at an outside location or a doctor's office. In this case, the service tries to push the caller up within half an hour. The rider pays whatever the meter reads plus $6. The county has developed a system of discount coupons based on income level for users of these special taxis.

Some residences have cars adapted to the handicapped driver, such as having the gas pedal, brake, or shift on the steering wheel for those who cannot use their legs or feet. Some have lifts which raise them into or lower them out of their van or car.

Those with hearing or visual impairments may be able to use public transportation with some careful barrier-free design, such as a bell at a traffic light in Jerusalem near the train station, which signals a light change for the blind. Lights can inform the hearing impaired when a train is coming. The hearing impaired can drive, and a number of the mentally handicapped at Inwood House owned and drove cars.

Within the buses and subways of Washington, D.C., Maryland, and Virginia there are seats reserved for the elderly or handicapped should they need them. However, this is not the case in all states.

9.5 SOCIAL RELATIONS

Although this issue may not seem to affect building design, it is important to know how residents interact with one another and whether different types of residents can be satisfactorily housed together or should be separated from each other in some way (Fig. 9.5). Newman (1973), for instance, does not feel teenagers and the elderly should be in close proximity, since the former tend to prey upon or harass the latter. On the other hand, Chapter 6 refers to the proximity of children and the aged in a community, so perhaps it works in some cultures but not in American culture.

Asked, "With whom do you get along well," most people got along well with others, but there were three conflicting groups.

1 Wheelchair Residents

Several wheelchair residents said they got along best with other residents in wheelchairs. Some residents not in wheelchairs complained about their noisy races, as mentioned. Certainly, the wheelchair handicapped have won more attention than many other groups of handicapped persons, both by their own and by others' efforts.

2 Physically and Mentally Handicapped

There was an interesting "class" distinction between some of the physically and some of the mentally handicapped at Inwood House. The physically handicapped usually considered themselves superior to the mentally handicapped, but some of the mentally handicapped, mostly young and in perfect physical condition, considered themselves superior to the physically handicapped. This was the attitude

Fig. 9.5 Residents of Revitz House interact in the summer at an entrance plaza.

among some of the two groups *inside* the building. However, their self-image and feelings about themselves when in public, outside the building, may be different.

When asked whether they considered themselves fully, partially, or not at all disabled, 90% of the respondents with physical handicaps said they were either not at all or only partially disabled, whereas 90% of the retarded said they were partially or fully disabled.

This may be partially or fully due to the treatment of the two groups by the public, outside the building. "Since I've been in a wheelchair, people make all kinds of allowances for me and will do anything for me," said a woman recently forced into a wheelchair by severe arthritis. On the other hand, the mentally retarded usually have been so since birth and are reminded repeatedly of this during training by the social services, in an effort to give them realistic expectations out of life. Also, they often appear normal in public, but are forced to constantly reveal their mental retardation over minor matters such as inability to read signs or prices and having to ask for help. There may be more public prejudice against the retarded than against the physically handicapped. Certainly those in wheelchairs have gained almost popular appeal, partially perhaps for reasons stated earlier, namely, often appearing youthful, war wounded, possibly heroic, and partially because they are, at least in Washington, D.C., comparatively well organized politically.

In designing buildings, the question remains whether they should be designed for various types of handicapped persons, as at Inwood House, or, as has been traditional, for single types of handicapped persons. The administration at Inwood House feels that the mix of handicap works well, and that there are comparatively few problems due to this. One could argue that this mix is more like real life than the more institutional type of building for one type of handicap only, such as the blind, the deaf, or the mentally handicapped.

3 Children

Inwood is also unusual insofar as most apartment houses for the handicapped do not usually house either families or children. Of the residents, 50% objected to having children in the apartment house. Some objected to the children of handicapped residents using for their play the grounds and bars outside the building, which were set up for the exercise of the handicapped residents. Of course, a separate play area for children could be built, although this would involve extra cost.

The other 50% of the respondents liked having children at Inwood House, saying "the children make the place seem more like a normal apartment house," and "the children remind me of my own childhood and family, and they make life here more interesting."

Although it may not always be possible to give incoming residents their choice, one could ask them whether they prefer to be near or not near children. Or, at the risk of accusations of segregation, families with children might be housed in a different part of the complex, where they can perhaps be freer to be noisy. Single persons wishing to live in this area can still have the choice of doing so if space is available. This necessarily involves design considerations as to the distribution of single- and multiple-occupancy apartments in a building, which depends to some degree on consideration of the building's anticipated residential makeup.

9.6 RELATIONSHIP BETWEEN BUILDING DESIGN AND SOCIAL RESEARCH FOR USER RESPONSE

Comparisons have been made of the similarities and differences of the two study groups, Inwood House for the handicapped and Revitz House for the elderly. Some suggestions have been made with regard to resident responses to barrier-free buildings, streets, shopping, working areas, and transportation, which designers may take into consideration when designing such buildings, their surrounding environment, and linkages, namely, transportation. It is hoped that designers will pay more attention to the responses of users of such buildings before, during, and after the buildings, environs, and transportation have been constructed. Those in the social sciences are well equipped to work alongside building designers, architects, and engineers to carry out such studies.

9.7 CONDENSED REFERENCES/BIBLIOGRAPHY

Blank, 1982, *A Social Psychology of Developing Adults*
Goffman 1961, *Asylums*
Haber 1977a, *Barrier-Free Environment for the Handicapped*
Haber 1977b, *The Impact of Tall Buildings on Users and Neighbors*
Haber 1980b, *Human Behavior in Fire in a Total (24 hour) Institution*
Haber 1986a, *Building Design for the Handicapped and User Response, a Study*
Haber 1986b, *Revitz House, a Survey of Resident Response to a Building*
Haber 1986c, *Response of the Handicapped to Living in a Barrier-Free*
Haber (unpublished), *Building Design for the Multiple Paraplegics in Cairo*
Newman 1973, *Defensible Space: Crime Prevention through Urban Design*
Salmen 1987, *Discussions at Architects Institute of America*

10

Access and Egress for Handicapped Persons in Public Buildings

10.1 CODES AND STANDARDS

Perhaps the greatest safeguard against being caught in a serious fire in a public building is not to enter the building in the first place. While this might sound like a strange suggestion, barring the entry of people with mobility difficulties (on the basis that their safety cannot be guaranteed) has been a predominant safety philosophy. As such, it has probably been the greatest political obstruction to the introduction of barrier-free design legislation. Now that public buildings are being made more accessible—in some countries years after innovative legislation in the United States such as the 1961 issue of ANSI A117.1 (ANSI, 1980) and the Architectural Barriers Act in 1968 (see Chapter 3)—building managers, fire authorities, architects, and life safety policy makers are faced with a worrying dilemma. While there is greater *access,* this does not necessarily imply that there is adequate *egress* in an emergency.

International fire legislation is based primarily on the principle of *unaided escape.* In other words, there is provision in terms of design parameters such as alarm systems, compartmentalization, fire resistance, travel distance, exit width, and exit choice for people who are capable of moving to safety without physical help and are assumed to move at similar speeds. There is little precedent in fire design legislation relating to public buildings for the kind of explicitly defined communication and evacuation procedures which are necessary for people who move particularly slowly or require assistance. This chapter attempts to outline some of the issues which barrier-free designs, at the point of access to a building and circulation around a building, raise for the establishment of principles of safe emergency egress of people with physical and sensory handicaps. Chapter 12 describes a very specific wayfinding system useful both for visually impaired and all persons in smoky conditions, and Chapter 11 discusses an approach that emphasizes nonegress as an option in emergencies, especially if mobility is impaired.

Much of this chapter will focus on the British experience with the provision of safe egress for handicapped persons. Let us first turn to a review of British standards related to access and egress.

In Britain the term *barrier-free design* is used far less than in North America

(Bednar, 1977), perhaps reflecting slower progress by the British. The expression building *access* is preferred and was incorporated into the title of the first British standard, BS 5810 (BSI, 1979), relating to new public buildings and intended as a guideline for the adaptation of existing buildings (offices, shops, hospitals, restaurants, theaters). BS 5810 was preceded in 1970 by the Chronically Sick and Disabled Persons Act (as amended in 1976). The latter requires that access and sanitary conveniences be provided for disabled people in public buildings ("wherever practicable and reasonable") but, like the British standard, and similar acts in other countries, discussed in earlier chapters of this volume, it does not contain any enforcement powers. The enforceable access requirements for disabled people (covering England and Wales), introduced first in Schedule 2 of the Building Regulations (DOE, 1985), apply to new offices and shops regardless of the number of stories. The provisions applying to new single single-story factories, educational establishments, and public buildings have now been extended in the Building (Disabled People) Regulations (DOE, 1987b) to multistory premises, but only with respect to the story of those premises which contains the principal entrance. The 1989 regulations also require that when a building is altered or extended, access and facilities for disabled people are not adversely affected. The approved document Part M, setting out how the requirement of "reasonable" provision for access is to be achieved, was recently introduced (DOE, 1987a) as part of a phased program aimed at improving access and mobility for disabled people in all new public buildings. Part M includes specifications relating to means of access (M2), sanitary conveniences (M3), and audience or spectator seating (M4). It is worth noting that *Guide to Fire Precautions in Existing Places of Entertainment and Like Premises* (Home Office, 1987) devotes one of 15 sections to access for disabled people. Reflected here is a growing sensitivity to the rights of access of the individual, whatever his or her physical capability.

While the United Kingdom has been slower than the United States in the initial introduction of access legislation applying to public buildings, the new *Code of Practice for Means of Escape for Disabled People,* British standard BS 5588 Part 8 (BSI, 1988), is innovative in actually detailing egress design parameters relating to the safety of the disabled. Taking it as axiomatic that buildings should be comprehensively accessible to disabled people, the new code of practice extends the life safety protection afforded through structural "means of escape." The standard applies to all buildings except private dwellings and includes recommendations concerning the provision of protected refuges and/or evacuation elevators, wheelchair spaces within protected stairways, and fire warning systems. An additional innovative feature of BS 5588 Part 8 is Appendix A, which includes advice to management. This advice is outlined in very general terms. Procedures have to be tailored to fit individual buildings. It is management's task to see that procedures devised are satisfactory in terms of the criteria contained in the code.

Compliance with a British standard does not itself confer immunity from legal obligations. However, British standards have historically figured prominently as the basis for design yardsticks eventually incorporated into fire regulations. To effect current requirements, the *Building Regulations: Mandatory Rules for Means of Escape in Case of Fire* (DOE, 1985) can only be complied with by adhering to certain sections of the appropriate BS 5588 codes of practice. It is clear from a recent communication from the Department of Environment (DOE, 1986) that the extension of enforceable access requirements to all buildings open to the public has awaited the resolution of how to deal with the means of escape problem and, in particular, the appearance of BS 5588 Part 8. The aim of this chapter is not to summarize the recommendations made in BS 5588 Part 8, but to use it as a starting point to consider broad conclusions about life safety for handicapped people which can be drawn from existing knowledge and research of people's behavior in public buildings on fire (such as offices, cinemas, shopping complexes, and hotels).

In the following argument the disabled are not isolated as a target group whose safety necessarily involves radically different building designs or evacuation procedures from the rest of a building's population. Attention to a broader category of mobility impaired people actually helps to raise fundamental safety issues affecting all building users. In this respect, if one is to add a set of design yardsticks and evacuation procedures to those that already exist, one has to be assured that the existing safety policy is optimum.

10.2 DEFINING THE HANDICAP

BS 5588 Part 8 defines access as "access to and use of facilities, and egress except in cases of emergency." Implicit in this definition is a conventional architectural separation of the access (entry) route in public buildings from the secondary emergency fire egress route. An exit choice is provided in the event of one of the routes being obstructed by smoke or flames. Depending on the number of stories and other factors such as floor area, secondary stairways are required in buildings such as offices and hotels. Access legislation and codes of practice to date have concentrated on the entry routes, and primarily wheelchair users, through the recommended provision of elevators, ramps, and doorways, with widths and floor areas wide enough to accommodate wheelchairs.

The most comprehensive advice in respect to access in the United Kingdom (serving as a guide to architects) is undoubtedly Selwyn Goldsmith's book *Designing for the Disabled,* first published in 1963 and now in its third revised edition. Goldsmith (1984, pp. 14–15) points out that although uncomfortable with the term disabled, since it tends to stereotype people in a derogatory fashion, he has continued to use the term in editions of the book as it is a recognizable term. He distinguishes between those people who are nonambulant (generally confined to wheelchairs) and those who are semiambulant. In many ways, he argues, the nonambulant should be regarded separately from both the ambulant and the semiambulant. The distinction can be important, since the disabled are often considered as a homogeneous group. Bearing in mind detailed design considerations relating to ramps and stairs, such as degree of incline, texture of surface, step dimension, and availability of handrails, he feels that ramps, which are often recommended as an alternative to stairs, may often be less easy for the semiambulant to use than stairways. This Monograph has raised similar points about ramps specifically, and more generally about the difficulty of designing in such a way as to take into consideration the diversity of disabilities for which one must account.

In 1969 a survey of people in the United Kingdom was conducted by the Social Survey Division of the Office of Population Censuses and Surveys (OPCS) (Harris, 1971). In the survey a distinction was made between those people who are impaired (in other words, people who had an impairment but were not at all handicapped in terms of physically caring for themselves) and those who are more appreciably handicapped. (This usage of handicapped vis-à-vis disabled should be compared to the related approach given in Chapter 3.) The handicapped group, at the time of the survey, was estimated to form 2.89% (1,329,000) of the U.K. population. The number estimated to be impaired or handicapped in the United Kingdom was 7.8% (3,071,000). The number of disabled people increases dramatically for older age groups (see Goldsmith, 1984, p. 20). Once one includes a range of other people whose movement is temporarily impaired (young, old, injured, pregnant), it is likely that 10% of the population (a number comparable to that described for most countries considered in this volume) would be a very conservative estimate of those likely to have marked difficulties in moving to safety at a speed consistent with current legislation.

This percentage is indeed very much an underestimate if one takes into account the findings of research which suggest that (1) people in public building fires, even in flight to an exit, do not necessarily move independently of each other, but often in social groups (Sime, 1983), and (2) the group will tend to slow down to the speed of its slowest member. People with severe handicaps are likely to be accompanied to the building and unlikely to be abandoned by their companions in an emergency. Taking into account the fact that occupancies will vary in the proportions of handicapped present, depending on the building's function or circumstances, a figure of 10% is a poor reflection of the degree of effort and funding that should be invested in the access/egress problem. It involves us all.

BS 5588 Part 8 defines disabled people as those "with a physical, hearing or sight impairment which affects their mobility or their use of buildings," putting more emphasis in this definition on the disability of a person than on the barriers to safe egress characteristic of a building. The reference in the definition to those with hearing or sight impairment is important. It is noticeable that the access codes of practice and the literature (in fact, BS 5588 Part 8 is no exception) tend to concentrate on design parameters affecting physical rather than sensory impairment. In this chapter the term handicapped is preferred to disabled, since it reflects the fact that difficulty in escaping is just as much a function of a building as a person's inability to move quickly.

Codes of practice and regulations in the United Kingdom have been based on the principle that the means of escape should allow people to physically reach safety unaided or unassisted. Since it is assumed that people who are mobility impaired or handicapped require assistance, it has been impossible to accommodate them into the existing safety philosophy. Attention to the needs of a group of people who self-evidently need assistance, because of a range of different kinds of physical and sensory handicaps, will ironically lead to a questioning of what is a handicap for *all* building users and what problems might be associated with the expression *unaided escape.* The current tendency is to isolate a group of people as requiring special treatment and facilities if their safety is to be guaranteed. This ironically perpetuates the difficulty in reconciling safety solutions appropriate to handicapped people with those dictated by the notion of unaided escape.

A difficulty in the philosophy underlining means of escape (as a design solution) is in regarding deviation from what the codes dictate, when people do not reach safety, primarily as a consequence of difficulties in movement. There may be an overlap between the tendency to equate crowd movement in fires with nonthinking objects in motion, and the tendency among safety engineers to look for technical-fix solutions to egress problems. This strategy, by definition, fails to recognize the active contribution people need to make to any effective evacuation. This is pertinent to wheelchair users who may be stigmatized even more in fires than others with the notion that they think in some inanimate fashion (Sime, 1985a).

Recent research of fires indicates that a significant problem for people reaching safety in time in large-scale fires is not simply how quickly they are physically capable of moving the travel distance to safety, but the delays that occur in information and warning. This has been termed the perceived time available, or the margin of safety in a fire (Sime, 1986a), in which "time to start" is just as important as "time to move." In this respect, all building users, regardless of their physical or sensory capabilities, are undoubtedly helped by certain features of a building (such as exit choice as legislated by fire codes), but handicapped by others. Perhaps if everyone could see through walls (often our best means of structural defense from exposure to a fire), we would not all be so handicapped. As long as some people are regarded as handicapped and others as not, there will be a misunderstanding of how building users with a range of mobility and sensory capabilities can best be accommodated into the mainstream of fire legislation.

10.3 REMOVING BARRIERS TO SAFE EGRESS AND ACCESS

The use of the terms handicapped and mobility-impaired should encompass not only undoubted problems that some people have in physical movement, which can be greatly helped by more accommodating designs, but also the people's use of a building under normal circumstances and in an emergency. In seeking a closer integration and even collapse of the terms access and egress, it is important to emphasize that fires are not an entirely different event from the normal use of a building. Indeed, studies of behavior in fires paradoxically provide considerable insight into the social and psychological rules of behavior that prevail in a building independently of as well as during the fire event. Any evaluation of a building's access and egress standards should take into account the following building-related factors which, depending on the circumstances, role of a person, and his or her physical and sensory capabilities, can be a handicap or an aid to movement in a building when there is not an emergency. These factors become more, not less, important as an emergency such as a fire unfolds.

Ease of physical movement   Physical barriers to circulation, entry, and exit routes in the building.

Social (prohibitory) rules   The social constraints which make entry into or egress from certain building spaces difficult, such as verbal instructions which demarcate certain areas as "out of bounds" and signs labeled "staff only" or even "emergency escape route only."

Information availability   The information about what is happening in different parts of a building, and access and egress potentially afforded by routes, by signage, and, with the advent of new technology, by different communication systems (alarm, intercom, public announcement, and the guidance devices delineated in Chapter 12).

Legibility and image of a building   The ease with which a building can be understood and spatially comprehended and, consequently, with which people can find their way around.

Constraints on access to particular spaces when the building is used are normally an added handicap in a fire. This applies to all building users. For example, research of fires shows not only that the early stages are often characterized by investigation of the fire, not escape from it, but that existing knowledge of a building layout is crucial. Provided that people do not receive alternative information, which dissuades them from using a particular route (for example through staff guidance, warning beacons, or fire obstruction), statistical analyses of evacuations suggest that movement will be most prompt in a familiar direction (Sime, 1985b; Kimura and Sime, 1988). Differing degrees of access for particular role groups will set up constraints in a fire. Research of fires in which large numbers of people have died shows that the movement by public and staff can differ in direction (the public to the familiar entrance, the staff to the emergency route more familiar to them) (see Chapter 11 and Sime, 1985b). The research shows that the timing of movement by the public can be seriously delayed if dual alarm systems (as are used in department stores) alert the staff first without there being a prompt fire warning to the public and carefully organized evacuation procedure. If there are existing problems in wayfinding in modern complex building, as mentioned in Chapters 4 and 12 (Passini, 1984), these difficulties will escalate in a fire.

Recognizing that all building users are handicapped is not a condemnation of codes and regulations relating to design, but a realistic recognition that there should be some form of assisted escape through efficient dissemination of information if people are to reach safety. Once this principle is accepted, life safety recommendations relating to mobility-impaired people (in the sense of people who move more slowly) can be understood as an extension of safety design features such as signposting applicable to all users. Thus the notion of macro as opposed to micro access design, in which as far as possible mobility-impaired people are not given separate tailor-made facilities (Goldsmith, 1985), is equally applicable to egress design. This, in fact, has tended to be the position adopted in drawing up the new BS 5588 Part 8, where alterations in the standard should increase the safety of anyone in a building.

Passini has recently extended his research on wayfinding difficulties in settings such as large-scale shopping complexes in Montreal to consider the factors influencing the spatial mobility of visually handicapped people (Passini, 1986a; Passini et al., 1986b). He refers to two types of information used for wayfinding: (1) reference points used to identify the person's position and destination, and (2) information used to maintain a wayfinding direction while proceeding toward a destination. Visually impaired people rely much more than sighted people on environmental features perceptible at a close range, such as sides of doorways and detectable surface treatment of floors (Sanford, 1985). It is important to note, however, that to a surprising degree visually handicapped people do comprehend spaces spatially (Passini, 1986a) and use reference points in a way similar to other people.

This is particularly pertinent in a fire, where information about a fire developing in another room is important for a person to know. In this sense, not only are fire-resistant doors and walls barriers to movement in an absolute sense (and indeed protection against fire spread), but doorways are points of access to information. Whatever an individual's physical and sensory capabilities, he or she acts according to previous experience of the building (and other buildings) as well as a subjective awareness of the changing environment which will eventually require evasive action.

The idea that people with visual or hearing impairment may well benefit from particular kinds of alarm warning systems (and prosthetic guidance devices; Preiser, 1985) helps to highlight the potential advantages to building users in general of information fire warning systems over alarm sirens. The new generation of smoke detectors linked to computer-operated "intelligent" fire warning systems

(Todd, 1985) could potentially provide more efficient warning of a danger to the public (provided they become economically viable). BS 5588 Part 8 quite rightly recommends that "some form of communications system should be provided to enable the rapid and unambiguous identification of those stories with disabled persons requiring evacuation, and the relaying of this information to the person operating the evacuation or firefighting lift car."

BS 5588 Part 8 recommends temporary refuge compartments similar to those cited in the next chapter, built according to specified degrees of fire protection and adjacent to a special safety evacuation or fire-fighting elevator. (This is a requirement some people would like to see in the U.S. NFPA *Life Safety Code*; Benjamin, 1982.) To keep persons in a temporary refuge or in their rooms, it may prove crucial to have a two-way communication system, whereby anyone waiting for assistance can not only be assured others know that he or she is there, but obtain and impart information about what is happening. All of these design facilities *depend on an efficient and well-practiced communication and evacuation procedure*. Training with the handicapped individuals who are most likely to be in the building will be more difficult in buildings with a predominantly transient population (such as shoppers) as opposed to regular users of a particular occupancy (such as office workers whose most likely location at different times of day can be predetermined, or residents of high-rise housing).

At a Committee Workshop in Chicago it was suggested that in high-rise hotels, fire-protected apartments should be considered as suitable refuges for mobile and nonmobile occupants alike, particularly if the bathroom could serve as an interim "pressurized life-support system" (Grosse, 1987). From the evidence available from U.S. *Fire Journal* reports, as Chapter 11 will point out, unless the fire starts in a particular person's room, the safest strategy may well be to stay put with the door kept closed. Field research by the U.K. Fire Research Station of 13 fires with fatalities in hotels and boarding houses, certificated under the Fire Precautions Act 1971 (Williams and Hopkinson, 1986), concludes that: "if trapped by a fire on an escape route, one's best chance of survival is to stay in the bedroom with the door closed and make one's presence known to fire brigade to achieve external rescue." Recent research of escape behavior in fires in occupancies such as hotels (Sime, 1987a) reinforces the argument that it may prove safer to stay in a room with the door closed and wait to be rescued by the fire service, rather than follow the normally recommended course of making one's way to an escape stairway. In this respect a greater emphasis on using compartmented fire refuges may well be sensible. (This is a common policy in new hospitals.) Putting a greater stress on refuges, in terms of building design and life safety management, would have to be balanced against the resources and ability of staff and the fire services to perform a supportive role in effective communications, fire containment, and rescues. For people to use the refuges appropriately requires efficient safety education and two-way communication systems, which link a refuge to strategic points in the building (entry to elevators, fire service, building access points, communications room).

10.4 EGRESS RESEARCH

While the comparative value of strategies that emphasize refuge in place versus those that optimize egress will continue to be debated (and, thus, exposition of both alternatives is presented in this and in Chapters 11 and 12), the fact remains that egress must be made as efficient and effective as possible so that it is a viable alternative to have available. Let us, then, turn to research on egress. The historical evolution of codes and standards relating to fire warning systems and means of escape is based to a limited extent on empirical research on behavior. Indeed, it is only in recent years that researchers have begun to turn their attention in a concentrated fashion to the potential difficulties faced by people who are unlikely to be able to move to safety rapidly in an emergency. While there have been laboratory studies of the physiological and biomechanical effects of people individually climbing stairs or ramps changing in slope (Corlett and Hutcheson, 1972; Turner and Collins, 1981), there has been little in the way of studies of people varying in their physical capabilities. There has been little research comparing nonambulant, semiambulant, and ambulant people or the effect of one group on another.

Fruin (1971) provides information on different speeds of movement up and down stairs by males and females under and over 50 years old, but, as in a field study by Boyce (1985) monitoring the speed of movement, where age was included as a factor, handicapped elderly people were not studied. Some evacuation research of wheelchair users' egress from theaters has been conducted in Sweden (Hallberg and Nyberg, 1984), but tends to be descriptive rather than statistical. In addition, the results are not widely available in English. While Johnson (1983) has outlined different evacuation techniques for physically assisting disabled people on stairs, there is no clear indication of how the effectiveness of these techniques was monitored in the form of a detailed research study. Passini et al. (1986b), in reviewing research on the mobility and spatial orientation of the visually handicapped (covering a quarter of a century), point out that it is difficult to assess which type of settings are accessible and which are inaccessible to the unaided visually impaired traveler—reflecting presumably the lack of an architectural tradition in research.

Following the American conferences on fire and life safety for the handicapped in 1979 and 1980 (Levin, 1980; Kennett, 1982), much of the attention has been directed by the National Institute for Science and Technology (NIST) (formerly the National Bureau of Standards) toward fire safety provision for people in residential board and care occupancies (Groner, 1982) and the development of the fire safety evaluation scheme (FSES) now forming appendices of the NFPA *Life Safety Code Handbook* for 1985 (Lathrop, 1985). One unique NBS-funded study by Pearson and Joost (1983) recorded the egress behavior response times of samples of typical college students, elderly persons (some with arthritic problems), blind people, and young adults who use wheelchairs in a simulated residential fire situation. It was concluded that while the able-bodied college students performed the actions more quickly, all the individual group members studied "were able to perform the actions in a timely fashion."

To begin to explore the potential difficulties in buildings used by the public, a recent study was conducted by Sime and Gartshore (1986b, 1987b) of the evacuation of a wheelchair user down a stairway. Although the new code of practice BS 5588 Part 8 concentrates primarily on the principle of holding people temporarily in a protected refuge, it was felt important to explore the difficulties in using a stairway. This route might be necessary to use in buildings in which a special safety elevator is inaccessible or not required; for example, new office and shop buildings in the United Kingdom below 18 m (59 ft) in height and old ones above this level (BSI BS 5810, 1983).

The focus of the study was on the pattern of movement of a wheelchair user evacuated from the sixth floor of a building containing offices and teaching areas and six floors above the ground floor. The building, 26 m (85 ft) in height, had two main stairways and elevators which switched off during an evacuation. The building occupants were unaware beforehand that an evacuation was going to take place. Using a video tracking procedure with a time clock, the time was recorded for the wheelchair user (PG) to be assisted by two companions down a staircase and out of the building.

PG (in essence a participant observer aware that there was to be an evacuation) began to move from his work or position with assistance 39 sec after the onset of an alarm siren. His final evacuation to an exit near a ramp at the bottom of one of the staircases took exactly 4 min. Carried by two male companions aged 20 to 25, his average speed of descent between each floor was 0.41 m/sec (1.3 ft/sec). This is slightly less than the 0.5 m/sec (1.6 ft/sec) recorded for able-bodied people on relatively crowded stairways in previous high-rise office block evacuations (at an average density of 2.0 persons per meter; Pauls, 1980, 1984). The wheelchair group increased its speed during the descent from floor to floor—0.27, 0.39, 0.44, 0.51, 0.42 m/s until the last flight of stairs. Of 359 people in the building, four (1%) left after PG, who was one of the last to leave the sixth floor. Detailed analyses of the progress of his movement, appraisal of the dimensions of the stairway in relation to U.S. and U.K. safety codes and standards and the video record itself, led to recommendations concerning stair width and "assisted escape" procedures (Sime and Gartshore, 1987b; Gartshore and Sime, 1987).

While admittedly a case study of a single building and movement by an individual wheelchair user, it is hoped that this study will serve as a precedent for future research. Studies could be conducted of the communication and evacuation procedures involved in the movement of people varying in their physical and sensory capabilities and in a range of different types of building occupancy. With the advent of innovative egress legislation and the emphasis on protected refuges, safety elevators, and new types of information warning systems, there is undoubtedly a need for research of building performance in the context of assisted escape procedures. There are currently the beginnings of international initiatives in this area in building safety legislation and research in countries such as the United States, Japan, the United Kingdom, and Sweden.

However, as ever, the funding of research lags seriously behind the resources directed toward building programs and fire service activities. In this respect, it is hoped that there can be as much international coordination and communication of findings as possible. With the introduction of egress codes and standards directed toward people who have mobility difficulties, there is likely to be far greater attention to the appraisal of fire safety design codes in relation to communication and evacuation procedures. The introduction into the U.S. NFPA *Life Safety Code Handbook* of a procedure for determining the evacuation capability in occupancies where people are predominantly physically dependent (Lathrop, 1985, App. F) and the acceptance of the need for carefully coordinated management evacuation procedures in the new British standard BS 5588 Part 8 (BSI, 1988) reflect what may be the beginnings of a major change in the philosophy of fire regulations.

Once it is recognized that everyone is handicapped in a fire, the concept of assisted escape could be broadened to encompass all building users. The safety of people with mobility difficulties is invariably considered to be an ergonomic problem of how to move them to safety or keep them protected until help is forthcoming. In contrast, research of behavior in fires suggests that efficient communications early on in an emergency are of paramount importance in *giving people time to reach safety*. In this respect there may have to be attention to the effectiveness of conventional fire sirens. There is still going to have to be extremely careful attention to the very real problems involved in guaranteeing the safety of people with mobility difficulties without putting other people's lives in jeopardy. While the provision of protected refuges will be feasible in certain types of building, their effective use depends on efficient communication and evacuation strategies. The relationship between technical design solutions and associated evacuation management will vary in different types of buildings and occupancy (such as department stores as opposed to offices or hotels). These difficulties need to be articulated, either as part of fire safety design codes or in back-up evacuation guidance documents.

The provision of barrier-free egress, as well as access, involves resolving economic and legal issues (life insurance premiums, potential liability in the event of an accident). In this respect building managers, the fire services, insurance companies, and the architectural profession need to be reassured about the consequences of removing the final obstruction to people's entry to public buildings, the provision of safe egress. Changes in the degree to which there are social, psychological, and physical barriers to emergency egress should be based not only on moral grounds, but on sound empirical research. The final plea of this chapter is for legislation to be based as far as possible on preemptive research rather than on findings after a disaster has occurred.

10.5 CONDENSED REFERENCES/BIBLIOGRAPHY

ANSI A117.1 1961, *American National Standard Specifications for Making Buildings and*
Bednar 1977, *Barrier-Free Environments*
Benjamin 1982, *Life Safety Codes—Current State of Regulations Providing Safety Consid-*
Boyce 1985, *Movement under Emergency Lighting: The Effect of Illuminance*
BSI BS 5810 1979, *Access for the Disabled to Buildings*
BSI BS 5810 1983, *Fire Precautions in the Design and Construction of Buildings, Part 2*
BSI BS 5588 1988, *Fire Precautions in the Design and Construction of Buildings, Part 8*
Corlett 1972, *Ramps or Stairs—The Choice Using Physiological and Biomechanic*
DOE 1985, *The Building Regulations 1985: Mandatory Rules for Means of Escape*
DOE 1986, *Building Regulations: Access and Facilities for Disabled People*
DOE 1987a, *Access for Disabled People: Approved Document Part M*
DOE 1987b, *The Building (Disabled People) Regulations Statutory Instrument*
Fruin 1971, *Pedestrian Planning and Design*
Gartshore 1987, *Assisted Escape—Some Guidelines for Designers, Building Managers*
Goffman 1959, *The Presentation of Self in Everyday Life*
Goldsmith 1984, *Designing for the Disabled*
Goldsmith 1985, *Micro or Macro—How Should We Treat Disabled People?*
Groner 1982, *A Matter of Time—A Comprehensive Guide for Fire Emergency*
Grosse 1987, *High-Rise Hotel or Apartment Fire Refuge Concept for the Mobile and Non-*
Hallberg 1984, *Evacuation of the Theater of Drokkningholm*
Harris 1971, *Handicapped and Impaired in Great Britain: Part 1*
Home Office 1987, *Guide to Fire Precautions in Existing Places of Entertainment*
Johnson 1983, *Evacuation Techniques for Disabled Persons*
Kennett 1982, *Proceedings of the 1980 Conference on Life Safety and the Handicapped*

Kimura 1988, *Exit Choice Behaviour during the Evacuation of a Lecture Theatre*
Lathrop 1985, *Life Safety Code Handbook NFPA (3rd edition)*
Levin 1980, *Fire and Life Safety for the Handicapped*
Passini 1984, *Wayfinding in Architecture*
Passini 1986a, *Visual Impairment and Mobility: Some Research and Design*
Passini 1986b, *Spatial Mobility of the Visually Handicapped Active Person*
Pauls 1980, *Building Evacuation: Research Findings and Recommendations*
Pauls 1984, *The Movement of People in Buildings and Design Solutions for Means*
Pauls 1987, *Are Functional Handrails within Our Grasp?*
Pearson 1983, *Egress Behaviour Response Times of Handicapped and Elderly Subjects*
Preiser 1985, *A Combined Tactile/Electronic Guidance System for Visually Impaired Per-*
Public Works Canada 1985, *Access to and Use of Buildings by Physically Disabled People*
Sanford 1985, *Designing for Orientation and Safety*
Sime 1983, *Affiliative Behaviour during Escape to Building Exits*
Sime 1985a, *Designing for People or Ball Bearings?*
Sime 1985b, *Movement towards the Familiar: Person and Place Affiliation in a*
Sime 1986a, *Perceived Time Available: The Margin of Safety in Fires*
Sime 1986b, *Assisted Escape of a Wheelchair User: An Evacuation Study*
Sime 1987a, *Research on Escape Behaviour in Fires: New Directions*
Sime 1987b, *Evacuating a Wheelchair User down a Stairway: A Case Study*
Todd 1985, *Intelligent Fire Alarm Systems*
Turner 1981, *Pedestrian Movement Characteristics on Building Ramps*
Williams 1986, *Factors Determining Life Hazard from Fires in Group-Residential*

11

Nonevacuation in Compartmented Fire-Resistive Buildings

In Chapter 10 the approach of remaining inside a building during a fire was raised and briefly discussed. This chapter provides considerably more detail and analyzes specific case histories where evacuation resulted in more deaths than would likely have occurred with appropriate refuge within the high-rise building. It should be remembered that in many of these cases the lack of information, cited in the preceding chapter as critical, may have been a crucial determinant. With more adequate information, perhaps either orderly assisted egress or nonevacuation could be more successful than either without the necessary information supplied during the fire. Still, the evidence found in the last chapter, and to be reviewed here, makes a persuasive case that, in many instances, at least in compartmented fire-resistive buildings, nonevacuation is a very appropriate choice that can save lives.

Compartmented fire-resistive buildings are used for hotels, motels, apartments, condominiums, dormitories, residential board and care, hospitals, and other health care facilities. A review of numerous fires in these buildings has shown the following.

Unless the fire is in one's own room or unit, it is safer to stay in the room or unit than to evacuate. The majority of people who die from fire and smoke in compartmented fire-resistive buildings die in the process of evacuation.

Evacuation of the fire floor in these occupancies increases the chance of death dramatically.

Self-closers for corridor doors are important tools to contain a room fire or control the spread of a corridor fire.

Several fires in compartmented fire-resistive buildings have been reviewed, but only those are presented in this study where reasonably accurate conclusions could be drawn as to whether the victims had evacuated or not. These fires are listed in Table 11.1. The main reference sources were articles in the National Fire Protection Association's (NFPA) bimonthly publication *Fire Journal*. In some instances the conclusions may conflict with the referenced article or other potential interpretations.

For an extensive treatment of fire in tall buildings, see Chapter CL-4 of the Council on Tall Buildings (1980) and *Fire Safety in Tall Buildings* in this series (Council on Tall Buildings, 1992).

Table 11.1   Compartmented fire-resistive building fire deaths

Location	Total deaths	Deaths on fire floor	Apparent decision of victims	
			Evacuate	Nonevacuate
1. Las Vegas Hilton, Las Vegas, Nev.	8	8*	5(3)	—
2. Inn on the Park, Toronto, Ont.	6	—	5	1
3. Westchase Hilton, Houston, Tex.	12	12	8	4
4. Holiday Inn, Cambridge, Ohio	10	10*	10	—
5. Conrad Hilton, Chicago, Ill.	4	4	4	—
6. Providence College, Providence, R.I.	10	10	8(2)	—
7. Baptist Towers, Atlanta, Ga.	10	9†	7	2
8. Howard Johnson, New Orleans, La.	6	6†	5	—
9. Cornell University, Ithaca, N.Y.	9	—	9	—
10. Orrington Hotel, Evanston, Ill.	—	—	—	—
11. Hartford Hospital, Hartford, Conn.	16	16	16	
12. Milford Plaza, New York, N.Y.	—	—	—	—
13. Bunker Hill Apartments, Los Angeles, Calif.	3	3	2	—
14. Howard Johnson Hotel, Orlando, Fla.	—	—	—	—
15. Conrad Hilton Hotel, Chicago, Ill.	2	2	2	—
16. East 50th Street, New York, N.Y.	4	0	4	—
	100	80	90	7
17. MGM Grand Hotel, Las Vegas, Nev.	61 high-rise (24 1st floor)	—	36	25
Total	161	80	126	32

*Multiple-floor fire.
†Guard or employee deaths.
Source: Fire Protection Unit, Travelers Insurance Co. Engineering Division.

11.1 REVIEW OF FIRES

1. On February 10, 1981, at the Las Vegas Hilton a fire occurred in an elevator lobby on the eighth floor around 8 P.M. The fire spread vertically on the outside of the building, involving, in varying degrees, floors 8 through 28. Eight people died, five in the process of evacuation and three who were apparently taking an elevator down when it stopped at an involved floor. The NFPA *Fire Journal* stated: "There were no fatalities in rooms where occupants had kept their door closed and waited out the fire or waited to be rescued" (NFPA, 1982).

2. On January 17, 1981, at the Inn on the Park in Toronto a fire occurred in a second-level meeting room around 2 A.M. Smoke spread to the upper levels by way of stairways, elevator shafts, and pipe chases (NFPA, 1981). Six people died, five due to evacuation. Four victims were found in a stairway and one in a corridor. The fire almost claimed 20 more victims in a stairway, but the people were able to force open a locked door to the roof.

3. On March 6, 1982, at the Westchase Hilton in Houston a fire occurred in a guest room on the fourth floor about 2:15 A.M. The door to the room of origin did not close when the occupants left. Twelve guests, all occupants of the fourth floor, died. It was estimated that eight of these people died as a result of their attempts to evacuate.

4. On July 31, 1979, at about 3:25 A.M., at the Holiday Inn in Cambridge, Ohio, a fire occurred in a corridor connecting two buildings. Fire spread in the building corridors and up the open stairs. There were 10 fatalities as a result of this fire. The NFPA *Fire Journal* stated: "The NFPA study at the time of the article was unable to locate any survivors who actually used the corridors for evacuation" (Demers, 1980). All those who died were occupants of rooms on the second floor of this two-story building. Seven victims were found in the second-floor corridor or in one of the stairs. Two were found in rooms with the doors open. One died four days later, but further information on this victim was not given. This fire demonstrated the problems of evacuation with a corridor fire and the need for self-closing room doors.

5. Shortly before 9 A.M. on May 23, 1982, at the Conrad Hilton Hotel in Chicago a fire occurred in a guest room on the 22nd floor. The door to the room of origin was left open. No self-closers were provided. Two victims were found in a room with an open door and one victim was found in the corridor (*The Hartford Courant*, 1982).

6. On December 13, 1977, a fire occurred at about 3 A.M. on the fourth floor of a dormitory at Providence College. Ten students died, two when they jumped from their room that was on fire and eight when they attempted to evacuate as the fire spread rapidly in the corridor on Christmas decorations. The corridor and a few rooms on one-half of the fourth floor were involved in the fire. On that half of the fourth floor where room doors remained closed, the rooms were clean and virtually undamaged. Here the corridor fire, the worst possible fire for floor evacuation, was survivable in rooms with the doors closed.

7. On November 30, 1972, at the Baptist Towers Housing for the Elderly in Atlanta a fire occurred in an apartment on the seventh floor around 2 A.M. The occupant of the unit of origin, upon discovering the fire, left her apartment,

leaving the door open (Willey, 1973). The fire subsequently spread to the corridor. Ten people died, nine on the floor of origin. Of these nine, eight were residents and one was a guard. Three victims were found in the corridor and one in an elevator. Five were found in rooms and four of them were probably in units with open doors.

8. On July 23, 1971, at the Howard Johnson Hotel in New Orleans a fire occurred in a guest room on the 12th floor at about 5 A.M. The fire spread to the corridor after the room of origin's door was forced open by a hotel guard. Six people died on the 12th floor. Five were guests staying on the 15th floor. They used the elevator to evacuate, and they died when the elevator stopped at the 12th floor. The sixth victim was the guard who attempted to fight the fire (Watrous, 1972). Had these guests not evacuated, they might have lived.

9. On April 5, 1967, in a dormitory at Cornell University a fire occurred in a basement lounge at approximately 4 A.M. Here the effectiveness of the enclosed stairs was negated because doors were wedged open or had been removed for shortening. Nine students died; seven victims were found in the corridors or in the first-floor lobby, two were found in rooms with open doors (Gaudet, 1967).

10. On March 11, 1981, at the Orrington Hotel in Evanston, Ill., a fire occurred in the third-floor elevator lobby and corridor at approximately 9 P.M. When the guests called the desk, the alarm was immediately transmitted to the fire department and guests were told to stay in their rooms. None of the 11 guests on the third floor became victims of evacuation (Juillerat, 1981).

11. On December 8, 1961, at the Hartford Hospital in Hartford, Conn., about 2:30 P.M. a fire originating in a trash chute burst out of the chute onto the ninth floor. It spread in the ninth-floor corridor due to combustible interior finish. Sixteen people died: seven patients, five guests, and four employees. Firemen on ladders were unable to reach the ninth floor "...but firemen at the top of the ladders gave instructions to people at the ninth-floor windows, advising them to keep the doors closed, use wet bed clothing around the doors, and remain calm until they could be rescued. Those who acted on this good advice lived to escape unharmed. Where doors to patients' rooms did not stay closed, the occupants perished" (Juillerat, 1962). The importance of nonevacuation and closed doors is seen here.

12. On July 11, 1982, at the Milford Plaza Hotel in New York City a fire occurred in a room on the eighth floor at about 9 P.M. The room door was open, allowing heat, smoke, and fire to enter the corridor. Fortunately no one died in this fire. Afterward the New York City Fire Department Manhattan Borough Command critiqued this fire. One of its four conclusions following the critique was: "Occupants of hotel rooms, other than those in the room that is afire, should be instructed to remain in their rooms, rather than self-evacuate and chance the atmosphere in the halls and stairways" (Mills, 1983). The New York City Fire Department's Manhattan Borough Command has developed fire safety guidelines for hotels. Their suggested instructions for hotel guests are:

    If the fire is in your room—leave.

    If the fire is not in your room—stay.

13. On October 29, 1979, at the Bunker Hill Apartment in Los Angeles a fire occurred in an apartment on the 11th floor of this 19-story fire-resistive building at approximately 3 A.M. The tenant of the apartment of origin awoke to find a

fire in his apartment. He left the apartment, leaving the corridor door open. He subsequently died in the corridor. The two tenants in the apartment across the hall apparently tried to evacuate and found that the fire from the apartment of origin had spread to the hallway during flashover. They retreated into their apartment but did not close their corridor door. Fire spread into their apartment, and they took refuge on a ledge outside the window, subsequently falling to their death. The need for self-closers on corridor doors is demonstrated here. This fire also shows the problem of opening a unit door even for a moment.

14. On January 28, 1984, at the Howard Johnson Hotel in Orlando, Fla., an incendiary fire occurred in the seventh-floor elevator lobby of the 14-story fire-resistive building at 1:51 A.M. Three guests on the seventh floor were seriously injured in the process of evacuation; fortunately no one died. This fire, which developed quickly, was also detected quickly by the corridor smoke detection system. The corridor smoke detectors, upon activation, did the following:

> Sounded an audible alarm on the fire floor and on the floors above and below
>
> Illuminated the zone of the alarm on the fire alarm panel
>
> Recalled the elevators to the ground floor
>
> Shut down the HVAC system
>
> Notified the fire department

The audible alarm sounded for 5 seconds, followed by 30 seconds of prerecorded verbal instructions telling occupants on the floors where the alarm activated to exit through the enclosed stairs and not to use the elevators.

A woman and her son sustained burn injuries over 25 and 15% of their bodies, respectively. This woman was alerted by the fire alarm system. "She opened her guest room door and finding no signs of fire in the corridor, moved with her son toward the elevators. However, conditions within the corridor began to deteriorate as they continued toward the elevators. They then turned and moved toward the west stairway, but were overcome by products of combustion before they reached it" (Timoney, 1984). To get a feeling for how rapidly the conditions in the hallway deteriorated, based on the diagram in the article, the distance from their room door to the center of the elevator lobby and hall intersection was less than 6 m (20 ft).

The article identified four significant factors as critical in preventing any loss of life. Item 3 was: "The protection provided by guest-room doors that prevented the penetration of heat and smoke into guest rooms on the seventh floor," but no conclusion was drawn that evacuation is a questionable concept. The article did say, however, that "this fire further documents the difficult problem of educating the public as to the proper actions to take in the events of a hotel fire" and "...guests still made fundamental errors such as attempting to exit by using elevators."

The "difficult problem of educating" and "still made fundamental errors" should be directed at the fire protection community rather than at the public who is relying on them for guidance.

15. On Sunday, January 25, 1970, at about 6:45 A.M. a fire was discovered in the ninth-floor elevator lobby of the 25-story fire-resistive Conrad Hilton Hotel in Chicago. The fire involved about 50 chairs being stored temporarily in the elevator lobby. The entire corridor system of the ninth story from ceiling to

floor was damaged by extremely heavy smoke and carbonized deposits. "...Room doors and trim were charred for about 30 m (100 ft) in both directions from the elevator lobby, but no penetration occurred, even in those doors opening directly to the lobby." Many guests on the ninth floor stayed in their rooms after having been reassured by the Chicago fire fighters fighting the fire that they should stay there (Grimes, 1970). Two occupants, deafmutes, died. They were found in the corridor about 6 m (20 ft) from a fire escape. Others in their group had to be rescued from a window ledge. Their two rooms were the only rooms affected by the fire as their doors were left open when the boys evacuated or attempted evacuation.

16. On Monday, January 11, 1988, at 8:19 P.M. a fire was reported in a 10-story high-rise apartment building in New York City. The fire involved an office on the first floor. Unfortunately the doors to both stairs that opened into the first-floor lobby were open. The stairs were filled with smoke in a short period of time. The stairwells were useless because of immediate smoke and heat penetration. The FEMA report *Summary of Key Issues*, in the area of *Refuge*, states: "Tenants who stayed in their apartments behind closed doors were unharmed" (Kirby, 1988).

   The NFPA published two articles and an investigative report on this fire. The first article, a one-page fact sheet, appeared in *Fire Command*, March 1988. The fact sheet noted: "...The four civilian deaths and nine civilian injuries appear to have occurred when escaping occupants entered smoke-filled corridors and stairways" (Isner, 1988).

   An interesting side light on this fire is the residential floor diagram in the *Fire Journal* (1988) article entitled *Smoky Fire Kills Four in New York High Rise*. This diagram is in the investigative report also. When the building was built in 1924, each residential floor, floors 2 to 10, had 12 apartments with five stairs and three fire escapes. Each apartment had access to two means of egress separate from the other. Each unit truly had two means of egress remote from each other. Unfortunately this system was abandoned and only two stairs remained in service.

   Of the 100 deaths that occurred in the fire described, it is estimated that 90 died in the process of evacuation. Also of the 100 deaths, 80 occurred on the fire floor or floors.

17. The MGM Grand Hotel fire is treated separately because of its size and because it was unique in many respects (Best, 1982). Of the 61 that died in the high-rise part of the building, 36 apparently died evacuating (they were found in corridors, elevator lobbies, stairs), while 25 were found in rooms. The 24 that died on the first floor were not counted since they were in a noncompartmented assembly occupancy. What should not be overlooked are the thousands that survived the MGM fire in the high-rise portion, even though total evacuation took about 4 hrs.

The final figures in Table 11.1 illustrate how deadly evacuation can be, particularly on the fire floor or floors. What is interesting is that most code officials or authorities having jurisdiction ask for evacuation of the fire floor and one or two floors above and below. Hopefully these figures show how wrong this procedure is.

Howard Emmonds from Harvard University analyzed the Beverly Hills Supper Club fire, and why so many people died in the Cabaret Room. Emmonds presented an educated guess to answer the question: "For some 15 minutes after discovery, little smoke went down a 46-m (150-ft) corridor from the Zebra Room (room where the fire was discovered) to the Cabaret Room (where the victims died), but then in a few minutes that corridor carried the fire the full length. Why?'' His theory is that the smoke and fire moved in that direction after exit doors were opened for guests to leave the Garden Room and the Cabaret Room. He points out: "The fire gases behaved just like the water in a water pipe. So long as the faucet is closed no water flows. As soon as a faucet is opened, water flows out. Thus, no flow occurred in the north-south corridor as long as the north end doors were closed. However, when the doors were open, the fire gases went down the hall." The open exit doors were the valves that allowed the smoke and fire to spread (Emmonds, 1983).

11.2 PRACTICAL APPLICATION: REASONS FOR NONEVACUATION

How can building and fire officials put this information to practical use in controlling smoke and fire spread, particularly in compartmented buildings? They can do this by having people stay in their rooms with the doors closed. This is particularly important on the fire floor to retard fire spread. Emmond's water pipe idea is even more interesting when one observes how the exits for compartmented fire-resistive buildings are generally designed (Emmonds, 1985). Dead-end corridors are discouraged as being unsafe. They may be unsafe with the present evacuation mind set, but they are safer in the nonevacuation mode. Since the dead-end corridors are discouraged, it is usual to have exit stairways at the ends of the corridors. In reality this provides a large chimney at each end of each corridor. With doors to the exit stairs open, particularly on the fire floor, the valve is opened and smoke spreads. There seems to be an impression that by putting an exit sign over the door to the stairway (chimney), smoke will not enter the stairway. However, smoke still follows the laws of physics and enters the stairway, with or without the doors open. However, the open stairway door accelerates the smoke spread via the stairs. The nonevacuation technique would keep these doors closed as much as possible.

Based on the foregoing study, the following advantages of the nonevacuation concept in compartmented fire-resistive buildings have been developed:

1. The chance for survival is better if the fire is not in one's room or unit. There are no guarantees that, should a fire occur in a given fire-resistive compartmented building, everyone will survive. But by nonevacuation, the occupants' chances for survival are much better, based on this study. If nonevacuation is adopted, fewer people will die in these buildings.

2. The nonevacuation concept provides for uniform handling of all occupants, handicapped and nonhandicapped alike. This is one of the most powerful reasons for nonevacuation. It allows the problem of the handicapped to be addressed in a logical manner, and it provides a uniform approach for all occupants. Since most elevators are returned to the first floor and use of the elevators is not recommended, having the handicapped stay put is easy and logical.

3. The room or unit offers many features for defense, as opposed to the halls, stairs, or other alternatives. These features are:

The door between the corridor and the room or unit is an effective deterrent to smoke spread. This was shown to be important in many fires.

Bedding, towels, and so on, are available for sealing openings to retard smoke penetration.

Running water is available to wet towels or sheets for sealing openings.

Windows are available for fresh air, if necessary.

A telephone is available to call the desk, the fire department, or other rooms.

All of these advantages are lost when someone leaves the room or unit. A key item to ponder here is that while people have an inherent fear of fire, they do not have an inherent fear of smoke. People often feel they can make it in a smoke-filled corridor or stairway. The following problems can be encountered in evacuation:

Flashover in a room with an open door can occur when the occupant is in the hall. This means almost certain death.

Seeing and breathing in smoke-filled corridors and stairs is very difficult.

People can become locked in stairways.

Going to the roof is a mistake, since not all stairs lead to the roof, and the roof door is likely to be locked.

It can be a long way down when one does not know where one is going. How many people will have trouble walking down 20 stories?

Accidents on stairs can be caused by problems due to age, medication, alcohol, or sleepy condition, as well as other hazards such as inadequate lighting, crowded conditions, people pushing or being pushed, fatigue, and smoke. Many aged persons could be seriously injured in evacuation.

In fact many of these problems will be particularly deleterious for elderly persons, who may have sensing and mobility problems as well as less stamina and lung capacity. Evacuation will also be more problematic for persons with a wide variety of handicaps, especially without the sophisticated wayfinding devices described in Chapter 12.

4. Closed doors, either room or exit, retard smoke and fire spread. As noted in Emmonds' study, closed doors limit fire and smoke spread. The spreading of smoke, like other fluids, is a function of orifice area. A closed door has greatly reduced the area for smoke spread around and under it relative to an opened door.

5. Closed room and exit doors allow smoke control systems to work properly. Stairway pressurization systems, for example, are designed to keep a stairway smoke-free with the door to the fire floor and a limited number of other doors open. When too many doors are opened, the stairway is no longer pressurized. If the pressurized stairway in a 40-story building is designed to have the door to the fire floor and three others opened, who decides which doors can or cannot be opened? The simple solution is nonevacuation. Occupants should leave the pressurized stairwells to the fire department. They have self-contained breathing apparatus. If they open too many doors, the smoky stairwell will not bother them.

6. This concept provides for uniform reaction by occupants whether they receive early or late notification. When occupants become aware of a fire is when their fire clock starts. However, they have no idea when the fire

started. When their fire clock starts, they do not know where the fire is, whether it is just starting, approaching flashover, or has burned out. They should be prepared to defend themselves in place. Many people place a great deal of reliance on early notification by sophisticated alarm systems. Will the alarm systems work when they are needed? Did they in fact ever work? This is a critical point, not only for the building occupant, but also for the building and fire officials.

7. This concept provides for uniform reaction to an accidental or incendiary fire. Is the cause of the fire important when a building occupant learns of it? Probably not, but many people have said that if there is an accidental fire and they have a chance to get out, they are going to leave. How will they know it is accidental? What they should be aware of is that if there is a life-threatening fire in one of these occupancies, the chances are that the fire is incendiary. The losses examined show this to be true. This means the fire will likely start fast and grow to the limits of its container very quickly. That fire growth can be controlled with closed doors, and the fire deaths reduced by nonevacuation.

8. This concept eliminates occupant reliance on inaccurate or incorrect information from building personnel. When building occupants call the desk or manager to report a fire, should they expect to get accurate information? If there is a fire, the switchboard is probably lit up like a Christmas tree. Confusion and stress is what will be happening. How can the operator possibly know what is happening and how bad it is? For example, at the Westchase Hilton fire, the first alarm, both automatic smoke detection and guest calling, came from the eighth floor. The fire was on the fourth floor.

9. This concept is in harmony with the accepted fact that in high-rise buildings, total evacuation is impractical. In the past a distinction has been made between high-rise building and low-rise building. The high-rise building is generally one where:

> There are floors beyond the reach of fire department aerial equipment. This means that evacuation and fire fighting on the upper floors have to be done internally.

> There is a potential for significant stack effect.

> Evacuation is impractical. This is due to the physical problems of a walk down many flights of stairs and of exit stair crowding, since exit capacity is designed to handle a single floor. In exit design, if the occupancy of the individual floors is equal or similar, a two-story, a 22-story, and a 62-story building may all have identical exit stairs.

Because of these limitations on evacuation due to building height, when a fire occurs, total evacuation is impractical and nonevacuation makes practical sense.

10. This concept provides a uniform approach to low- and high-rise buildings. All high-rise buildings are also low-rise buildings. Since nonevacuation makes sense in high-rise buildings, it also makes sense in low-rise compartmented fire-resistive buildings. The validity of this reasoning was demonstrated in the fires reviewed. The Holiday Inn, Providence College, and Cornell University fires were in low-rise buildings. Similar results are seen when comparing high-rise and low-rise buildings. The Westchase Hilton had 13 stories, the Providence College dorm had 4 stories; each had a fire on the fourth floor, and in each 8 people died attempting to evacuate.

11. This concept provides for greater employee safety by not having them respond to evacuate occupants or fight the fire. Often hotels, apartments, or similar buildings will have their employees respond to the suspected fire floor to do a variety of jobs. These response plans are often drafted in conjunction with or at the direction of the local authority having jurisdiction. Some of the activities that an employee may be expected to do are:

> Assist occupants to safety, with special attention to aged, infirm, or otherwise incapacitated persons
>
> Search rooms to be sure all occupants have escaped
>
> Extinguish or control the fire, using available first-aid equipment

One assumption that seems to underlie these items is that the fire will be small and nonthreatening. Another is that employees can do all of this without self-contained breathing apparatus since maintenance of and training in the use of self-contained breathing apparatus is not something that hotels or apartments should be doing. Having employees do these things is not realistic, particularly with the high chance of incendiary fires. The chance for employee injury is substantial and unnecessary. Nonevacuation addresses this problem very nicely.

12. This concept handles the problem of a limited night staff. All of the problems discussed are compounded by limited staffing during the evening and night shifts. The greatest chance for a multiple-death fire occurs when the most problems exist for the limited staff. Some of these problems are:

> Guests are asleep with their security locks locked. The pass key will not work.
>
> There will probably be only one to three staff people available. Do they use the buddy system or go alone on the search and rescue mission? Someone has to stay at the desk to answer phones and other duties.
>
> Without breathing apparatus they are expected to go to the fire floor, where there is the greatest chance of being killed, and put their lives on the line to evacuate guests who are already safe in their rooms.

The nonevacuation concept provides an easy solution to these problems.

13. This concept provides a uniform response to new and existing compartmented fire-resistive buildings. Does the building you are staying in, living in, or reviewing for code compliance comply with the latest codes? How old is it? These are questions that cannot be answered by occupants just by looking around. Also, building code and fire officials cannot always get improvements made because of retroactive features of some codes. However, when the nonevacuation approach is considered, the differences due to age become less significant and new solutions to problems become available.

14. This concept provides a uniform approach in sprinklered and nonsprinklered buildings. Buildings with automatic sprinkler systems have an unblemished record as far as life safety is concerned. Nonevacuation fits like a glove. Nonevacuation in nonsprinklered buildings makes sense for all the other reasons mentioned.

15. Buildings using the nonevacuation concept will be more likely to call the fire department for help at the first alarm of fire. The employee responsible for sounding the alarm and calling the fire department may feel a need to investigate the alarm prior to calling the fire department if the call necessitates

evacuation of the building, or a portion of it, at 3:00 A.M. If, however, the building is using the nonevacuation approach, the fire department can be called with less fear on the part of the responsible employee of doing something wrong and upsetting the occupants.

16. In buildings where security is a problem, occupants are reluctant to evacuate. Where security is a problem, people are concerned for their own safety and the safety of their possessions. Nonevacuation addresses this problem and improves their safety, whether a fire alarm is real or false.

17. It is simple. In fire-resistive compartmented buildings, much money has been spent in making them fire-resistive. These buildings have been divided into tens, hundreds, or sometimes thousands of compartments, and the overall fire load has been divided into many smaller ones. Many barriers have been put in to limit the spread of fire and smoke. With all that has been done, it does not make sense to eliminate these advantages by telling people to evacuate. The present evacuation mind set is probably a holdover from the combustible hotel buildings of many years ago and from fire-drill training in grade school. The construction of these buildings has changed but the evacuation approach has not.

In looking at some recent fires in combustible buildings, the same non-evacuation approach may be the way to go here also. In the Dorothy Mae fire in Los Angeles, another corridor fire, the Los Angeles Fire Department seemed quite positive in saying that if the 24 people that died "...had stayed in their rooms, they'd still be alive" (Dektar, 1983).

11.3 LESSONS LEARNED

Although no guarantees can be given that there will be no injury or loss of life, should a fire occur in a compartmented fire-resistive building, the studies and statistics related here support these conclusions:

1. In a fire-resistive compartmented building, unless the fire is in an individual's unit, it is safer to stay rather than to evacuate.

2. Evacuation of the fire floor increases the chances of deaths dramatically.

3. Self-closers for corridor doors are an important tool to help contain a room fire or control the spread of a corridor fire.

11.4 CONDENSED REFERENCES/BIBLIOGRAPHY

Best 1982, *Investigation Report on the MGM Grand Hotel Fire Las Vegas, Nevada*
Council on Tall Buildings 1980, *Tall Building Criteria and Loading*
Council on Tall Buildings 1992, *Fire Safety in Tall Buildings*
Dektar 1983, *24 Killed in Apartment Fire*
Demers 1980, *Familiar Problems Cause 10 Deaths in Hotel Fire*
Emmonds 1983, *The Analysis of a Tragedy*
Gaudet 1967, *Dormitory Fire Kills Nine*

Grimes 1970, *Hotel Fire Chicago*

Isner 1988, *Fact Sheet: High Rise Apartment Fire New York City, January 11*

Juillerat 1962, *The Hartford Hospital Fire*

Juillerat 1981, *Prevention and Planning Avert Hotel Disaster in Evanston*

Kirby 1988, *Apartment Building Fire East 50th Street, New York City*

Mills 1983, *The Milford Plaza Fire...A Post Fire Critique*

NFPA 1981, *Inn on the Park Hotel Fire*

NFPA 1982, *Investigation Report on the Las Vegas Hilton Hotel Fire*

NFPA 1988, *Smokey Fire Kills Four in New York City High Rise*

The Hartford Courant 1982, *Four Killed in Chicago Hotel Blaze*

Timoney 1984, *Howard Johnson's Hotel Fire Orlando, Florida*

Watrous 1972, *Fatal Hotel Fire New Orleans*

Willey 1973, *FIRE Baptist Towers Housing for the Elderly*

12

Locator System with Voice Guidance for Emergency Evacuations

The purpose of this chapter is to consider some proposed concepts for efficient emergency egress from smoke-filled or burning buildings by utilizing a four-part interactive system composed of:

1. Fire-locator system
2. Personnel-locator system
3. Central computer processing unit
4. Voice-beacon system which facilitates egress by giving preprogrammed directional messages to stranded individuals

An efficient evacuation system is greatly needed, given the well-known problems in emergency egress from high-rise buildings, especially for the handicapped or the elderly. It can be available as a complement to the nonevacuation approach outlined in the preceding chapter when fire personnel deem that circumstances warrant. In those cases it is critical to ensure that the most vulnerable tenants are not impaired beyond their ability to cope.

The proposed approach is built on the lessons learned from a combined tactile/electronic guidance system for the visually impaired, which was invented by Preiser and Small and tested as a prototype (Preiser et al., 1981). Relevant portions of the system are described here in some detail.

A worldwide review is proposed of the scientific literature on the psychological aspects of effective and efficient voice instructions for building evacuations. The goal of the effort is to determine the optimum timing and repetition of messages, the most appropriate content of messages, and the quality of the voices that people will respond to, particularly when in panic situations or physically or psychologically impaired.

This is to be followed by the development of appropriate technological concepts. Building on the previously developed computer-chip voice synthesis beacon system, different messages for various parts or types of buildings may be needed to direct people to appropriate emergency exits in the most orderly and efficient manner. Provisions must be made to locate individuals who are incapable of responding or left unassisted so that help can be provided to them.

Next, pilot data gathering must involve simulated emergency egress under various situations that approximate those likely to be encountered during a fire in a laboratory with on-line video recording capabilities, observation, and path tracking of subjects, comparing expected evacuation route configurations with the occupants' actual egress behavior and routes. This is to be followed by debriefings with in-depth interviews.

The establishment of performance criteria for the proposed emergency evacuation system and guidelines for emergency situations in buildings will be based on the previous project phase. Data concerning the location and distribution of guidance beacons and the distances and relationships to emergency egress doors, stairs, and such will be assessed. A taxonomy of descriptors of building features will be created which are commonly understood, easily recognizable, and essential in guiding persons through, and out of, buildings in emergencies.

12.1 BACKGROUND

Research and development of guidance systems for the visually impaired have been developed at the University of New Mexico over the past 10 years. The ideas presented here are currently conceptual, or hypothetical, as none of the elements of the system outlined have yet been used or tested in fire emergency egress situations. It is hoped, however, that this Monograph will stimulate new ideas and discussions by those engaged in the development of emergency egress technologies and potential owners or operators of the proposed evacuation system. It is also hoped that one day a prototype of the system will be designed, built, tested, and perhaps implemented on a broader basis.

The notion of utilizing elements which were developed in the context of a guidance system for visually impaired persons in a system that would benefit the general public in fire emergency egress situations is based on the fact that under certain circumstances all occupants of buildings (including the sighted) may become temporarily blinded or disoriented due to panic or smoke-filled spaces. This implies that under emergency conditions egress may be made even more difficult because exit signs may not be visible and therefore rendered useless.

In order to guide building occupants to obscured emergency exits, it is thought that one or maybe two elements of the already developed guidance system for the visually impaired may be adapted and developed further to suit the requirements of fire egress for the general public.

Before proceeding to a detailed discussion of the technologies involved, it is useful to keep in mind the real cost of technological innovation. For example, it is certainly possible to construct buildings which are completely fireproof. If buildings contained no materials other than concrete and glass, they would not burn, but they would also be unacceptable for human occupancy.

Similarly, fires could be quickly stopped if sprinkler heads were installed at 1-meter grid intervals throughout the ceiling, wall, and utility spaces of a building, but both the monetary cost and the aesthetic price of such a scheme are unattractive.

Other more subtle approaches are certainly possible. One might construct highly sophisticated radarlike devices, which could be embedded in a building. In the event of emergency, or just someone's curiosity, the location of all living persons could quickly be determined. Aside from the police-state aspects of such a system, the cost would again be very high.

Any potentially expensive system should be justified on the basis of a believable cost-benefit analysis. Benefits, in the case of safety, are based on both perceptions and demonstration of reduced risk. The system architect ultimately has to deal with the sensitive subject of the monetary cost of reducing risk. It may reduce to a question as simple as: "What is the monetary value of preventing two deaths in 500 years?" For expensive systems, risk analysis is essential.

The four-part interactive system described in this chapter must also conform to a cost-benefit assessment unless it can be kept very inexpensive. If the cost is very low compared to other costs in a building, then almost no one will care to ask the difficult questions of risk analysis. Although the research and the understanding of some of the critical issues are preliminary, it is hoped that many features of the interactive system may, in fact, be quite inexpensive to implement.

12.2   DESCRIPTION OF COMBINED TACTILE/ELECTRONIC GUIDANCE SYSTEM

The primary purpose of the combined tactile/electronic guidance system is to help improve orientation, direction finding, and mobility of visually impaired persons in complex buildings and public places where travel is difficult. These include wide-open, undefined spaces, multilevel spaces, and curved or angular pathways without "shorelines," in other words, orienting aids such as borders or tactile differences in pavements. Traveling problems encountered by the visually impaired are caused in part by the spatial features of contemporary architecture, relating to such trends as open-plan schools and offices or nonrectangular grids in building design.

Specifically, the intent was to develop and test tactile building directories to be used for familiarization with an area (through creation of mental maps) and trip planning, and further, to develop and test an electronic guidance system which permits safe tracking of pathways from an origination point to predetermined destination points.

The latest addition to the guidance system is a prototype electronic voice beacon with directional word messages. This type of beacon, which has yet to be systematically tested and evaluated, may hold the greatest potential for aiding in fire emergency egress.

The system consists of three elements: tactile building directory, electronic guidance device, and electronic voice beacons.

1   Systems

Tactile Building Directory.   Recent research indicates that visually impaired persons, similar to sighted person in unfamiliar buildings, as shown in Chapter 4, have more difficulty negotiating the interiors of buildings than they have going from one building to another. The work of Brecht and Preiser (1982) led to the development of a first-generation tactile directory for building interiors with tactile, architecturally accurate representations of building plans in raised images (Fig. 12.1). Evaluation data were collected both in the laboratory and in field

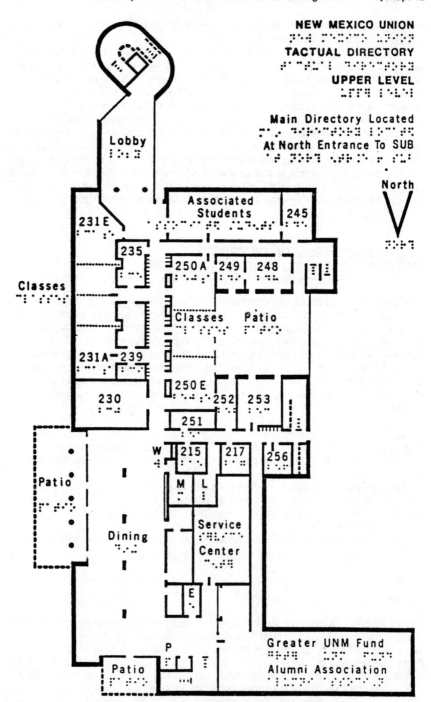

Fig. 12.1   First-generation tactile building directory (1979).

tests. They pertained to symbol discrimination, observation and mapping of subjects on travel routes, timing of travel, and self-report measures in extensive debriefings. This type of directory was basically a failure. Subsequently, based on the mostly negative findings, considerable progress was made in the conceptualization and design of an improved second-generation tactile directory, which was highly schematized, with a minimum of necessary information. It followed the analogy of circuit diagrams, showing only route configurations in buildings and key orienting features along pathways such as stairs, emergency exits, and restrooms. The directory map was topological; route segments were not necessarily depicted to scale. Directory simplification was facilitated by the electronic guidance device described in this section.

An example of the innovative third-generation tactile building directory showing the main level of the Student Services Center at the University of New Mexico is given in Fig. 12.2. For low-vision persons, words were shown in print, overlaid by tactile two-letter Braille codes or full-length legend descriptors, respectively. No symbols are used. The tactile directories are posted in standardized places and locations adjacent to the handicapped entrances for a given building.

Based on this research, the lessons to be applied to situations of emergency egress for the general public and especially for elderly and disabled inhabitants with limited mobility or sensory acuity may pertain to the notion that the creation of mental maps of potential egress routes may aid in accelerating evacuation, just as mental maps of potential travel routes aid visually impaired persons in trip planning and the negotiation of difficult pathways.

Electronic Guidance Device.   Important progress has been made in the design, development, and testing of an electronic, safe tracking device for the visually impaired. The device is inexpensive to install and easy to use. A transmitter (115 volts, ac-powered, and operating on a frequency of 550 kHz) has been constructed with an amplitude which is modulated by a continuous audiofrequency tone. The signal is received by a conventional transistor radio and is felt as a vibration given off by a converted small loudspeaker which is mounted below the handle of a specially designed electronic cane. This vibration can be felt by the visually impaired traveler by placing the index finger or thumb on the vibrator. If desired, an audio display mode can be heard from an earphone or from a small radio worn by the traveler. The sensor for the AM radio signal emanating from a wire loop antenna in the floor is contained in the tip of the electronic cane.

In the present design and state of development of the device, the null effect is used to establish electromagnetic pathways for the visually impaired. Antenna loops may be placed beneath carpets or other floor materials, or beneath outdoor pathways. The pathways may be straight or curved, and they may be followed by the cane described to an accuracy of a few centimeters. They are tracked by moving the receiver from side to side, in a manner similar to a blind person's use of a standard white cane. The antenna may take the form of a long rectangular loop with flat wires spaced approximately 200 mm (8 in.) apart and up to many hundreds of meters in length. As one approaches the wire loop antenna with the cane or a hand-held receiver, a signal of increasing strength is detected within a few meters of the antenna loop. However, when passing the precise center of the loop wires there is a sharp null in the signal strength, which in turn gives appropriate orientation for the receiver antenna in the tip of the cane.

The ability of the guidance device to precisely and spatially pinpoint a pathway is critical for wayfinding and orientation in obscured environments.

Electronic Voice Beacon.   The same transmitter with a different antenna configuration can be used as a point-source beacon, indicating points of interest or key orienting features of environments along pathways. Such features may include names of building areas, the locations of fire exits, intersections, stairs, and restrooms. They can be announced by point-source beacons, such as voice synthesis devices with microprocessors. When using a circular wire loop antenna of approximately 100-mm (4-in.) diameter, the transmission may be received at a

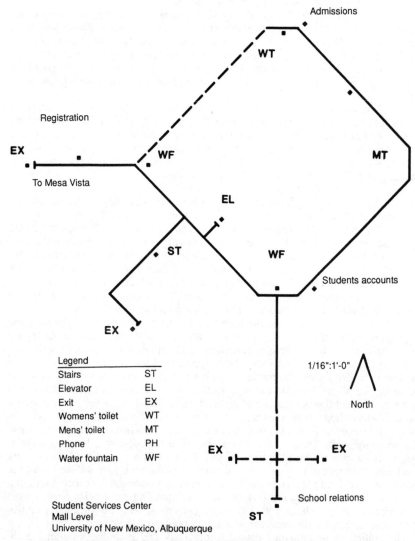

Fig. 12.2   Third-generation tactile building directory (1984). Braille text not shown.

distance of 2 m (6.5 ft) or less. In this embodiment, the electronic voice beacon is a point-source beacon transmitter of very short range.

2 Tests and Applications

Pilot installations and tests on the campuses at Indiana University, the University of New Mexico, the New Mexico School for the Visually Handicapped, and the Department of Veterans' Affairs Blind Center at the Medical Center in Palo Alto, Calif., indicate the potential benefits of the new guidance system in indoor and outdoor situations, primarily through safer travel and greater ease of direction finding for visually impaired users.

A pilot study was conducted at the Federal Polytechnic Institute in Lausanne, Switzerland, in 1984 using a Tolman maze with a full-scale mock-up of 3-m (10-ft) high walls (Figs. 12.3 and 12.4). Blind subjects were asked to navigate through the maze under three different conditions:

1. No assistance was provided.
2. Verbal instructions on how to reach the end of the maze were given, in addition to the subject having the opportunity to study a tactile map of the maze showing the route configuration.
3. Subjects used the electronic guidance device.

Travel time for subjects using the electronic guidance device was considerably shorter than for the other subjects. Subjects indicated their satisfaction with the observation of how easy the electronic guidance device was used without prior

Fig. 12.3   Subject negotiating Tolman maze with electronic guidance.

Fig. 12.4   Testing of prototype guidance system in completed building.

training. On the contrary, subjects receiving no assistance expressed great frustration (some of them aborted the trip, got lost, or turned around) and typically succeeded in negotiating the maze only after having traced all walls and surfaces, including blind alleys. Debriefings indicated that subjects in general found the electronic guidance device to be useful for certain applications to complex environments, including department stores. The same was said for the experimental electronic voice beacon that was demonstrated at the time of the pilot study.

As outlined, parts of the system could be adapted for use by sighted persons in complex, crowded, unfamiliar, and obscured environments, especially fire egress situations.

12.3 REQUIREMENTS FOR A GUIDANCE SYSTEM TO AID IN EMERGENCY EGRESS

The primary objective is to guide persons through obscured environments and dense smoke toward emergency exits. This should be accomplished in as short a time as possible without encountering obstructions in order to minimize injuries. Injuries may be caused by building occupants encountering objects, barriers, or other persons, by occupants falling, or by objects falling on occupants.

Another objective is to identify and be able to follow with minimal training a clearly identified pathway that is spatially and directionally precise. This will permit evacuees to easily pinpoint the appropriate evacuation route at a given point in time.

It should be possible to vary evacuation routes, depending on conditions in the building, location of the fire, obstructions to egress, and the locations of building occupants.

The system should permit disabled persons such as wheelchair-bound, deaf, or blind persons, to evacuate on their own power.

Further, the system should allow monitoring personnel to detect the location of persons who are unable to evacuate for whatever reason. The system should not be destroyed by excessive heat or smoke, it should survive electrical blackouts, and it should be powered independently. It should provide unambiguous guidance.

Potentially, the system would be able to track and locate individual building occupants who would have electronic IDs with individualized, recognizable frequencies or codes.

The system should respond to varying conditions of fire, fumes, and smoke and provide appropriate evacuation guidance. This implies preprogrammed evacuation instructions, which would be issued in response to the monitored location of building occupants versus the location of the obscured environments and egress routes, and it would compute "least loss of life" routes of evacuation. The system would be an audio system with voice instructions to evacuees.

12.4 CONCEPTS FOR TECHNOLOGY DEVELOPMENT

Based on past work on guidance for the visually handicapped, we have learned much about how people guide themselves. We have learned what they look for and what cues and help they are willing to accept. For example, humans are very independent. They resist being told where to go. They want to be presented with information and want to decide themselves whether or not to go in those directions. In an emergency egress situation it is unlikely that the evacuees will be specially equipped, so we must construct systems which exploit natural human responses and which are intuitive and obvious to the casual and first-time user. In the following, four concepts are presented in outline format.

1 Safe-Path Concept

Humans rely primarily on sight and secondarily on sound for guidance cues. Since warm smoke tends to rise and first fill the upper portions of a passageway, we would propose pathways at the floor level. The simplest path we can imagine would be mounted in baseboards along the floor of the hallway and would consist of sequenced flashing lights which simply lead the person in a given direction. For example, the emergency guidance lightstrips in airplanes might be baseboard-mounted at 2-meter intervals, which might be a reasonable distance in a smoky corridor. The lights could be programmed to flash sequentially, starting at one end of the corridor and going toward the other end, forming a rather obvious pathway toward the exits.

One form of this guidance system is already implemented at major airports during poor weather conditions. The landing approach for the main runway is preceded by a row of stroboscopic lights, which flash in sequence. When seen from the air it looks like a little rabbit racing toward the runway approach. In a practical building environment, stroboscopic lights may not be necessary. Also, this approach will require some research to determine reasonable light intensity levels, flash rates, spacing between lights, and repetition of the flash patterns.

Sequenced flashing lights would be most effective when integrated with a total building monitoring system. For example, a long hallway might have an exit at each end; however, if one of the exits is hot due to a local fire, an integrated monitoring system could direct the light sequence to lead occupants away from the hot exit and toward the safe exit. In all cases, the electronic pathways should be powered independently from the back-up battery, similar to the emergency lighting systems presently installed. It is also possible to have default light flashing patterns or default directions which would automatically switch on in the event that the system were somehow to decouple from the main building monitoring system. It would still indicate exits, and in that case perhaps multiple exits rather than a single preferred exit for a given corridor.

2 Acoustic-Path Concept

A simple extension to sequenced flashing lights would be sequenced sound-makers, perhaps little beeps—possibly even colocated with the flashing lights. Generally, humans prefer to use sight rather than sound, but in a totally smokey environment a clearly defined sequence of sounds coming down the hall toward one and going on beyond might also give reasonable cues. As with a sequenced light system, a sequenced sounding system would require a modest amount of research ahead of time to identify the most effective sounds, pulse repetition rates, and placements of the sound sources. It may also be appropriate to install voice beacons at exit points and perhaps at corridor intersections and ends to give plain-language instructions to the occupants that there is a fire in the building and that they should follow the lights and the sounds. Such a voice beacon could also be intercepted by fire department personnel upon their arrival to give specific instructions to individuals beyond just what a preprogrammed computer could produce.

3 Occupant-Locator System Concept

It is possible to install radarlike systems which could look down a corridor and detect persons in the corridor and the directions in which they are moving. Such a system would probably be based on small ultrasonic sonarlike transducers mounted in the ceiling tiles above the corridors (Fig. 12.5). Acoustic sensing works very well through smoke-filled spaces. It is not dependent on any visual paths and will work in darkness or in smoke.

Both microwave radar and related sonar devices are currently used for such mundane tasks as opening doors when persons approach. There is a popular snapshot camera on the market which uses a sonar device built into the camera to measure the range from the camera to the subjects of the picture and to set the camera focus appropriately. Those cameras have a working range of perhaps 6 to 9 m (20 to 30 ft), and a slightly more enhanced version could produce an acoustic sonar through the atmosphere which could easily detect humans walking about in a corridor at ranges of perhaps 15 m (50 ft).

Based on the technology demonstrated in the snapshot cameras, the amount of electric power to run such an acoustic ranging device is rather low and could easily be supported by back-up batteries with an operating lifetime of perhaps 1 hr or more in the event of power failure. The acoustic ranging device could be used to produce a corridor-by-corridor electronic display at a centralized building monitoring point (Fig. 12.6). A simple oscilloscope-type display would indicate a horizontal line with vertical blips at the locations of persons or obstructions in the corridor. Moving persons would be represented by blips which move left or right along the hall. Nonmoving persons or other obstructions would also be visible on the display from the central monitoring position. This information could be of

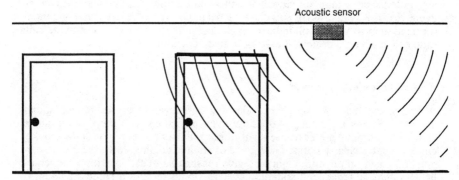

Fig. 12.5   Ultrasonic personnel sensor could be mounted in ceiling units. It would emit short pulses of ultrasonic sound waves to persons by echo location. The low-powered devices could easily be operated on battery power. The received echoes can be sent to a central building monitor over wires or by low-powered radio transmissions.

substantial use to the rescue and fire personnel as it would immediately indicate how many persons were moving about in public areas.

The system would not be capable of penetrating walls, say into a hotel room, and so there would be no privacy issues as long as the guests remain in their rooms. Personnel monitoring such a display could speak with persons in the hallways through loudspeakers mounted in the hall. They would be able to tell them: "You are moving in the wrong direction, turn around and go back, we can see you clearly on our radar." The human contact could go a long way toward reducing panic in emergency situations.

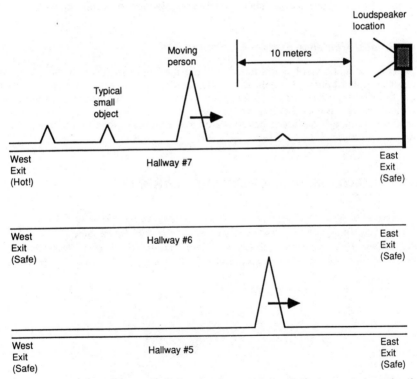

Fig. 12.6 A possible acoustic sensor display. In Hallway 7, for example, one person is moving the wrong way toward a hot exit. Two low nonmoving objects can also be seen. Rescue personnel could talk to occupants through wired loudspeakers and could observe their reactions. A nonwired system could also be constructed using battery-powered short-range radio transmitters and receivers.

12.5 RESEARCH NEEDS

1 Systematic Testing and Evaluation

The guidance system elements described should undergo vigorous and systematic testing in a variety of applications before being adopted as a standard.

2 Voice Message Studies

It is necessary to research, assemble, and evaluate the appropriate vocabulary and messages that are clear, effective, and fast to transmit, and also to establish how many times a message should be transmitted without being redundant.

3 Simulation Studies

Simulation studies of the evacuation behavior of people in burning buildings should be carried out to establish whether people would follow verbal instructions better than other cues, such as beepers, beacons, or strobe lights.

4 Graphic Guidance System Evaluation

Special applications of color-coded graphic systems are found in hospitals or other complex buildings where differently colored bands are mounted on either the floor or the wall surface, guiding the traveler from the building entrance to various destinations. This is particularly true in complex buildings where over time the building's additions have created a virtual maze for the uninitiated visitor.

12.6 CONDENSED REFERENCES/BIBLIOGRAPHY

Association of American Geographers 1983, *Proceedings of the First International*
Brecht 1982, *Testing and Evacuation of the Tactile Directory for the New Mexico*
Preiser 1981, *Guidance Systems for the Visually Handicapped—Progress Report No. 1*
Preiser 1982a, *Guidance Systems for the Visually Handicapped—Progress Report No. 2*

13

Techno-Housing and the Future: Prospects and Cautions

Consider this scenario. It is the year 2030 A.D. Almost one-fifth of the total U.S. population is over the age of 65, with nearly 10% of those over 85. Most live in their own homes in urban areas, as in the 1980s. However, the home itself has undergone a major transformation. Since before the turn of the century, most new housing has been constructed to be computer-controlled. Conditions of the house and its residents are monitored continuously, and necessary modifications are then made to temperature and air-quality control as well as to lighting and other energy consumption. If the status of the system requires external modification (for example, an electrical repair is required or a resident's condition requires attention by a health care professional or social service provider), the appropriate source for such attention is contacted and apprised of the situation automatically. Such mundane tasks as meal preparation, cleaning, and communication with other persons are completed with the touch of a button. Virtually any kind of information is also available in the home through computer networks. Back-up systems have increasingly made fears about what happens when the computer goes down a thing of the past.

First in larger buildings, including specialized housing, and by 2020 in virtually all new homes, the computerization combines with robot helpers to make the environment suitable to support persons with limited personal ability. Cleaning, cooking, and simple repairs are routinely done by robots, whereas most other activities can be remote-controlled. In combination with the widespread use of both transplants and advanced prosthetic devices implanted or attached to one's body, this sort of "techno-housing" ensures that systematic physical declines in mobility and sensory ability and the limitations in control over one's housing environment which they entail are pretty much a thing of the past (adapted from Blank, 1988).

If this scenario seems farfetched, or at least something far in the future, consider also that the National Association of Home Builder's *Smart House* project of fully computer-controlled, networked housing not only has prototype units available, but expects to have units available in the early 1990s and predicts an increasingly progressive demand for such housing over the coming decades (Geremia, 1987). Likewise, robotics is progressing swiftly toward a regular place in American working and living environments (Engelhardt and Edwards, 1986). Using these technologies, in combination with barrier-free design (Bednar, 1977; Raschko, 1982; Struyk and Zais, 1982), can mean that housing units may be designed or equipped to forestall many of the problems of accomplishing everyday tasks that may result from declining personal competencies or disability in such areas as strength, ability, sensory sensitivity, mobility, and memory. An understanding of this—what changes are occurring, how they affect and are responded to by those who enter those environments—is an important avenue to being prepared for aiding persons who are dealing with such changes in their housing environments. In this chapter we will consider an overview of the components of techno-housing and their potential benefits (and problems). This information can complement the main portions of this volume, which deal with the environments that now exist, and other chapters, such as those on wayfinding and electronic monitoring, which explore other facets of the future of design for the disabled and that portion of the elderly who has problems dealing with housing that does not have "smart" characteristics.

At the outset we should consider that the benefits of such housing design, while attractive to and useful for the population as a whole, are perhaps most obviously likely to benefit both persons with disabilities that limit mobility or sensation whatever their ages and older persons in general, many of whom have at least some limitation in their ability to control and manipulate their environments. The thrust of much of the techno-housing developments is a great increase in both safety from danger within the house and security from outside threats; fears about safety and security, in turn, are major worries in the older population (Lawton, 1985; Blank, 1988).

All told, it is very likely that the rush toward technology and computerization already felt will accelerate in coming decades. If presented properly and accepted by those they may benefit most, high-technology solutions may provide the answer to many of the problems of living in one's own home associated with disability or aging, some of which have been highlighted in other chapters. However, as with any other innovation or new idea, if such solutions are presented without regard for attitudes and readiness of the recipients to accept them and without concern for potentially negative side effects, they are likely to confuse and frustrate both those intended to use them and those who wish to produce and market them (Rogers, 1983). It is therefore critical that planning, development, and availability of technologically sophisticated housing be done in a context of design responsive to two very different levels of consideration. On the one hand, techno-housing will only succeed as it is related to the attitudes, expectations, evaluations, and concerns of those who are targeted to be users. Thus knowledge of those attitudes and perspectives is critical prior to full-scale implementation. Of special relevance both to society and readers of this Monograph are the attitudes and expectations of older and disabled persons. On the other hand, techno-housing, rather than improving the lives of persons with disabilities or special needs, may be counterproductive if it results in either frustration or "overservicing"; both of those possibilities, as well as positive impacts, can be analyzed in terms of Lawton and Nahemow's (1973a) ecological model described elsewhere in this volume.

This chapter will consist of three parts. First, several aspects of techno-housing that are likely to be contained, in whole or part, in housing for older and disabled users in the coming decades are surveyed in a broad, nontechnical fashion. Second, although no studies to date have addressed directly the attitudes and expectations of either current or future cohorts of older or disabled persons, a few related studies will be used to develop hypotheses that may be pursued to relate possible design features to likely attitudes and felt needs of elderly or disabled persons. Finally, several potential results of introduction of techno-housing will be explicated using the ecological model as a base.

13.1   WHAT IS TECHNO-HOUSING?

First, it is important to recognize what is encompassed by the category of high technology. This discussion is based on descriptions of high-technology solutions in Blank (1988), which, in turn, is based on information available in the gerontological and disability literature (Dunkle et al., 1984; Haber, 1986) and in magazines and journals (Engelhardt and Edwards, 1986; Harb, 1986; Kubey, 1980; Mann, 1978), as well as in presentations of developers of many of the technologies (Geremia, 1987; LaRocca and Turem, 1978; and several recent workshops on technology and aging).

The techno-housing, or smart-house, approach is based on the electronic revolution, especially microchip technology and computer design. Smart houses, automatically or in interaction with users, can perform many maintenance aspects of buildings and can also continually monitor the status of the building and its components and, if desired, its occupants. Functions or systems that are regularly included in an integrated techno-housing design are security, air-conditioning, and air quality based on actual moment-to-moment demands of occupants and of what is good for the building (humidity levels, temperature, and exhaust systems are examples), lighting (possibly automatically responding to occupant placement and activities as well as energy demands), and a host of appliances for cooking, cleaning, and entertainment. Every electrical appliance in a house can be controlled from any location and can be made to respond by sending the proper signals. One can turn off any appliance from anywhere in (or outside) the house by signaling the system at any entry point. As systems become more sophisticated, one can go beyond simple on-off control to complete control as though one were physically present with the appliance.

Instantaneous, constant monitoring of resident needs and response to many of those needs will be entirely possible in such an environment. The system can also include sensors that notice and react to a variety of conditions, such as movement. When these sensors are integrated with other components of the system, the techno-housing can do a variety of tasks, such as turning lights on when someone moves into an adjacent room (or sounding an alarm and calling the police if no one is "supposed to be" in that room) or shutting down or turning up a system if there is too much or too little humidity or activity or noise. The smart house, of course, can tell someone in one part of the house (or with a remote tie-in) if someone is calling out or gasping for air or whatever else is being monitored in some other part of the house. This is obviously very handy in a house in which one is giving care to either a child or a frail older person.

Techno-housing can enhance safety, security, and comfort, as well as convenience. This process holds great promise, especially for persons with mobility or sensory limitations, for it makes housing and other buildings more flexible and supportive of use by a wide variety of users. The monitoring functions may allow persons who cannot be fully trusted to monitor themselves, such as those with

Alzheimer's disease, to remain in their homes. Danger situations can be sensed quickly. Once sensed, they can either be alleviated automatically (by turning off the stove, for example, if it has been left on without cooking anything, or providing ventilation if the air quality is stale), or outside intervention can be called automatically (such as the fire department in case of smoke). In other words, techno-housing has great potential for enhancing the independence and quality of life of older persons in general and disabled persons of all ages.

Robotics (Engelhardt and Edwards, 1986) is a different but related aspect of the future of technology for housing. Robots are already beginning to take on certain activities in many work settings. It is likely that coming decades will see their expansion into homes, just as we have seen with such devices as telephones and, more recently, computers. Robots are best at functions that entail constant monitoring and response to specified changes. They can also perform tasks often considered menial, because of their regimentation, such as cleaning and simple maintenance.

Of course, it is these sorts of tasks that often become particularly burdensome to disabled persons and those struggling to remain in their own homes as they age. In many ways, then, robots are ideal for enabling persons with deficits of one sort or another to remain in place (by taking on some of the activities made difficult by the deficits and by monitoring potential problems and either responding to them directly or contacting service providers) (Engelhardt and Edwards, 1986; Haber, 1986).

Several other related devices are discussed in other chapters of this Monograph. For example, Chapter 12 (Chapter 10 to a lesser degree) describes wayfinding devices that, on the upper end, are clearly "smart" aspects of housing. Elevators, communication devices, fall monitors/protectors (Myers, 1989), and security devices that are responsive to the needs of particular users are other developments that are into or beyond the prototype stage.

Although all aspects of integrated techno-housing may be quite far in the future or remain prohibitively expensive for single-home housing of older and disabled persons, at least some level of computerization and robotics will be a matter of course in housing in the future, even at the single-family home level. Indeed, the ubiquity of technologically sophisticated individual products already available at low cost—clap-sensitive appliances, movement sensors, automatic dialing telephones, and a range of monitoring/response/security systems, as reported by Hikoyeda and David (1989), for example—means that some aspects that will be incorporated into an integrated design are already widely advertised and used.

It is even more likely that relatively integrated computer-based techno-housing will have great impact on various levels of congregate housing for older and disabled persons (such as high-rise housing for the elderly and disabled, retirement communities, nursing homes, group homes, and the array of alternative settings already available).

Given all the obvious potential benefits of techno-housing, and the application of electronic technology to the control and monitoring of housing environments, especially for older or disabled persons, those involved in this area have been very persuasive in arguing for the advancement of technology to provide those benefits. Does this mean that this technology is trouble-free or the answer to all of the problems older persons may have with their housing? It does not. There may be several "down" sides to advancing technology that must be considered along with the benefits. These problems have to do with both the matching concepts considered in the preceding and some potential attitudinal factors. Let us consider each briefly.

13.2 ATTITUDES AND POTENTIAL FOR USE

In light of its great potential, and of the emphasis by proponents of techno-housing, for benefiting disabled and elderly users, it is important to understand how today's older persons and nonolder ones (who, of course, will be tomorrow's older persons) view these emerging technologies. Attitudes and evaluations are important factors in the acceptance or rejection of new products and services (see, for example, Rogers, 1983). Thus these innovations should be compared carefully to interests, abilities, and needs of older and disabled persons, both now and for the future. Evaluations of existing "pieces" of techno-housing should be pursued along with an investigation of attitudes toward the larger, more integrated approaches being developed. In particular it is important to understand how older persons with and without disabilities compare to each other and to younger ones with disabilities, to discover both similarities and differences prior to dealing with either or both populations.

The most obvious attitudinal factor that may inhibit demand for or use of techno-housing is fear of technological control. Many persons of all ages have one degree or another of distrust or fear of at least some technologies, especially computerization. Not the least of a range of fears is the concern that computers are tools of control, taking away the key to one's ability to make choices. By monitoring and adjusting everything automatically, they make it more and more difficult for people to feel in charge. Many persons just do not feel comfortable using very technical devices.

People of all ages have such fears. Yet, older persons may be particularly prone to fears and the resultant negative attitudes. One major way to overcome fear, of course, is not to have it in the first place. The young are in that situation, since they have grown up within an environment in which computerization and electronic control are commonplace. Although very little research has been done, it stands to reason that older persons, who did not grow up or become educated in such a world, would be more likely to be wary of high-technology devices and approaches. Kerschner and Hart (1984), in fact, indicate some evidence that older persons of today are particularly prone to fears and general and specific negative attitudes, and clearly they are much less likely to seek out and embrace new technologies such as automatic teller machines and computers (Schwartz, 1988). The end result of such factors is that older persons of today may, in general, have less positive evaluations of high-technology approaches to housing, especially insofar as control and ease of usage are involved.

On the other hand, several recent studies indicate that older people, given the opportunity to experience new technologies, become more positive and have attitudes quite similar to those of other groups (Danowski and Sacks, 1980; Jay and Willis, 1989; Kerschner and Hart, 1984; Krauss and Hoyer, 1984). Jay and Willis, in particular, found a lessening of fears of "dehumanization," interestingly, not only in their group who used computers, but even in a waiting-list group that simply may have become more aware of computer technology as they anticipated receiving training at a later date. These results indicate that there may be an openness of older persons to at least some relatively high technologies. Of course, in none of these studies was anything approaching a fully integrated smart housing a major focus. In fact, Ansley and Erber (1988) did not find a positive "carryover" effect of computer use by older adults to their broader attitudes toward technology, nor did Jay and Willis find effects on questions that focused on broader social utility or enhancement/diminution of personal control by advancing technology. Yet the result, especially in comparison to what may be expected in terms of cohort development, points directly to the need for very focused research to examine whether specific types of technological solutions may be at least as positively viewed by older as by younger adults and which, if any, may be viewed more negatively because of factors such as those noted.

Furthermore, many of the studies show that attitudes toward computers, and perhaps to broader technology, are more positive in groups familiar with high-technology solutions. This may lead to an as yet untested hypothesis that persons, older as well as younger, who are disabled may respond more positively than those without disability to an integrated techno-house, since they are necessarily involved on a daily basis with at least relatively high-technology equipment in rehabilitation settings (and thus are likely to have access to and use of technologically sophisticated assistive devices such as motorized wheelchairs, lifts, and closed-caption devices). Also, the disabled are more likely to see the need for assists of various sorts than the nondisabled. This special motivation may lead them to overcome fears of control by computerization simply because it is less problematic than the already experienced problems of being disabled, leading to a lack of a sense of control.

Since experience is one major way of reducing the fear of use of an object or product, it is likely that the disabled may be less concerned about many specific aspects of high technology with which they are already familiar. Also, the previous experience may reduce a general "fear of the new" and increase interest in and positive evaluation of as yet untried technological solutions. The lack of generalization noted in one or two of the studies mentioned, if found consistently, may moderate the positive effects of exposure to aspects of the technology, however. Much more clearly directed study is needed in this area.

This brief review indicates both the necessity for a clear understanding of attitudes toward technology in a broad sense, and toward specific aspects of technology that are clearly contained in the techno-housing approach, and the relative lack of such understanding about the elderly and the disabled. Some of the current knowledge is more positive, though, than the broader stereotypes of resistance to change in general and to technology in particular by older persons often portrayed in the popular literature.

13.3 EFFECTS OF TECHNO-HOUSING: POTENTIAL HITS AND MISSES

Is techno-housing a winning solution for older and disabled persons who are having difficulty dealing with the "failings" of a "stupid" house? Is the only potential for pessimism to be found in attitudes that block usage, so that if those can be surmounted, techno-housing should be developed and implemented as fully and as quickly as possible to the benefit of these populations? Or are there some potential dangers to techno-housing that must be considered alongside the development of the technologies and search for more and more ingenious solutions to housing problems?

In an area as important at this, all sides must be examined, not only for diamonds but also for land mines. For example, when something goes wrong with such a highly integrated system, what is normally a very simple, undemanding environment can suddenly and without warning become an exceedingly difficult one. One can easily become imprisoned in a very difficult, if not impossible, home setting. Alternatively, the integrated nature and the ability of techno-housing to both provide services and monitor conditions can provide an environment that is not matched with its inhabitants because they have higher personal competence than is allowed expression in such a setting. Lawton (1985) and others have noted that a "too easy" housing situation can be as maladaptive as one that is too difficult, leading to atrophy from disuse and boredom and restlessness. In a way, the home situation can become the analogy of an institution, and an institution is not an appropriate housing situation for any but those with very few personal skills to control their environments.

One way to envision and evaluate the effects of the variety of high-technology solutions on persons in general and, especially, on older persons and those with disabilities is to relate those to a model of the relationship of persons to housing situations. Several gerontologists and rehabilitation researchers have developed such models. Perhaps the best known is the competence-press ecological model of Lawton and Nahemow (1963; Lawton, 1980). Since this model is both well known and described at several other places in this Monograph, it will be reviewed here very quickly.

Lawton and Nahemow indicate first of all that the abilities of persons to control or live well within a broad set of housing types can range from very low to very high. An example of a very low "personal environmental competence" is a person in a coma; one with very high competence is a very agile, strong, intelligent person oriented toward activity and control. Correspondingly, housing can range from very demanding to very undemanding. An example of the former is life in the middle of the desert with no "creature comforts," whereas a very undemanding housing situation (for residents at least, not for staff) is a hospital or nursing home. In the latter, virtually everything is done *for* the person, with little need for activity *by* him or her.

Important in regard to the present concerns is that the optimal situation for persons is to be situated in a housing environment that more or less matches with their capabilities and competence. Thus persons with low competence are best housed in very undemanding situations, and those with high competence in demanding ones. Those researchers and others, furthermore, have indicated that, in general, older persons and those with disabilities of any age are likely to have generally lower personal competence than younger, nondisabled ones. Thus a disabled person, and to some degree a nondisabled older person, is likely to match with a fairly undemanding environment compared to a nondisabled person. Although there are wide variations within each group, these average differences are of great significance in designing and providing housing for older person (see, for example, Lawton, 1975). At the same time, since people change (and so do environments, of course), the ideal match is really an environment that is supportive and yet flexible, optimal and yet able to adapt to its users as much as the users adapt to it.

What does all this have to do with the matters at hand, that is, with an understanding of the impacts of techno-housing on disabled or older persons? Clearly, quite a bit. First of all, use of the model makes it clear why techno-housing holds great promise for users with lower personal competence. A major reason behind developing techno-housing is to make the housing environment an easier one to control, to make it less demanding. In fact, the combination of monitoring and automatic control can make it a very undemanding environment, one that requires only a minimal amount of input to "change its program," so to speak, to fit changing needs of its inhabitants. Further, because of computer control and monitoring capacities, techno-housing should also be flexible and adaptive to changing needs of its users. Because of these factors, it should be able to provide particular benefits to individuals and groups low in personal competence. Since the processes of aging are likely to make a person somewhat slower, less strong and mobile, and less in full sensory contact with environmental stimuli, older persons are likely to find techno-housing an answer to an environment that has become too demanding. Obviously, persons with disabilities, regardless of age, should also be benefited, as long as the characteristics of the techno-housing are the ones that compensate for the disabling conditions.

The model also indicates why caution in planning and care in implementation are perhaps more critical when techno-housing is involved than in other conditions. The nature of the housing turns errors easily and quickly into disasters, simply because of the power and integration of the approach.

First, a fully integrated techno-house has within it the potential for boomeranging its inhabitants into a truly difficult, even hazardous environment in the time it takes for a circuit to click off. If a breakdown occurs, residents of the housing are, quite literally, imprisoned. Most obviously, a computer-controlled environment, or, indeed, any environment that is heavily dependent on automatic control and on complicated equipment, can be devastatingly difficult to deal with if and when something goes wrong. Although a perfectly working smart building is in fact a very simple, undemanding environment, its very complexity and automaticity become impossible to deal with, at least by nonexperts, in the rare instances when the system does not work. All of this is familiar to any of us who have begun to depend on the computerization of data or on automatic controls. In fact, nonworking elevators in high-rise buildings and broken air-conditioning in the thousands of newer buildings that do not have operable windows are similar complications that predate computerization. Having to wait a half-hour to check out of an automated supermarket when the computer-guided cash registers go down is a fairly common example of a problem induced by reliance on—indeed, dependence on—a computer. After having been lulled into complacency by the computer-guided match of environment to personal competence, one can suddenly be left in the equivalent of a car with power steering when the steering fluid runs out—in great danger.

Such problems are likely to be with all of us until better ways of providing backup are developed. When the environment is one's home, obviously the problems of reliance on complicated, impersonal systems for even relatively simple tasks can become exceedingly severe, especially if the controlling system is not operable and one cannot easily leave the situation. Of course, the latter is particularly likely to be the case for older persons who may have limitations of movement or financial ability to move, or any combination of the possible limitations in the range of choice. It is clear, though, that well-designed techno-housing can be—and is being—built in a redundant way, so that loss of one segment or controller does not doom the entire system. Still the rare possibility must be adequately considered, and the greater likelihood of resident and potential resident fear of being trapped in an impossible situation must be faced directly.

Unfortunately this is not the only potential disaster area of techno-housing. Sometimes the perfect working of the system is itself a problem. This is the case when the system does so much for and to the resident that skills atrophy and one is bored and restless. In the Lawton-Nahemow model an environment that is too undemanding is as damaging, at least psychologically, as one that is too demanding. Negative affect, aimless or listless behavior, or even sabotage may result from a feeling of being overly protected and understimulated. When technology is fully applied, a techno-house can easily be so overdesigned to care for the person that it becomes a *de facto* institution. Yet, often the person is not in an institution, precisely for the reason that he or she is too capable, too personally competent to be matched well with such a low-demand environment. In an effort to assist persons to remain independent and free to live as they choose, zealots of technology may slip easily into an overreliance on technological solutions that discourage that very same independence and freedom.

Therefore care must be taken to place an even greater emphasis on flexibility and, indeed, on responsiveness to inhabitants in a technologically sophisticated environment. The well-designed techno-house, in essence, must be *so* intelligent that it "knows" when to back off and allow those who reside in it to take care of themselves. At the same time it should ideally be educable in such a way that older and disabled inhabitants would be able to reprogram (teach) it to tailor itself to their particular needs and capabilities. Emphasis must be placed on assuring that the services and functions of the house itself complement and foster self-control and self-maintenance, not replace them.

At a more interpersonal level, technological solutions may make it less likely that residents will be able to maintain personal one-on-one contact with other human beings. Family members, friends, neighbors, social service workers, and others who regularly visit older persons in their homes to perform functions for them (shopping, cleaning, assistance with self-care) and to monitor their status may feel less obliged to stop by if they know that the housing environment itself takes care of those work and monitoring functions. At the same time, even for those who continue to visit, the nature of the time spent together can be quite different in the common cases in which that time has been organized around specific functional activities. Older persons and their visitors may not feel comfortable simply sitting and talking if their mutual time has previously been devoted to household tasks that no longer require attention. Of course, there is no requirement or demand of the technology that disallows social interaction, visiting, and so on, but the social impact must nonetheless be considered. Technology influences and affects the nature of one's relationships to other persons as well as to inanimate objects of all sorts. In this case, introduction of technology must make it clear that the services performed by machine are not to replace those that are part of the interpersonal milieu of the residents, but that, in fact, the techno-housing frees visitors and inhabitants alike to interact on a truly personal basis rather than a colder, more functional one demanded by a housing situation that requires constant attention and effort.

13.4 SUMMARY

Techno-housing is coming. Pieces of it have already arrived. Further, it clearly holds great promise for all of us, especially those who are having difficulty dealing with housing situations that are not adaptive, do not maintain themselves or monitor needs of their users, and keep their users from taking adequate care of themselves. In many ways, older persons and those with disabilities are justifiably a potentially benefited part of the population.

Concurrently techno-housing introduces new problems, new complications, and a potential for making life more difficult rather than easier. Those who propose and develop advances in "smart" houses must pay more attention than has thus far been paid to the likely reception of target populations to what techno-housing has to offer by examining attitudes and perceptions prior to the introduction of the technologies and actual usage patterns and attitudes following introduction. Some data on the reaction to and use of computers by older persons are hopeful but send mixed signals.

Techno-housing also must be developed and introduced with an eye to the needs of those who may best be able to use it—the elderly and the disabled—and to the potential problems inherent in such a major change in the basis for environmental relations. Flexibility, responsiveness, and openness to change must be maximized along with the ability to perform basic necessary functions for residents of the housing of the future.

13.5 CONDENSED REFERENCES/BIBLIOGRAPHY

Ansley 1988, *Computer Interaction: Effect on Attitudes and Performance in Older Adults*

Bednar 1977, *Barrier-Free Environments*

Blank 1988, *Older Persons and Their Housing—Today and Tomorrow*

Danowski 1980, *Computer Communication and the Elderly*

Dunkle 1984, *Communication Technology and the Elderly: Issues and Forecasts*

Engelhardt 1986, *Increasing Independence for the Aging: Robotic Aids and Smart Tech-*

Geremia 1987, *Smart House*

Haber 1986, *Technology in Aging*

Harb 1986, *No (Beep) Place Like Home (zzzt) (A Smart Home Technology Reviewed)*

Hikoyeda 1989, *Evaluation of a Home Response System*

Jay 1989, *Influence of Direct Computer Experience on Older Adults' Computer Attitudes*

Kerschner 1984, *Aged Users and Technology*

Krauss 1984, *Technology and the Older Person: Age, Sex, and Experience as Moderators*

Kubey 1980, *Television and Aging: Past, Present and Future*

LaRocca 1978, *The Application of Technological Developments to Physically Disabled*

Lawton 1973a, *Ecology and the Aging Process*

Lawton 1975, *Planning and Managing Housing for the Elderly*

Lawton 1980, *Environment and Aging*

Lawton 1985a, *Housing and Living Arrangements of Older People*

Mann 1978, *Technologies for Human Rehabilitation*

Myers 1989, *Fall-Safe*

Raschko 1982, *Housing Interiors for the Disabled and Elderly*

Rodgers 1983, *Diffusion of Innovations*

Schwartz 1988, *The Computer Market*

Struyk 1982, *Providing Specialized Dwelling Features for Elderly with Health and Mobility*

14

An Assessment

This Monograph is the only one in this series which deals with human behavior in the built environment in nonemergency and emergency conditions, and is the only one concerned with two target groups of extreme importance today, the aged and the handicapped. When referring to the built environment, all kinds of buildings and infrastructure (see Section 14.5), as well as transportation, which includes roads, signs, and lighting, are considered. Thus building design for the elderly and handicapped person has to include consideration of buildings and transportation, and the participation of all levels of government and the community itself. Since the government and the community have become involved in dealing with the elderly and the handicapped (who are now recognized as part of the community), one may well ask: "Why the sudden interest in the behavioral aspect of building design for the elderly and handicapped in the last ten to twenty years, when very little was manifested earlier?" Some possible answers are suggested in the following sections.

14.1 WHY ARE BEHAVIORAL ISSUES FOR THE HANDICAPPED AND THE AGED COMING TO THE FORE?

1 More Elderly

There is a huge increase in the number of aged in most countries, which has been well documented in all of the chapters in this volume.

2 Increase in Handicaps with Age

There is frequently an increase of handicaps with extreme age. Many examples given in Chapter 3 of the elderly in the United States illustrate the increase of handicaps with age. However, statistics commonly show that only 5% of the elderly are so incapacitated that they require full-time care in a nursing home. This means that 95% are able to operate somewhat independently. With better adjustment of their built and transportational environment, their level of independence should increase tremendously, to the advantage not only of themselves but also of the entire society.

3 More Awareness of Handicapped Persons

There is an increasing awareness, particularly in the industrialized countries, of the disabled, possibly because of the following reasons.

There are more disabled persons now. This is due both to improved medical procedures and to the lingering effects of World War II and other wars. Many soldiers who formerly would have died from their injuries are now being saved, but are left handicapped or severely disabled. These men or women are more likely to appear in public than in the past. The public sees them more often and is more likely to be aware of them; due to increased numbers, deinstitutionalization policies in many countries, and increased emphases on independence and autonomy, and, subsequently a somewhat more barrier-free, less unfriendly environment.

4 Change in Societal Structure

There has been a change in societal structure in the West from an agrarian or family-oriented society in which the family took care of the elderly or disabled at home to an industrial and now a postindustrial society (Bell, 1976), dominated by impersonal (in the West, more often) services. This is particularly obvious in the United States, but evident in all countries represented in this volume. For example, Chapter 7 observes that in Singapore, in the past, the disabled person would most likely have been taken care of by the family or by an institution, whereas the goal nowadays is the attempt, as in the West, to mainstream the elderly or handicapped into society. In Israel, too, the family still maintains primary responsibility for the care of the elderly and disabled among both Jews and Arabs (see Chapter 6). This has had the effect of giving special attention to adapting housing already in use by the elderly and handicapped, to meet each such person's individual needs so that these persons can continue to live with their families or spouses or alone. This is not to say that changes have not been made in public buildings or in transportation for the elderly and handicapped, but much emphasis is on retrofitting building or apartment design for specific elderly and handicapped in housing.

On the other hand, there is more governmental legislation in Israel (which has thousands of young disabled war veterans) than in other countries, requiring new government-supported housing as well as public places to comply with Eshel-designed guidelines. In all such buildings, provisions must be made by designers and builders for barrier-free access and egress, and for toilets accessible to the elderly and the handicapped.

In the Netherlands (Chapter 5) a strong concern with the human rights of individuals, particularly those with vulnerabilities, makes society anxious to provide the best possible familial and community responsibility for the aged and the handicapped.

In the Western and increasingly westernized world, however, these three countries tend to be the exception rather than the rule. In the more industrialized countries such as the United States, the role of the family in caring for the elderly and handicapped is being reduced dramatically.

5 Institutionalization

Along with a lesser family role in caring for these two groups, there is also a stronger movement against institutionalizing those not being cared for by the family. Numerous social and psychological studies in the United States and elsewhere repeatedly demonstrate that in many cases the condition of the person often deteriorates rapidly, to the point of early death, when living in the sort of large, depersonal, "total" institution described by Goffman (1961). Thus as the family or the institution, which earlier were the two main ways of caring for the elderly and the disabled, have become less available or less desirable, this trend may have contributed to the desire to build structures in which the elderly or the disabled person needs neither the family nor the institution.

6 Building Technology

With increasing urbanization and building technology there as been a large increase in the number and complexity of buildings, particularly tall buildings, perhaps especially in countries with very small land mass such as Japan (Chapter 2), Singapore (Chapter 7), and Israel (Chapter 6), and with a growing population, particularly of the aged. Some of these have been particularly well adapted to the aged and disabled when accessibility, egress, and internal structural needs are taken into account. An unintended consequence is that the tall building, by being densely populated, also provides a good social life for residents who might otherwise be lonely, but who now have many neighbors who watch out for each other (Haber, 1989). At the same time, designers and builders of tall buildings are becoming more aware of the humans occupying these buildings, as well as the structural concerns.

14.2 DEFINITION OF THE ELDERLY AS USED IN THIS VOLUME

Most frequently accepted definitions of the elderly refer to persons aged 65 and over. Some differentiate the aged as being 85 or over. For purposes of this volume we usually have referred to the elderly as 65 or over, primarily because most policies that treat elderly differently (for example, in access to specialized housing) use somewhere between 60 and 65 as the minimum age.

It should be remembered that the likelihood of minor problems becoming major handicaps naturally tends to increase in a person's sixties and beyond. Such handicaps are most frequently loss in speed or agility in mobility, some loss in vision, and some in hearing. Various other losses in health may occur that have not been systemically related to building design or structure, barrier-free environment, or transportation, such as heart disease or epilepsy. Only recently have designers and builders been attempting to include in building environments design for hearing or vision handicaps, which particularly affect the elderly.

14.3 DEFINITION OF HANDICAPPED, DISABLED, IMPAIRED, AND HAVING SENSORY DEPRIVATIONS

It is hard to know which term to use as a general term when discussing the handicapped, disabled, impaired, or those with sensory deprivations. Some object to using such categories altogether and wish to refer to elderly persons or handicapped persons as individuals rather than as categories of people. However, again for purposes of an operational definition, the general term handicapped has been used in this Monograph where the implication is that the person has some difficulty in mobility or sensory deprivation. The term sensory deprivation is used in reference to those with visual or hearing impairments. The term disability tends to be used implicitly in discussions on difficulty in mobility experienced in the built environment, particularly by those in wheelchairs.

Virtually no discussion has as yet taken place regarding those who are disabled or impaired due to some chronic but not necessarily visible handicap such as arthritis, heart disease, or mental illness. Some treat these terms not as medical alone, but as handicaps due to faults in the environment that is not fitted to the needs of these persons (see Chapter 3), an interesting alternate approach. However, most contributors to this volume have recognized a realistic degree of age or physical impairment as some kind of physiological situation which can often be alleviated, if not totally handled, by altering the built environment.

The definitions of handicap and disability have necessarily changed over time with increasing refinement and sophistication, and have reflected the influence of ideas on the definition from one country to another. (Compare the definitions given for the different countries in Part 1 of this Monograph.) Definitions are very important, as they establish the perception of the group and its needs: usually they are followed by attempts at regulations and legislation. Such definitions could be useful to countries which are still formulating policies and programs to assist persons who fall into these defined categories. Building, transportation, and community design programs can then be tailored to incorporate the requirements of such citizens, so that they may participate in society fully and independently.

14.4 TYPES OF DISCIPLINES INVOLVED

The totality of this volume illustrates that a number of disciplines other than those dealing simply with the aged, with the handicapped, or with building design have become involved with building design and construction for the elderly and handicapped. Some of the disciplines and professionals involved are:

Political and law-making bodies

Lobbying groups for aged and disabled, including wounded war veterans such as the lobbyist Page for the Paralyzed Veterans of America

Code- and standard-making bodies

Supervisors and enforcers of codes and standards

City planners and local governments

Architects and designers

Engineers

Builders

Services such as health, education, welfare, housing, employment, and transportation

Social scientists

The aged

The handicapped

14.5 TYPES OF BUILDINGS FOR THE AGED AND THE HANDICAPPED

This volume also illustrates the wide range of built environment that must be carefully designed for the aged and the handicapped if they are to function as closely to the nonaged and nonhandicapped as possible. Such types of buildings are:

Public and governmental buildings and those under government aegis such as public monuments, museums, and zoos

The workplace

Buildings for services such as those for health, education, welfare (for the aged, welfare cases, immigrants, unemployed)

Shopping areas, stores, and malls, including restaurants and theaters

Housing, such as single-home dwellings, small apartment houses, or high-rise apartments

Total institutions used in Goffman's sense as 24-hr establishments, such as hospitals, nursing homes, and prisons (Goffman, 1961)

Religious and communal buildings

This has also been put well in Chapter 7, where we have observed that city or other societal planning must be made around three foci:

1. Private life—home
2. Public life—commercial, recreational, and social
3. Linkages—transportation, both air and ground

The study of Inwood House (Chapter 9) brings forth one example of how the everyday lives of the handicapped are affected by prior planning for their specific needs.

14.6 LEGISLATION AND AWARENESS FOR BARRIER-FREE DESIGN

The United States became aware of the handicapped, as suggested earlier, through the returning disabled veterans of World War II and particularly after the Vietnam War, when medical advancements saved more lives of the wounded, but left them with disabilities. The continued growth of the elderly population as well has been obvious with each U.S. Census. National concern for a barrier-free environment began in the early 1960s, but only in the last few years has there been any sanction power. The American National Standards Institute (ANSI) released recommended standards for building design for the handicapped and the elderly beginning in 1961. These specifications are largely voluntary for the private sector and often enforced only where federal or state funds are used by builders.

An important new law, passed in the summer of 1990, is known as the Americans with Disabilities Act, which substantially enforces building requirements for the accessibility of the handicapped in both public and private buildings over a period of time, from 1990 to 1993. Public buildings must comply soonest, then large businesses, followed by smaller businesses.

In Japan (Chapter 2) awareness of the disabled began about 1949 with the Disabled Persons Welfare Law of 1950. The government eventually introduced slopes and elevators for the disabled in its own structures. However, no requirements have been made for privately owned buildings, nor do architects or designers fully understand barrier-free design; for instance, although there may be a slope in front of a building, there may be steps in front of the slope.

Similarly, in Canada (Chapter 4) concern for barrier-free design began in early 1960 with the development of building standards paralleling that of the United States. As these two countries demonstrate, activity in one country is often followed by another country, absorbed, assimilated, and copied with variations suitable for that country.

Although Singapore (Chapter 7) may have initiated study on barrier-free design earlier, the 1977 HDB (Housing and Development Board) study on barrier-free design was one of the first to facilitate accessibility for the physically disabled within the master plan for the New Town. The guidelines and accessibility features have been improved annually.

The Netherlands (Chapter 5) and Israel (Chapter 6) have a somewhat different attitude, way of life, set of values, and economic and political system from the other countries discussed. This has given them a somewhat different way of dealing with the needs of their elderly, handicapped, and disabled. The present state of legislation and design of buildings and environments for the elderly and the handicapped should be seen in the Netherlands as a phase and ongoing process, as it is in the countries discussed in this Monograph. The Netherlands, however, is a welfare state, as is much of western Europe (represented in this volume only by the Netherlands) and Israel. In a welfare state all citizens, and in some countries even visitors, have a guaranteed right to health care, food, and housing, whether or not they can afford it, paid for out of a tax system.

While the demand for specially designed buildings grows, there is as yet no legislation in the Netherlands that regulates the design of public buildings for the elderly, the handicapped, or the disabled. To deal with the problem, however, there are guidelines, now in the seventh revised edition, with the purpose of creating a society accessible to everyone, developing the necessary criteria for new and existing facilities.

In Israel all new government-supported housing projects are required to comply with Eshel-designed guidelines. These must be observed in all apartments, public places, toilets, and offices. However, besides these guidelines, there is much activity at the local, community, and individual-needs levels, tailored to the individual needing the building changes for functioning. Also, as in the Netherlands, family, friends, and neighbors are encouraged to help.

Thus it appears that the smaller, less affluent, but humane welfare state has a somewhat different approach to helping the elderly, the handicapped, and the disabled mainstream into normal society, which seems to be the goal of all. More is done to help through personal intervention, and through adaptation of the built environment to each individual's needs.

Which, if either, of these two methods is more desirable? Is one approach "right" and one "wrong," or are both useful, but in different societies? In the United States the society may be so advanced in barrier-free building design specifically because it cannot be "burdened" with weak groups. It wants these individuals to be independent, and does this best by providing them with prefabricated building designs created so that they can by and large look after themselves. In the smaller societies, such as the Netherlands and Israel, a more personal and individualized approach regarding changes in the built environment seems to exist. In either case, the solutions attempted may be the only ones possible for those societies at the moment. The two types of societies might also be said to have greatly different value systems, which in turn affect how they deal with the elderly, the handicapped, the disabled, and those with sensory deprivation.

It is nonetheless interesting to ask what gets a country "off of the ground" from the stage of sensitive recognition of the design needs of the elderly, the handicapped, and the disabled to actual legislation of such requirements. Whatever the reason, the technological solutions often proposed may well be good solutions, particularly if tempered with the more humane attitudes toward the elderly and the handicapped that seem to prevail in countries like the Netherlands and Israel, and the new attitudes against institutionalization in the United States.

Thus, each of these countries developed an awareness, then codes, regulations, and, mostly, legislation beginning from about the 1950s, after World War II, and continuing into the present. The legislation largely comes from the government and often is enforced only in public places. However, the process of refinement of the definitions of elderly, handicapped, disabled, and sensory deprived continues to evolve, and with that, new refinements and additions to legislation are passed and sometimes even enforced on private designers and builders. The more industrialized or post-industrialized service (especially self-service societies rather than the more humane, personal care societies, may have evolved the most legislation and sophistication in building barrier-free designed buildings and transportation. The Netherlands and Israel seem to have developed more personalized attention to individual needs, in individual apartments and housing, with a greater emphasis on personal care where needed from family, neighbors, and people in the community. It is a Gesellschaft versus a Gemeinschaft approach, perhaps, as to how to deal with people with special needs, with the U.S. impersonal efficiency toward their independence, or with the Netherland-Israel approach: some building design mixed with personal physical attention. The other countries contributing to this volume appear to fit in between these two extremes.

14.7 RESPONSIBILITY FOR BARRIER-FREE ENVIRONMENT

Throughout the countries discussed in this Monograph, the multiplicity and spread of public and private responsibility appear common at this stage of planning for barrier-free design for the elderly and the handicapped. Responsibility rests with many different types of departments, which often change from one year to the next. Hopefully departmental responsibility will soon be standardized within each country. Ideally, in the near future, the same department in every country worldwide would be responsible for barrier-free building design and enforcement, for both public and private designers and builders, making compliance easier for internationally active professionals. But this is unlikely, unless obtained by an international body such as the United Nations.

14.8 POSSIBLE REASONS FOR NONCOMPLIANCE OF PRIVATE INDUSTRY WITH GOVERNMENTAL CODES AND GUIDELINES

Complaints about the designer failing to understand the needs of the elderly and the handicapped surface in many places in this Monograph and other reference volumes. If this statement has any veracity to it at all, it may be partially because the designer considers himself or herself primarily an artist, and the engineer considers only what buildings must "perform." The designer, too, is often not responsible in any way, as yet, for governmental permission, even less so than are the engineers or the construction company for the construction codes of a building. Also, perhaps, the designer works for the "client," and the client is usually defined as the one who pays for a building, not the occupants, who are the "users."

If research on the needs of the building's end user, in this case the elderly and the handicapped, is to be carried out, it might well be done *before* million dollar structures are put up, and not after. Such findings could then also be used by others without having to go through so much of the trail and error and costly retrofitting which now exist.

Indeed, concern over costs is a major factor in the design of all buildings. However, most estimates are that the costs to accommodate the needs of the handicapped are very small, amounting to only about 1% in addition to the total cost. Further, many of these additions or changes are of benefit to the general public. In discussing cost, one might consider that an elderly or a handicapped person with autonomy, who has the ability to function in the workplace and to be independent, represents great savings in taxes as compared to those who are dependent on others, particularly on government funds, for support. So barrier-free design may be very cost-effective.

Another objection by designers to the inclusion of barrier-free design might be the sheerly esoteric fear that such factors as ramps or other barrier-free structures might detract from the beauty of the building. So far no arbitrators on standards of beauty have been established; however, codes which include equal rights of all humans to have access to buildings without discrimination have been growing fast in every country. The experience of Canada in retrofitting architectural masterpieces such as the Parliament Building successfully illustrates that neither beauty nor access need be sacrificed when sufficient sensitivity and innovation are brought to bear. Obviously these rights are denied if one person is able to enter a building whereas another person is unable to enter it at all. For those users of buildings and transportation whose money has contributed to construction but whose use of the structures is limited, their equality and ability to earn a living is likewise limited. Poor access to means of work, choice of shopping, or even of recreation is among the several reasons for a lower economic status of the disabled, which in certain cases could be enhanced significantly by barrier-free buildings and transportation.

14.9 BASIC DESIGN OF BARRIER-FREE ENVIRONMENT IN FREQUENT USE

In this section designs are presented that are used frequently and are common to many countries.

1. Access to buildings via cuts in the sidewalk to eliminate steps, which permits wheelchair occupants or those using small motorized units to use sidewalks or get into buildings.
2. Ramps besides steps leading up or down to a building.
3. Doors which do not have to be pulled toward the individual to enter since the feet of those in wheelchairs project further forward than their hands, impeding access.
4. Automatic doors which open before a person gets near them. These are also useful for the elderly or for those with arm or upper-body handicaps.
5. Doors wide enough for wheelchair entry and exit.
6. Clear signs indicating the location of numbered or lettered hallways, rooms, and, in particular, elevators and exits. Some propose signs in more than one language where there is a major group speaking a second language in a country, and others propose international symbols.
7. Lowered telephones and water fountains.
8. Toilets and bathrooms with doors and entrances large enough so that wheelchairs have room to both enter and turn around inside, as well as seats low enough for the aged or handicapped person to slide from wheelchair to seat. Also needed are handlebars on either side of toilets and on the sides of baths.
9. The size of many elevators has been increased to make room for people in wheelchairs. On the lower sides of the elevator there may be a detector so that the doors do not close on a slower person in the process of entering or leaving.

14.10 EGRESS IN EMERGENCIES

Most barrier-free design considerations refer to access rather than egress. Yet egress, particularly under emergency conditions, is important to all. Time is crucial for warning both normal persons and the handicapped and elderly to take action in a fire emergency. Chapter 10 describes how in Britain, although there are design guidelines for alarm systems, compartmentalization, fire resistance, travel distance, and exit width and choice, these guidelines are for people who move at normal speeds, as is evacuation down the stairs. But the elderly and the handicapped move more slowly than others, and some cannot move at all.

In Chapter 11 a strong argument is made, especially appropriate for the handicapped and the elderly, for not leaving one's room unless it is itself on fire, or going only as far as a compartmented safe area close to one's own room but safe from the fire. Closing off a fire area with fire doors also decreases risk to life and reduces the amount of movement necessary for the elderly or handicapped or those in hospitals, nursing homes, and prisons.

The common knowledge that elevators should not be used in fire, as they are liable to open precisely on the floor of the fire, impacts the elderly and handicapped people, especially as they cannot traverse stairs to escape as fast as others. In a high-rise building, total evacuation for everyone may be impossible within the time constraints of fire spreading, possibly within as short a time as 2 minutes. In buildings where many elderly or handicapped are housed, prompt and correct action by staff in closing the doors on fires also saves lives.

Chapter 12 contains ingenious design ideas for emergency evacuation of the visually or hearing impaired, while some of the devices described in Chapter 13 can aid greatly in monitoring the location and movement of persons incapacitated either on a permanent basis or temporarily by smoke or other dangerous conditions.

There is apparent contradiction between Chapters 10 and 12 which both emphasize methods of egress for the mobile as well as the handicapped and the aged from buildings during fire, and Chapter 11 which advocates against evacuation during fire wherever possible. The latter argues for safe places within a building, for people to stay during a fire—a compartmentalized area with the door shut—as a better safety alternative.

After having visited the scenes of many fires in nursing homes, hospitals, homes for the aged, and prisons, where multiple fatalities occurred, and having done intensive research on causes of death, Haber has verified that many people who tried to escape through smoke-filled corridors did, in fact, die, while those who remained behind their doors, with the doors closed, even though very close to the fire itself, survived. This research was done for the Department of Fire Research at the National Bureau of Standards to determine human behavior in fire, and causes for fatalities in fires in heavily occupied or tall buildings, especially by the handicapped and the aged (Haber, 1980a).

The fire department itself has long been trained in helping people escape, as have the staff of most institutions as well as individuals, so the idea of staying in place behind a closed door, unless one is in the room of the fire, is at first extremely difficult to accept.

This idea of compartmentalization appears good where fires break out in rooms with doors or areas set aside for compartmentalization during fire, and where people know the layout of the building. It is important, however, for someone to shut the door of the room where the fire broke out, if in a room, so that it does not spread smoke, and of course to immediately alert the fire department for professional help.

However, Chapter 11 and, in particular, Chapter 12 do note that people are not always in a building with which they are familiar, and they may have visual problems, as does everyone subjected to dense smoke. In such a building, particularly those with the open spaces favored by modern architecture, people may well need guidance on where to go, certainly to be steered *away* from smoke-filled areas. This guidance can be in various forms, as proposed in Chapters 11 and 12, through public announcements, blinking lights showing the directions to follow, or even electronically guided passages of high sophistication. All of this presupposes a working electrical system (and a backup should the first fail), and the remaining presence and clear training of management while fire may be raging around them. There is barely any mention of panic factors, which figure largely in catastrophic fires. Every single experiment on time for escape was done under normal circumstances.

Chapter 10 addresses methods of escape before disasters. Some of the best results on what to do and what not to do have resulted from in-depth observation by the NFPA and others, and the research done by Haber (1978) and others immediately after multiple-death fires.

A third alternative to either evacuation or compartmentalization of the aged or the handicapped has not been given serious consideration for legalization because of strong opposition due to costs. Sprinklers reduce fires, in most cases quickly and effectively. Also, much more could be done to reduce the toxins in building furnishings, carpeting, and ceilings, which, when heated, emit the poisonous gases that are the primary reasons for death in fire.

Also, management of all tall buildings needs intensive training on how to respond to fire fast by such elementary rules as shutting the door of the room that has the fire (after emptying it of people), calling the fire department instead of trying to fight it themselves, and compartmentalizing people in safe rooms or areas where this is possible, or providing clear guidance to safe areas by mechanical means where this is not possible, until the fire department arrives. Fire fighters themselves are prone to smoke inhalation and have the highest rate of occupational deaths besides police officers. They, too, have been trained to evacuate, and are also in the process of rethinking the best alternatives for avoiding fatalities. The public, too, needs far better information on the situations described as part of its basic education. A useful part of wartime training when entering a large, unfamiliar building was always to look upon entering to see where the exits are located.

Legislation requiring sprinklers (and that they are always active), solid doors on rooms, clear exit routes that are not barred and are well lit, reduction in toxic materials in buildings, management procedures, and public awareness of the terrible swiftness of fire and the two alternatives toward safety, egress or compartmentalization, are all areas which need to be developed, particularly for the aged and handicapped in tall buildings.

14.11　OTHER ISSUES AND QUESTIONS

Finally there are some key issues on which there are disagreements or conflicts among those interested in barrier-free design.

1. Some say the elderly or handicapped should not be grouped together but be treated as two totally separate entities, even though in some areas the design needs of the two overlap. These design needs are in regard to ambulatory needs and visual and auditory handicaps.

2. There are those who object even to referring to the elderly or the handicapped as groups at all, and who prefer the term handicapped or elderly *persons,* addressing individuals rather than as groups. These group names are often considered to incur stigmatization. However, they have their use in providing a description of the needs of this population.

3. Some object to grouping all handicapped together, as there are many different kinds of handicapped people. This is true to a degree, and it is critical to alert designers to the variety within such a global category. However, in attempting to diagnose situations, or to design buildings, it may be useful to consider a number of people with similar needs for which one can design useful changes in the built environment or in transportation or traffic patterns.

4. In designing for one type of handicap, nevertheless, one sometimes comes into conflict with, or causes problems for, those with another type of handicap or for nondisabled people. For instance, while a ramp may be very useful for a person in a wheelchair, it may cause great difficulties for an elderly person or someone with muscular dystrophy, or for anyone who can walk but has weak legs. This person may fare better with steps.

Another example is the door which opens automatically if a special button for the handicapped is pressed. This same door, if opened manually, is very heavy to pull open, and while not allowed, the nonhandicapped may also take to pressing the button. A change made for the hearing impaired, such as lights instead of bells, may cause problems for those with visual impairments if both visual and auditory messages are not given.

5. There is still the argument as to whether the elderly or the handicapped should be maintained in their own homes wherever possible, changing the design of their individual homes, or for that matter, their individual work environment, or whether they should be grouped and have the entire building designed for their express use.

6. While most public and government buildings have laid down guidelines for barrier-free design, these are not enforced in many countries. Should they be enforced in all places accessible to the public, and if so, how?

7. Private buildings have been free of the obligation to build with barrier-free design. Should they, too, be required by law to conform to governmental guidelines, and how should sanctions be imposed?

8. Is it possible, in each country, or even throughout all countries, to get the same department to consistently be responsible for barrier-free building design? At present, responsibility is with many different types of government departments and shifts from one department to another; it is different in every country. Could some consistency be achieved, at least within the same country?

9. A primary objection, it is believed, to implementing barrier-free design is the fear of the cost by designers and builders. Can one educate private builders as to the often quoted cost of 1% of the total estimated cost of the building going to the barrier-free design of the building? What incentives can be offered, or should the law just state that (as in the United States) almost all private buildings will have to include designs for the elderly and handicapped by 1993?

One cannot overemphasize the tax savings in changing a person who is totally dependent on society for survival to one who can take care of himself or herself and who also is employed due to adequate transportation and building design.

10. Do the handicapped and the disabled have a *right* to equal access to a building and equal opportunity as others to work (or live, or shop) in that building? Many disabled, barred from entering buildings because of their inability to do so, are in the process of prosecuting the owners of such buildings.

11. Although the elderly and the handicapped or disabled are often housed in structures specifically designed for them, they are not consulted nearly often enough before a building is designed, nor asked their response to it afterwards. Should preoccupancy surveys and postoccupancy evaluations be required to obtain construction permits?

12. Is it sufficient to design only the building for the elderly or handicapped? Since they want to leave the building, the surrounding streets, traffic lights, buses, shopping centers, libraries, hospitals—in fact the entire community and surrounding transportation system—must be taken into account.

These are just a few issues for consideration when designing buildings and transportation for the elderly and the handicapped.

14.12 CONCLUSION

This Monograph envisions (in Chapter 13) a techno-housing future where computers and robots will take care of the needs for barrier-free design in the homes of the elderly. Automatically provided sensors will anticipate the needs of targeted recipients through constant monitoring of their location, responses, and needs, and provide both maintenance of such services as well as protection for safety, both within and outside the home. This would allow many elderly to continue to live in their homes.

There are negative aspects to such a solution, such as the danger involved if the system breaks down, the possibility of inability to learn the new system, atrophy of existing skills, boredom in an environment which is too undemanding or challenging, or reduced visits by relatives or friends who no longer feel necessary. "Smart" or techno-housing, then, is not to be used as a substitute, but to complement other forms of care.

Also emphasized is the evergrowing need for housing for the elderly (Chapter 8), but the importance should be noted of *not* moving them from assisted independent living to a long-term dependent environment where many may deteriorate. Good alternatives, such as congregate housing, where a number of elderly and handicapped can live in independent units but with some minimal supervision, must be expanded.

These and many of the other concepts explored in this Monograph of building design for the handicapped and aged are applicable to both kinds of persons, and are intended to raise their quality of life. Much has been done to improve the built environment for the elderly and handicapped. Needless to say, much more can be done and is being done every day. Hopefully those who are just beginning to become aware of such developments will find some of these discussions useful.

14.13 CONDENSED REFERENCES/BIBLIOGRAPHY

Bell 1976, *The Coming of Age in Post-Industrial Society*

Goffman 1961, *Asylums*

Haber 1977b, *The Impact of Tall Buildings on Users and Neighbors*

Haber 1978, *Human Response to Fire among the Aged and Handicapped in Health Care*

Haber 1980a, *Human Behaviour in Fire, Depending on Types of Occupancy*

Haber 1980b, *Human Behavior in Fire and in a Total (24 hour) Institution*

Haber 1989, *A Survey of Occupants' Satisfaction for an Apartment House Built for the*

Haber 1991, *Changes in Arab and Bedouin Israelis*

Haber 1990, *Issues in the Definition of Disability and Use of Disability Survey Data*

Research Needs

1. **Potential advantages of tall buildings for the handicapped and aged.** Research has shown that tall buildings can be of benefit to the handicapped or aged given certain conditions. Socially, the denser the population the more contacts are afforded to residents who might otherwise be lonely. In most of these buildings (for example, Revitz House, Inwood House, and most facilities reviewed in the Netherlands and Israel), there is a resident manager. Also medical, recreational, religious, and cultural facilities and programs are either internal or close-by. More research should be done on how to maximize the social, cultural, medical, religious, and other benefits available to the handicapped and aged.

2. **Where to locate facilities for resident handicapped and aged?** More research could be carried out on whether to locate these facilities inside the building, as in the case of Inwood, or both inside and also close-by as in the case of Revitz House, or in the center of the community as in the case of Israeli aged housing units. When a gathering place exists (such as a lobby), research could explore the best place for meeting people without disturbing other residents nearby as was the case at Inwood House.

3. **Where to locate buildings for the handicapped or aged?** The problem of a large highway between Revitz House and shopping illustrates how important it is to study accessibility prior to construction. This raises the question as to where the building for aged or handicapped persons should be located. Some object to grouping them altogether, preferring to spread them normally with, and among, family and friends where possible, together with community and/or local or government assistance. Some say that housing for the aged should not be near teenagers, but this is not found to be the case in Israel, where the culture respects its elderly. Community attitudes toward such buildings and its occupants as well as the location of the building in relation to other facilities should be studied.

4. **Social research on community attitudes to special use buildings before construction.** Before commencing a building for either elderly or handicapped it would be useful to study the attitudes of the potential neighbors toward this new population.

A process of planned education of the community toward acceptance of these groups is needed, informing the sometimes hostile community about those who will be living in the area, allowing response and questions from the communities involved (including business people in the area), and the possible benefits and the ways in which the community can help integrate such people into the community. It could help overcome the fear or hostility before the building is constructed.

Incorporating ample greenery can make facilities less conspicuous. Shopkeepers and transportation people can be informed as to the needs of the handicapped and aged and how to make them active shoppers and transportation users. Working with school programs can lead children to help rather than abuse the elderly and handicapped.

5. How to encourage social scientists, architects, and engineers to work together to meet these special needs? The different disciplines often have a different perception of the problems. Architects and engineers speak of the "performance" of a building, which has almost no meaning to social scientists who understand that people, not buildings, perform. Buildings are inanimate. Architects and engineers often do not consider the opinions of the occupants of these special buildings, but make decisions as to how the occupants "ought" to behave. Social scientists may not understand the realities of structures and costs. Legislators, in their demands for barrier-free environments, may be interpreted as interfering by adding to the already high cost and, at times, uncertain ventures of tall buildings. Fire inspectors, likewise, may be perceived as adding to those high costs by demanding more exits and fire precautions.

More exchange and intermingling between social scientists and architects and engineers, in particular, is needed. The social scientists have the skills to determine the needs of specific types of users. The architects and engineers have the skills to design for the needs of these people. The two disciplines need to get together in the early stages of the project.

6. Survey future of potential residents of tall buildings on their needs. Suggestions are needed for location, performance, and services of such buildings and the immediate surroundings, including transportation, shopping, medical, religious, and recreational needs. After a building has been occupied for some time, regular surveys of residents would be useful, to find out how the building is working for them, and what suggestions they have for improvement.

After a building has been occupied for some time, regular surveys of residents should be used as part of postoccupancy evaluation (POE) to find out what suggestions they have for improvement. Even when it is not possible to make changes in the existing building, the ideas can be used on future buildings. Certainly one country can learn from the experiences of another, especially since many countries are only newly aware of building design for the handicapped and/or aged. There is an increasing number of aged in the population and an increasing number of handicapped as well. Formerly, many who would have died now go on to live functional lives. Buildings must maximize the possibilities of normal functioning for such populations. Tall buildings are attempting to do this.

7. Research on legislation and building codes in each country for building design for the handicapped and aged. More research is needed, beyond access. Comparison is needed of legislation in each country, and how it changes over time, including the publishing of these results.

8. How to modify buildings and urban transportation systems for the sensory deprived, or those with simple slowness or weakness due to age or other handicap? Much effort has gone into access, ramps, elevators, and also to such factors as lowered telephones, water fountains, toilets, stoves, cabinets, freezer compartments, even peepholes on doors. However, the majority of the changes made, while highly useful, are largely oriented toward those in wheelchairs. Little research has been done on how buildings and transportation interfaces can be modified for those with sensory deprivation such as visual or hearing impairment, or simple slowness or weakness due to age or some other handicap.

9. How do the hearing impaired know when there is a noise such as a fire alarm? How do the visually impaired know how to find a particular building or how to find their way around in it? So far, except for a few exceptions reviewed in this Monograph, researchers and designers have considered only normal situations when dealing with changes necessitated by disability, not those such as fire, where the handicapped and aged are under severe hazard, far more than the young or healthy person.

10. How can designers resolve conflicting solutions in building design? Will designing a building for one kind of handicap cause a problem for another kind of handicap—or for those with no handicaps? The ramp, useful to the wheelchair occupant, can be difficult for the ambulatory but older person, or one who can walk but with difficulty. There can be a push button for wheelchair occupants to open doors automatically as they approach. However, these same doors can be so heavy to open by hand that a healthy but less strong senior citizen cannot easily open them. They, too, may be forced to use a push button, making them feel more dependent than they really are.

11. Wayfinding. Given the ever increasing size of tall buildings, how can the designer ensure that the building users will know where exits and safe zones are located under normal as well as emergency conditions?

12. How to improve the reliability and performance of elevators? A major point of user dissatisfaction is elevators. Except in luxury buildings, there are regular complaints of elevator breakdowns. Since these are crucial for the handicapped and aged in tall buildings, research on improving the performance of elevators is essential.

13. Research on building egress. Most studies on building design for the handicapped and aged have centered on access and barrier-free environment. Relatively little research has been done on egress. Further study of emergency egress under fire and smoke conditions, in particular, must be considered in building for the handicapped and aged.

14. Research on whether to evacuate or compartmentalize the handicapped and aged. The issue of whether to evacuate or compartmentalize the handicapped and aged (or those who are neither) is critical because the escape time is so limited. Flashover can occur within two minutes of the onset of a fire. The most likely cause of death is exposure to smoke, which is largely toxic.

15. More research on how to build safe areas in all buildings If egress is too slow or not possible at all. The best plans can go wrong. Alarms do not go off, the deaf do not hear, the phones may be jammed or out of order, the fire department may be delayed, firefighters cannot reach the floor, access to the building may be blocked by impediments, or the firefighters themselves can be overcome by smoke. A voice system may not work or the back-up system itself may fail. Electronic systems which lock prisoners in their cells may cease operation, resulting in smoke inhalation and death.

An ignorant or careless person can open a door on a fire and let the fire rage out into the hallways where people escaping are overcome by smoke. The exits may have been locked, may be covered by curtains, may not be lit, or may be obscured by smoke. Some who have escaped may run back to retrieve objects or to be heroes and fight the fire. All these actions put others, in particular, the handicapped and elderly, in jeopardy if they try to move. Thus, it is important for all to know how to behave in fire so as not to jeopardize themselves and the lives of others.

16. How should management staffs of tall buildings be trained for emergencies?

17. Research on reducing the rate of combustion in building materials and furnishings and reducing (or eliminating) their level of toxicity when heated.

18. How can strong doors, so effective against fire, be designed to be lighter and more cost-effective?

19. How can designers reduce overall costs? Costs of protecting the building from fire and the overall cost of designing for the particular needs of the handicapped and aged are high. Research is needed to determine ways to reduce cost without reducing safety.

20. What alternative methods can firefighters use to assist in evacuating the handicapped?

21. How to improve fire inspection to eliminate blocked or locked emergency exits? It would be useful to develop a system to enable automatic activation of exit doors without risking fire spread. For some inexplicable reason fire inspection is extremely lax in many buildings. Innumerable cases of exit doors which are covered over, not lit, or worse, locked, crop up repeatedly in serious fires with resulting multiple fatalities. Systems must be developed to provide doors that open automatically in case of fire or other emergency. Of course this must not come into conflict in cases where one wants doors kept closed in cases of other emergencies.

22. Exchange of information. A research newsletter from different countries would be helpful on building access, wayfinding, and egress in normal and emergency situations; transportation solutions; and legislation that is working. How can social scientists, engineers, architects, developers, managers, and others reach the kinds of goals outlined above? How can research agendas be formulated so as to be most effective? How can the results of research be translated and made available so that mistrust is minimized and, instead, mutual respect of different points of view and areas of expertise made the rule rather than the exception?

One method is to increase the rate and flow of information. One approach may be a Research Newsletter that is international in scope and provides an exchange of ideas on such issues as access, wayfinding, egress, and the other topics covered in the Monograph. It could foster many improvements in life for the handicapped and elderly and also result in designs and approaches that would benefit all users of tall buildings that are "handicap conscious." The combination of research in areas such as those indicated in this section and adequate dissemination of results of that research would make tall buildings both attractive, cost-effective, and useful for everyone, particularly those who are vulnerable to the handicapping effects of insensitive design and construction.

Nomenclature

Accessibility. Characteristic of buildings that allows for free access to a building for all purposes for which it is intended by all, including those with disabilities; often narrowly defined to focus on mobility for wheelchair-bound persons.

Activities of daily living. Checklist of major activities of self-care designed to pinpoint areas in which persons are unable to accomplish such self-care; examples of activities are grooming, dressing, eating, use of toilet.

Acuity, sensory. Ability to make fine discriminations among environmental stimuli; sharpness in sensory processes.

Adaptability (adaptable environment). Characteristics of design features of physical settings that allow them to be added to or altered so as to accommodate the needs of their users.

Adaptation level. Point at which a person is capable of behaving appropriately and having high affect. (*See also* Affect.)

Adapted housing. Housing that has been retrofitted so as to be customized to needs of specific disabled user. (*See also* Retrofitting.)

Affect. Psychological "feeling" state or emotional state. Can be positive or negative related to environmental pressures.

Aging in place. Change in needs of older persons as they live in the same housing in spite of reductions in ability to care for themselves.

Alzheimer's disease. Most common form of organic brain syndrome, a progressive irreversible disease ultimately resulting in loss of control of bodily function, speech, and cognition, and finally death.

Ambulatory (ambulant). Related to ability to move about freely.

Americans with Disabilities Act. A 1990 law that greatly broadens the scope of definition of disability, the range of requirements for accessibility and penalties related to failure to provide access. (*See also* Accessibility.)

ANSI A117.1. Standard for accessibility developed by the American National Standards Institute and forming the basis for codes for handicapped access in United States.

Anthropometrics. Precise measurement of size, proportion, and musculature of persons, such as reach or angle of movement, so as to design work spaces that allow most effective use of that space.

Assisted escape. Use of information and physical assistance to enable persons with disabilities to exit buildings in an emergency situation.

Assisted housing.   *See* Congregate housing.

Autonomy.   Independent right to make one's own decisions and be able to carry out those decisions.

Balustrade.   Set of closely spaced vertical supports and railing adjacent to stairways or around the perimeter of porches.

Barrier-free design.   Careful design and construction of the exterior and interior built environment—pathways, doors, toileting facilities, kitchens, and so forth—so that they are accessible to persons with mobility and/or sensory deficits.

Beacon system.   Voice, light, or audible signal system that provides information about place and/or route when a person cannot use normal visual cues.

Braille.   System of raised dots in patterns to indicate letters, numbers, and words to provide information to blind users.

Chronic condition.   Long-term, usually irreversible disease state or result of injury or accident.

Closed caption.   System that provides subtitles for hearing-impaired television viewers by using a decoding device.

Compartmented fire-resistive building.   Building designed with compartments that may be as small as each room but never larger than several per floor so that fires will be confined to one or a few such compartments.

Congregate housing.   Form of *sheltered housing* (see also) that provides many on-site social and medical services, including food preparation and housekeeping, to enable persons to remain out of institutions; also called assisted housing.

Cost-benefit analysis.   Comparison of total costs (direct and indirect) of a course of action to its benefits; usually made in comparing several alternative approaches to solving a design problem.

Curb cuts (curb ramps).   Grading of curb areas of sidewalks at corners so that persons do not have to step up or down and wheeled devices can move freely across roadways.

Decentralization.   Movement away from central governmental authority to control by local authorities of specifics of policy-making and implementation.

Disability.   Characteristic of a person that is a limitation or loss of use of a part of the body or mental capacity that significantly limits his or her ability to carry out some activities of independent living.

Ecological model.   Model of person-environment relations developed by M. Powell Lawton and Lucille Nahemow; states that there is a direct relationship between the environmental competence of individual persons and the environmental demands, or press, such that only some combinations of person and environment are positively adaptive; also called press-competence model.

Egress.   Exiting from a building.

Elderly.   Aged segment of a society; usually measured in chronological age, using an age such as 60 or 65 as entry to the category of elderly.

Environmental Design Research Association.   Organization of planners, architects, and social scientists interested in research on relationships of design factors to person-environment relations.

Environmental docility.   State of being under the control of environmental characteristics, in which behaviors are highly influenced by physical design elements.

Environmental press.   Within the ecological model, the demands or pressures placed on inhabitants of a physical setting; high environmental press means the environment is difficult to use and control. (*See also* Ecological model.)

Environmental fit.   Within the ecological model, the situation in which a person's competence level is well matched with the press or demands of the environmental setting. (*See also* Ecological model.)

Ergonomics. Study of the relationship between human beings and machines or furniture, especially in terms of physiological, psychological, and technical requirements.

Eshel. Association for Planning and Developing Services for the Elderly in Israel; planning agency to ensure coordination of design and services for elderly in Israel.

Fire clock. Time between becoming aware of a fire and becoming trapped by it.

Flashover. Sudden expansion of scope of a fire when air becomes superheated.

Frail. Loosely used term to indicate that a person is at risk of not being able to continue to care for him- or herself or live in independent housing.

Gerontological. Of or pertaining to the study of aging processes or old people.

Gesellschaft versus Gemeinschaft. Two types of societies or organizations, the former very formalized, impersonal, and "objective," the latter based more on a strong sense of community, tradition, and sentimental attachments.

Grab bar. Bar placed around a bathtub, toilet, or other device to enable a disabled person to lift or move him- or herself as from a sitting to a standing position.

Handicap. Result of environmental factors that do not allow all persons to use the environment effectively; a handicapped person is one that has difficulty in a handicapping environment.

Hemiplegic. Person who has lost use of arm and leg on one side of the body.

Home equity conversion. "Reverse" mortgage arrangement with a bank that allows a home owner, usually elderly, to receive a monthly annuity payment based on return of the owner's built-up equity while the owner retains full use of the home.

Hostel. *See* Sheltered housing.

House mother. On-site manager of sheltered housing in some countries. (*See also* Sheltered housing.)

Housing and Urban Development, Department of. U.S. governmental unit responsible for policy and programs that include most of the activities related to disabled and elderly, especially in, but not limited to, housing itself.

Immigration. Permanent movement into a country for purposes of residency.

Incendiary fire. Fire that results from intentional ignition, often using flammable liquids.

Independent housing. Usually an individual's home or apartment within a regular residential area, as distinguished from sheltered housing or institutionalization. (*See also* Sheltered housing.)

Infrastructure. Roads, sewer and water systems, and other physical elements of an area that support construction and maintenance of buildings.

Knurled handles. Handles that have grooved turnings in them to distinguish handles of doors that lead to specialized or restricted areas from most door handles.

Life safety. Integrated focus on ways to enable persons to be protected in buildings during emergency conditions; may include maintenance in place or egress from the building.

Long-term care. *See* Nursing home.

Medicaid. Program of payment for health care of low-income persons in the United States, which pays for approximately 50% of all nursing home care in the U.S.

Mental map. Internal representation of the placement of objects in a space and routes to use to move about or exit from that space.

Mobility deficits. Inability to move within or between physical environments effectively.

Model code. Set of "generic" design regulations that are recommended for use as the basis of customized codes in individual jurisdictions.

Morbidity rate. Rate or likelihood of incidence of a particular disease in a population or subpopulation in a given unit of time.

Mortality rate. Rate or likelihood of death in a population or subpopulation in a given unit of time.

New Town. Jurisdiction within Singapore that is planned and developed in an integrated way.

Normal aging. Changes in the body that appear to be inevitably related to the aging process; major aspects are slowing of reflexes, loss of flexibility in tissues and organs (including sense organs), and loss of acuity in sensation. (*See also* Acuity.)

Normalization. Process of ensuring that persons with disabilities are not handicapped by environments but can use them for all the purposes for which they are intended.

Nosing. Edge of a step or other raised surface.

Nursing home. Institution that provides 24-hour nursing care and residency for persons who have major difficulty in caring for themselves; also known as long-term care.

Old old. Persons who are elderly and have serious problems with activities of daily living; often identified with being above age 75 or 85, but is actually a functional determination based on daily living skills. (*See also* Activities of daily living; Elderly.)

Optimal level of performance. Maximum or best performance possible for an individual.

Osteoporosis. Diseases of the bones, especially prevalent in elderly women, that weakens bone structure and can lead to breaks.

Paraplegic. Person who has lost use of both legs.

Pathological aging. Loss of full functioning due to disease states that are associated with being older, but not a universal part of aging; examples are problems due to arthritis, cataracts, heart disease, and diabetes.

Personal competence. Within the ecological model, the combination of abilities, skills, and motivation that a person brings to his or her dealings with the physical environment. (*See also* Ecological model.)

Pilaster. Architectural element projecting from a wall as a supporting column or decoration.

Press-competence model. *See* Ecological model.

Prosthetics (prostheses). Artificial devices, such as heart pacemakers, hearing aids, canes, leg-braces, that allow a person to compensate for loss of or reduced ability in use of sensory systems, limbs, or muscles.

Quadriplegic. Person who has lost use of all four limbs.

Refuge compartments. Areas within tall buildings that provide a secure haven from fire and other environmental hazards.

Retardment policy. Direct policy to minimize institutionalization and maximize normalization of persons with disabilities, to move away from segregation into separate living and working arrangements. (*See also* Normalization.)

Retrofitting. Restructuring an existing unit, building, or building element so that it can be used by persons with disabilities.

Robotics. Development of mechanical devices to perform acts usually associated with human action, such as assembly of products, cleaning, and cooking.

Section 8, Section 202, Section 236. United States programs that provide federal funds for construction and/or ongoing rent for housing for low-income persons, especially the handicapped and elderly.

Semiambulant. Able to move about relatively freely, but more slowly and with some more limitations than fully ambulatory persons.

Sheltered housing. Housing designed or retrofitted to house a category of persons with disabilities, such as developmentally disabled, mobility deficit; usually a relatively small number of such persons coreside in the housing with service providers.

Signage. Visual or auditory cues to direct persons within environments or along pathways or roads.

Slope. Slant; angle of grading in ramp design; recommended inclination of slope for accessibility is usually 1/20.

Smart house. *See* Techno-housing.

Sponsor. Nonprofit organization or local governmental authority that develops and manages subsidized housing. (*See also* Subsidized housing.)

Stack effect. Movement of fire from floor to floor through stairwells or elevator shafts.

Stroboscopic. Lamp capable of producing extremely short, brilliant burst of light.

Subsidized housing. Housing for elderly or disabled in which the rent paid by the individual is a relatively small, fixed portion of the cost of the housing, with the remainder paid for by governmental sources.

Tactile warning system. Use of texture changes in pathways, walls, and other building components to indicate use changes to persons with visual impairments; for example, using rough versus smooth surfaces to indicate the areas of walkways versus roadways.

Techno-housing. Computer-controlled, integrated housing that provides for security, monitoring, communication, and other functions through a single integrated system; may also include robotics. (*See also* Robotics.)

Tolman maze. Artificial maze with many blind alleys and one correct path, used in research to investigate mental mapping and speed of exit under various conditions. (*See also* Mental map.)

Total institution. Institution that maintains its inhabitants 24 hours a day, with rigid control over their activities; includes prisons, nursing homes, and hospitals.

Transducer. Device that receives energy from one electrical system and retransmits it in a different form to another device.

Unaided escape, principle of. Notion that all users of a particular building should be able to leave the building on their own, even in an emergency; effect is to limit access to disabled who may not be able to get out on their own in a timely fashion.

Usable space. Total area of a physical setting that is fully accessible and can be used for completion of tasks appropriate to that setting.

Warden. Term used in the British Commonwealth countries. *See* House mother.

Wayfinding. Explicit use of signage or specialized devices to lead people through complex or dangerous environments. (*See also* Signage.)

World Health Organization. International agency of the United Nations that has responsibility to improve health status and prevent or control diseases throughout the world through various technical programs and projects.

ABBREVIATIONS

ANSI	American National Standards Institute
ATBCB	Architecture and Transportation Barriers Compliance Board (U.S.)
BSI	British Standards Institute
CMHC	Canada Mortgage and Housing Corporation
CSA	Canadian Standards Association
DoD	Department of Defense (U.S.)
EDRA	Environmental Design Research Association (U.S.)
GSA	General Services Administration (U.S.)
HDB	Housing and Development Board (Singapore)
HUD	Department of Housing and Urban Development (U.S.)
IHDA	Illinois Housing Development Authority (U.S.)
JNR	Japanese National Railways
MRTC	Mass Rapid Transit Corporation (Singapore)
NFPA	National Fire Protection Association (U.S.)
PWC	Public Works Canada
PWD	Public Works Department (Singapore)
SCSS	Singapore Council of Social Services
UFAS	Uniform Federal Accessibility Standards (U.S.)
URA	Urban Redevelopment Authority (U.S.)
USPS	United States Postal Service

UNITS

In the table below are given conversion factors for commonly used units. The numerical values have been rounded off to the values shown. The British (Imperial) System of units is the same as the American System except where noted. Le Système International d'Unités (abbreviated "SI") is the name formally given in 1960 to the system of units partly derived from, and replacing, the old metric system.

SI	American	Old metric
	Length	
1 mm	0.03937 in.	1 mm
1 m	3.28083 ft	1 m
	1.093613 yd	
1 km	0.62137 mile	1 km
	Area	
1 mm^2	0.00155 in.^{2}	1 mm^2
1 m^2	10.76392 ft^2	1 m^2
	1.19599 yd^2	
1 km^2	247.1043 acres	1 km^2
1 hectare	2.471 acres[1]	1 hectare
	Volume	
1 cm^3	0.061023 in.^{3}	1 cc
		1 ml
1 m^3	35.3147 ft^3	1 m^3
	1.30795 yd^3	
	264.172 gal[2] liquid	
	Velocity	
1 m/sec	3.28084 ft/sec	1 m/sec
1 km/hr	0.62137 miles/hr	1 km/hr
	Acceleration	
1 m/sec^2	3.28084 ft/sec^2	1 m/sec^2
	Mass	
1 g	0.035274 oz	1 g

SI	American	Old metric
1 kg	2.2046216 lb[3]	1 kg
	Density	
1 kg/m^3	0.062428 lb/ft^3	1 kg/m^3
	Force, Weight	
1 N	0.224809 lbf	0.101972 kgf
1 kN	0.1124045 tons[4]	
1 MN	224.809 kips	
1 kN/m	0.06853 kips/ft	
1 kN/m^2	20.9 lbf/ft^2	
	Torque, Bending Moment	
1 N-m	0.73756 lbf-ft	0.101972 kgf-m
1 kN-m	0.73756 kip-ft	101.972 kgf-m
	Pressure, Stress	
1 N/m^2 = 1 Pa	0.000145038 psi	0.101972 kgf/m^2
1 kN/m^2 = 1 kPa	20.8855 psf	
1 MN/m^2 = 1 MPa	0.145038 ksi	
	Viscosity (Dynamic)	
1 N-sec/m^2	0.0208854 lbf-sec/ft^2	0.101972 kgf-sec/m^2
	Viscosity (Kinematic)	
1 m^2/sec	10.7639 ft^2/sec	1 m^2/sec
	Energy, Work	
1 J = 1 N-m	0.737562 lbf-ft	0.00027778 w-hr
1 MJ	0.37251 hp-hr	0.27778 kw-hr
	Power	
1 W = 1 J/sec	0.737562 lbf ft/sec	1 w
1 kW	1.34102 hp	1 kw
	Temperature	
K = 273.15 + °C	°F = (°C × 1.8) + 32	°C = (°F − 32)/1.8
K = 273.15 + 5/9(°F − 32)		
K = 273.15 + 5/9(°R − 491.69)		

(1)Hectare as an alternative for km^2 is restricted to land and water areas.
(2)1 m^3 = 219.9693 Imperial gallons.
(3)1 kg = 0.068522 slugs.
(4)1 American ton = 2000 lb.   1 kN = 0.1003612 Imperial ton.   1 Imperial ton = 2240 lb.

Abbreviations for Units

Btu	British thermal unit	kW	kilowatt
°C	degree Celsius (centigrade)	lb	pound
cc	cubic centimeters	lbf	pound force
cm	centimeter	lb_m	pound mass
°F	degree Fahrenheit	MJ	megajoule
ft	foot	MPa	megapascal
g	gram	m	meter
gal	gallon	ml	milliliter
hp	horsepower	mm	millimeter
hr	hour	MN	meganewton
Imp	British Imperial	N	newton
in.	inch	oz	ounce
J	joule	Pa	pascal
K	Kelvin	psf	pounds per square foot
kg	kilogram	psi	pounds per square inch
kgf	kilogram-force	°R	degree Rankine
kip	1000 pound force	sec	second
km	kilometer	slug	14.594 kg
kN	kilonewton	U_o	heat transfer coefficient
kPa	kilopascal	W	watt
ksi	kips per square inch	yd	yard

References/Bibliography

Advisory Council on the Disabled, 1988
EMPLOYMENT, ACCESSIBILITY AND TRANSPORTATION FOR DISABLED PEOPLE, Report of the Committee on Employment, Accessibility and Transportation for Disabled People, August.

ANSI A117.1, 1980
AMERICAN NATIONAL STANDARD SPECIFICATIONS FOR MAKING BUILD-INGS AND FACILITIES ACCESSIBLE TO AND USABLE BY PHYSICALLY HANDICAPPED PEOPLE, American National Standards Institute, New York.

Ansley, J., and Erber, J. T., 1988
COMPUTER INTERACTION: EFFECT ON ATTITUDES AND PERFORMANCE IN OLDER ADULTS, *Educational Gerontology,* vol. 14, pp. 107–119.

ATCB, 1982
MINIMUM GUIDELINES AND REQUIREMENTS FOR ACCESSIBLE DESIGN, 36 CFR, Part 1190, August 4.

Association of American Geographers, 1983
PROCEEDINGS OF THE FIRST INTERNATIONAL SYMPOSIUM ON MAPS AND GRAPHICS FOR THE VISUALLY HANDICAPPED, Washington, D.C., pp. 86–99.

Barnea, T., 1990
AGING AND DEVELOPMENT OF HEALTH SERVICES FOR THE ELDERLY IN ISRAEL, Paper presented at the WHO/EURO Seminar on Community Based Reha-bilitation, Jerusalem, January.

Bednar, M. J. (Ed.), 1977
BARRIER-FREE ENVIRONMENTS, Stroudsburg, Pa.: Dowden, Hutchinson and Ross.

Beer, S., and Factor, H., 1989
LONG-TERM CARE INSTITUTIONS AND SHELTERED HOUSING: THE SITUA-TION IN 1987 AND CHANGES OVER TIME, Research Report PR-10-89, Brookdale Institute of Gerontology, Jerusalem.

Bell, D., 1976
THE COMING OF AGE IN POST-INDUSTRIAL SOCIETY, New York: Harper and Row.

Bendel, J. P., and King, Y., 1985
A MODEL OF COMMUNITY, AGE INTEGRATED LIVING FOR THE ELDERLY, Discussion Paper 105-85, Brookdale Institute of Gerontology, Jérusalem.

Benjamin, I. A., 1982
LIFE SAFETY CODES—CURRENT STATE OF REGULATIONS PROVIDING SAFETY CONSIDERATIONS IN BUILDINGS ACCESSIBLE TO THE HANDI-CAPPED, in E. W. Kennett (Ed.), *Proceedings of the 1980 Conference on Life Safety and the Handicapped,* Report NBS-GCR-82-383, U.S. Department of Commerce, Na-tional Bureau of Standards, Washington, D.C.

Berkowitz, M., 1974
COST BURDEN OF DISABILITIES AND EFFECTS OF FEDERAL PROGRAM EX-PENDITURES, Final Report, Disability and Health Economics Research, Bureau of Economic Research, Rutgers University, New Brunswick, N.J.

Bernstein, J., 1982
WHO LEAVES—WHO STAYS: RESIDENCY POLICY IN HOUSING FOR THE ELDERLY, *Gerontologist,* vol. 22, pp. 305–313.

Best, R., and Demers, D., 1982
INVESTIGATION REPORT ON THE MGM GRAND HOTEL FIRE LAS VEGAS, NEVADA, NOVEMBER 21, 1980, National Fire Protection Association, report revised January 15, 1982.

Blank, T. O., 1982
A SOCIAL PSYCHOLOGY OF DEVELOPING ADULTS, New York: Wiley-Interscience.

Blank, T. O., 1988
OLDER PERSONS AND THEIR HOUSING—TODAY AND TOMORROW, Springfield, Ill.: Charles C. Thomas.

Blonk, C. J., and Hoekstra, E. K., 1984
AT HOME IN AN INSTITUTION? (Thuis in een inrichting?), Stichting Architectenonerzoek gebouwen gezondheidszorg, Amsterdam.

Bowe, F., 1978
HANDICAPPING AMERICA—BARRIERS TO DISABLED PEOPLE, New York: Harper and Row.

Boyce, P. R., 1985
MOVEMENT UNDER EMERGENCY LIGHTING: THE EFFECT OF ILLUMINANCE, *Lighting Research and Technology,* vol. 17, no. 2, pp. 51–71.

Brecht, M., and Preiser, W. F., 1982
TESTING AND EVACUATION OF THE TACTILE DIRECTORY FOR THE NEW MEXICO UNION, in *Proceedings of the 12th Annual Environmental Design Research Association Conference,* EDRA, Inc., Washington, D.C.

Brill, M., Lang, J., et al., 1977
EVALUATING BUILDINGS ON A PERFORMANCE BASIS, in *Designing for Human Behavior: Architecture and the Behavioral Sciences,* Stroudsburg, Pa.: Dowden, Hutchinson and Ross.

Brookdale Institute of Gerontology, 1982
AGING IN ISRAEL, a Chart book, Jerusalem.

BSI BS 5810, 1979
ACCESS FOR THE DISABLED TO BUILDINGS (Code of Practice) (revised version of CP96 1967), British Standards Institution, London.

BSI BS 5810, 1983
FIRE PRECAUTIONS IN THE DESIGN AND CONSTRUCTION OF BUILDINGS, PART 2 (Code of Practice for Offices), British Standards Institution, London.

BSI BS 5588, 1988
FIRE PRECAUTIONS IN THE DESIGN AND CONSTRUCTION OF BUILDINGS, PART 8 (Code of Practice for Means of Escape for Disabled People), British Standards Institution, London.

Building Division of Construction Department, 1977
A DESIGN GUIDE OF STATION FACILITIES FOR USE BY THE DISABLED USERS (Shintai shougaisha no riyou wo kouryo shita ryokyaku eki setsubi sekkei shiryoushuu), in Japanese, Japanese National Railways, 137 pp.

Byerts, T. O., 1978
ELDERLY HOUSING: CHALLENGE AND OPPORTUNITY, *Inland Architect,* November/December.

Calkins, M., 1988
DESIGNING FOR DEMENTIA, New York: Van Nostrand Reinhold.

Canada Mortgage and Housing Corporation, 1982
HOUSING DISABLED PERSONS, NHA 5467 82/12, Cat. no. NH21-8/1982/E, Ottawa, Ont., Canada.

Canadian Human Rights Commission, 1983
OFFICE CONSOLIDATION OF THE CANADIAN HUMAN RIGHTS ACT, Ottawa, Ont., Canada.

Canadian Standards Association, 1980
SAFETY CODE FOR ELEVATORS, DUMBWAITERS, ESCALATORS, AND MOVING WALKS, SUPPLEMENT NO. 2-1980 TO CSA STANDARD B-44, APPENDIX E, Rexdale, Ont., Canada, May.

Canadian Standards Association, 1981
SAFETY CODE FOR ELEVATING DEVICES FOR THE HANDICAPPED, CAN3-B355-M81, Rexdale, Ont., Canada, April.

CD Publications, 1987
HOUSING THE ELDERLY REPORT, Silver Spring, Md., vol. 3, p. 1.

CD Publications, 1988
HOUSING THE ELDERLY REPORT, Silver Spring, Md., vol. 8, p. 1.

Central Bureau of Statistics, 1988
STATISTICAL ABSTRACT OF ISRAEL, Central Bureau of Statistics, Jerusalem.

Chen, A., and Abend, A., 1985
DEVELOPING RESIDENTIAL DESIGN STATEMENTS FOR THE HEARING-HANDICAPPED ELDERLY, *Environment and Behavior,* July.

Conway, D. J. (Ed.), 1977
HUMAN RESPONSE TO TALL BUILDINGS, Stroudsburg, Pa.: Dowden, Hutchinson and Ross.

Corlett, E. N., and Hutchinson, C., 1972
RAMPS OR STAIRS—THE CHOICE USING PHYSIOLOGICAL AND BIO-MECHANIC CRITERIA, *Applied Ergonomics,* vol. 34, pp. 195–201.

Council on Tall Buildings, 1978–1981
PLANNING AND DESIGN OF TALL BUILDINGS, a Monograph, 5 vols., ASCE, New York.

Council on Tall Buildings, Committee 56, 1987
DESIGN FOR THE HANDICAPPED, Proceedings of a workshop held January 6, 1986, at the 3d International Conference on Tall Buildings, Chicago, Ill., Council on Tall Buildings and Urban Habitat, Lehigh University, Bethlehem, Pa.

Council on Tall Buildings, Group CL, 1980
TALL BUILDING CRITERIA AND LOADING, vol. CL, Planning and Design of Tall Buildings, ASCE, New York.

Council on Tall Buildings, Group PC, 1981
PLANNING AND ENVIRONMENTAL CRITERIA, vol. PC, Planning and Design of Tall Buildings, ASCE, New York.

Council on Tall Buildings, Committee 8A, 1992
FIRE SAFETY IN TALL BUILDINGS, Tall Buildings and Urban Environment series, McGraw-Hill, New York.

Cranz, G., and Schumacher, T. L., 1977
THE IMPACT OF HIGH-RISE HOUSING ON OLDER RESIDENTS, in D. J. Conway (Ed.), *Human Response to Tall Buildings,* Stroudsburg, Pa., Dowden, Hutchinson and Ross.

Danowski, J. A., and Sacks, W., 1980
COMPUTER COMMUNICATION AND THE ELDERLY, *Experimental Aging Research,* vol. 6, pp. 125–135.

De Jong, G., and Lifchez, R., 1983
PHYSICAL DISABILITY AND PUBLIC POLICY, *Scientific American,* June 24.

Dektar, C., 1983
24 KILLED IN APARTMENT FIRE, *Fire Engineering,* January.

Demers, D., 1980
FAMILIAR PROBLEMS CAUSE 10 DEATHS IN HOTEL FIRE, *Fire Journal,* NFPA, January.

Diutemeyer, 1981
ENCYCLOPEDIA OF SOCIAL WORK (Encyclopedia van sociale arbeid), 5th edition, 's-Gravenhage: VUGA.

DOE 1985
THE BUILDING REGULATIONS 1985: MANDATORY RULES FOR MEANS OF ESCAPE IN CASE OF FIRE, Department of Environment and the Welsh Office, HMSO, London.

DOE 1986
BUILDING REGULATIONS: ACCESS AND FACILITIES FOR DISABLED PEOPLE, circulated letter from Department of Environment, unpublished.

DOE 1987a
ACCESS FOR DISABLED PEOPLE: APPROVED DOCUMENT PART M, in *The Building Regulations 1985,* Department of Environment and the Welsh Office. HMSO, London.

DOE 1987b
THE BUILDING (DISABLED PEOPLE) REGULATIONS STATUTORY INSTRUMENT 1987, No. 1445, Department of Environment and the Welsh Office, HMSO, London.

Doorn, J. van, 1978
THE WELFARE STATE IN PRACTICE (De verzorgingsstaat in de praktijk), in J. van Doorn and C. Schuyt (Eds.), *De stagnerende verzorgingsstaat,* Meppel.

Dunkle, R. E., Haug, M. R., and Rosenberg, M., 1984
COMMUNICATION TECHNOLOGY AND THE ELDERLY: ISSUES AND FORECASTS, New York: Springer.

Eldar, R., and Solzi, P., 1986
FROM DEPENDENT TO INDEPENDENT LIVING, Paper presented at the IAPS 9th International Conference on Environments in Transition, Haifa.

Emmonds, H., 1983
THE ANALYSIS OF A TRAGEDY, *Fire Technology,* National Fire Protection Association, May.

Englehardt, K. G., and Edwards, R., 1986
INCREASING INDEPENDENCE FOR THE AGING: ROBOTIC AIDS AND SMART TECHNOLOGY CAN HELP US AGE LESS DEPENDENTLY, *Byte,* pp. 19–23.

Feller, B. A., 1982
HEALTH CHARACTERISTICS OF PERSONS WITH CHRONIC ACTIVITY LIMITATION, Vital and Health Statistics, series 10, data from the National Health Survey 137, DHHS Publ. PHS 182-1565.

Fruin, J. J., 1971
PEDESTRIAN PLANNING AND DESIGN, Metropolitan Association of Urban Designers and Environmental Planners, New York.

Gartshore, P. J., and Sime, J. D., 1987
ASSISTED ESCAPE—SOME GUIDELINES FOR DESIGNERS, BUILDING MANAGERS AND THE MOBILITY IMPAIRED, *Design for Special Needs,* vol. 42, January to April, pp. 6–9.

Gaudet, R., 1967
DORMITORY FIRE KILLS NINE, *Fire Journal,* National Fire Protection Association, July. Gelderse Council, 1984

Gelderse Council, 1984
SYMPOSIUM FOR ADAPTED LIVING AND ADAPTABLE BUILDINGS (Symposium aangepast wonen en aanpasbaar bouwen), Provinciale Raad voor het gehandicaptenbeleid, Arnhem, May.

Gennep, A. T. G., 1985
REMEDIAL EDUCATION ON HOUSING (Residentiele rothopedagogiek: Theorieen en onderzoek relevant voor de praktijk), *Nederlands Tijdschrift voor Opvoeding, Vorming en Onderwijs*, vol. 1, no. 3.

Geremia, K., 1987
SMART HOUSE, Smart House Venture Development, Upper Marlboro, Md.

Goffman, E., 1959
THE PRESENTATION OF SELF IN EVERYDAY LIFE, New York: Anchor Books.

Goffman, E., 1961
ASYLUMS, New York: Anchor Books.

Goffman, E., 1985
TOTAL INSTITUTIONS (Totale instituties, original edition 1961), Rotterdam.

Goldsmith, S., 1984
DESIGNING FOR THE DISABLED, 3d revised edition, London: RIBA Publications.

Goldsmith, S., 1985
MICRO OR MACRO—HOW SHOULD WE TREAT DISABLED PEOPLE? *Design for Special Needs,* vol. 38, September/December, pp. 6–9.

Gouldner, A. 1971
THE COMING CRISIS OF WESTERN SOCIOLOGY, London.

Government Building Department, 1975
A DESIGN GUIDE FOR DISABLED USERS, PART 1 (Shintai shougaisha no riyou wo kouryo shita sekkei shiryou, in Japanese), Ministry of Construction, 150 pp.

Government Building Department, 1976
A DESIGN GUIDE FOR DISABLED USERS, PART 2 ((Shintai shougaisha no riyou wo kouryo shita sekkei shiryou shusei, in Japanese), Ministry of Construction, 114 pp.

Government Building Department, 1981
DESIGN GUIDELINES OF GOVERNMENT BUILDINGS WITH SPECIAL CONSIDERATION TO DISABLED USERS (Kanchou eizen ni okeru shintai shougaisha no riyou wo kouryo shita sekkei shishin, in Japanese), Ministry of Construction, 24 pp.

Green, I., Fedewa, B. E., Deardorff, H. L., Johnston, C. A., and Jackson, W. M., 1975
HOUSING FOR THE ELDERLY: THE DEVELOPMENT AND DESIGN PROCESS, New York: Van Nostrand.

Grimes, M. E., 1970
HOTEL FIRE CHICAGO, *Fire Journal,* National Fire Protection Association, May.

Groner, N. E., 1982
A MATTER OF TIME—A COMPREHENSIVE GUIDE FOR FIRE EMERGENCY PLANNING FOR BOARD AND CARE HOMES, Report NBS-GCR-82-408, National Bureau of Standards, Washington, D.C.

Grosse, L. W., 1987
HIGH-RISE HOTEL OR APARTMENT FIRE REFUGE CONCEPT FOR THE MOBILE AND NON-MOBILE OCCUPANTS, in G. M. Haber, A. Churchman, and T. O. Blank (Eds.), *Design for the Handicapped,* Bethlehem, Pa.: Council on Tall Buildings and Urban Habitat.

Guffens, Th., 1983
ACCESSIBILITY AND USABILITY OF NETHERLANDS RAILWAY STATIONS FOR HANDICAPPED PEOPLE (Bereikbaarheid en bruikbaarheid van N.S. stations voor mensen met een handicap), Centraal Overleg, Provinciale Revalidatie Stichtingen, Haarlem.

Guffens, Th., 1985
EVALUATION OF THE DISTRICT PROJECT FOR HANDICAPPED PEOPLE IN
THE NETHERLANDS (Theoretische achtergronden bij het E.G.-Districtenproject
voor gehandicapten in Nederland), Evaluatieproject Sociale en Economische Integratie
Gehandicapten, Nijmegen.

Guffens, Th., 1988
YOU TEND TO TAKE IT FOR GRANTED, EXPERIENCES OF HANDICAPPED
PEOPLE IN PUBLIC SPACE (Je staat er niet bij stil, ervaringen van gehandicapten in
de openbare ruimte), Eurosound OSBN 9068050052, Nijmegen.

Haber, G. M., 1977a
BARRIER-FREE ENVIRONMENT FOR THE HANDICAPPED, Paper presented at
the American Sociological Society Annual Convention, Chicago.

Haber, G. M., 1977b
THE IMPACT OF TALL BUILDINGS ON USERS AND NEIGHBORS, in T. Conway
(Ed.), *Human Response to Tall Buildings,* Stroudsburg, Pa.: Dowden, Hutchinson and
Ross.

Haber, G. M., 1978
HUMAN RESPONSE TO FIRE AMONG THE AGED AND HANDICAPPED IN
HEALTH CARE FACILITIES, in *Proceedings of the International Conference on
Fire,* University of Surrey, England.

Haber, G. M., 1980a
HUMAN BEHAVIOR IN FIRE, DEPENDING ON TYPES OF OCCUPANCY: A
HOME FOR THE AGED, A PRISON AND A NIGHT CLUB, National Bureau of
Standards.

Haber, G. M., 1980b
HUMAN BEHAVIOR IN FIRE IN A TOTAL (24 HOUR) INSTITUTION, in D. Cantor
(Ed.), *Fires and Human Behavior,* Chichester: Wiley, Chap. 9.

Haber, G. M., 1985
USE OF TALL BUILDINGS BY THE AGED AND HANDICAPPED, in *Tall Buildings
and the Urban Habitat,* Council on Tall Buildings.

Haber, G. M., 1986a
BUILDING DESIGN FOR THE HANDICAPPED AND USER RESPONSE, A
STUDY OF INWOOD RESIDENTS, Paper presented at the International Association
of Applied Psychology, Jerusalem.

Haber, G. M., 1986b
REVITZ HOUSE, A SURVEY OF RESIDENT RESPONSE TO A BUILDING DE-
SIGNED FOR THE ELDERLY, Paper presented to the Montgomery County Depart-
ment of Housing.

Haber, G. M., 1986c
RESPONSE OF THE HANDICAPPED TO LIVING IN A BARRIER-FREE ENVI-
RONMENT, in *Advances in Tall Buildings,* New York: Van Nostrand Reinhold.

Haber, G. M., 1989
A SURVEY OF OCCUPANTS' SATISFACTION FOR AN APARTMENT HOUSE
BUILT FOR THE ELDERLY, unpublished.

Haber, G. M., 1991
CHANGES IN ARAB AND BEDOUIN ISRAELIS, in progress.

Haber, G. M., unpublished
BUILDING DESIGN FOR THE MULTIPLE PARAPLEGICS IN CAIRO, AND IN
BETH MALOCHEM FOR ISRAELI WAR WOUNDED.

Haber L., 1990
ISSUES IN THE DEFINITION OF DISABILITY AND USE OF DISABILITY SUR-
VEY DATA, in D. L. Levine, M. Zitter, and L. Ingram (Eds.), *Disability Statistics—
In Inventory,* Washington, D.C.: National Academy Press.

Haber, P., 1986
TECHNOLOGY IN AGING, *Gerontologist,* vol. 26, pp. 350–357.

Habib, J., and Factor, H., 1987
THE NEEDS OF DISABLED ELDERLY IN THE COMMUNITY AT PRESENT AND IN COMING YEARS, Social Security 30.

Hallberg, G., and Nyberg, M., 1984
EVACUATION OF THE THEATER OF DROKKNINGHOLM (Utrymning av Drottningholmsteatern), Department of Building Function Analysis, Royal Institute of Technology, Stockholm, Sweden, unpublished.

Harb, J. A., 1986
NO (BEEP) PLACE LIKE HOME (ZZZT) (A SMART HOME TECHNOLOGY RE- VIEWED), *Nation's Business,* p. 34.

Harris, A. I., 1971
HANDICAPPED AND IMPAIRED IN GREAT BRITAIN: PART 1, Office of Popula- tion Censuses and Surveys, Social Survey Division, HMSO, London.

Harrison, J. D., 1988
DESIGNING FOR THE DISABLED IN SINGAPORE: A UNIQUE OPPORTUNITY, *Singapore Institute of Architects Journal,* January/February.

The Hartford Courant, 1982
FOUR KILLED IN CHICAGO HOTEL BLAZE, *The Hartford Courant,* May 24.

Heek, F. van, 1972
WELFARE STATE AND SOCIOLOGY (Verzorgingsstaat en sociologie), Valedictory Lecture 7-11.

Hendricks, J., and Hendricks, C. D., 1986
AGING IN MASS SOCIETY—MYTHS AND REALITIES, Boston, Mass.: Little, Brown and Co.

Heumann, L. F., and Boldy, D., 1982
HOUSING FOR THE ELDERLY: PLANNING AND POLICY FORMULATION IN WESTERN EUROPE AND NORTH AMERICA, New York: St. Martins Press, 223 pp.

Heumann, L. F., 1985
A COST COMPARISON OF CONGREGATE HOUSING AND LONG-TERM CARE FACILITIES IN THE MIDWEST, Housing Research and Development Program, University of Illinois, Urbana, 139 pp.

Heumann, L. F., 1987
THE RETENTION AND TRANSFER OF FRAIL ELDERLY LIVING IN INDEPEN- DENT HOUSING, Housing Research and Development Program, University of Illi- nois, Urbana, 226 pp.

Hikoyeda, N. N., and David, D., 1989
EVALUATION OF A HOME RESPONSE SYSTEM, Paper presented at the Gerontological Society of America Meeting, November 16.

Hoglund, J. D., 1985
HOUSING FOR THE ELDERLY: PRIVACY AND INDEPENDENCE IN ENVIRON- MENTS FOR THE AGING, New York: Van Nostrand Reinhold.

Holshouser, W. L., 1986
AGING IN PLACE: THE DEMOGRAPHICS AND SERVICE NEEDS OF ELDERS IN URBAN PUBLIC HOUSING, Citizens Housing and Planning Association, Bos- ton, Mass.

Home Office, 1987
GUIDE TO FIRE PRECAUTIONS IN EXISTING PLACES OF ENTERTAINMENT AND LIKE PREMISES, Draft Document, Home Office, London, unpublished.

Hooyman, N., and Kiyak, A., 1991
SOCIAL GERONTOLOGY: A MULTIDISCIPLINARY PERSPECTIVE, 2d edition, Boston, Mass.: Allyn and Bacon.

House of Commons Special Committee on the Disabled and the Handicapped, 1981
OBSTACLES, Cat. no. XC 2-321/5-03E, Ottawa, Ont., Canada, February.

Hout, A. C. van den, 1983
DISCHARGED PSYCHIATRIC PATIENTS (Ontslagen psychiatrische patienten), Dissertation, Nijmegen.

Howell, S. C., 1980
DESIGNING FOR AGING: PATTERNS OF USE, Cambridge, Mass.: M.I.T. Press.

Howell, S. C., 1984
ELDERLY HOUSING: WARPING THE DESIGN PROCESS, *Progressive Architecture,* July.

Isner, M. S., 1988
FACT SHEET: HIGH RISE APARTMENT FIRE NEW YORK CITY, JANUARY 11, 1989, *Fire Command,* National Fire Protection Association, March.

Japan Federation of Architects and Building Engineers Association, 1982
DESIGN STANDARD OF BUILDINGS WITH SPECIAL CONSIDERATION TO DISABLED USERS (Shintal shougaisha no riyou wo kouryo shita sekkei hyoujun, in Japanese), with editorial supervision of the Building Guidance Division of the Ministry of Construction, 87 pp.

Japanese Standards Association, 1983
JIS A4301: SIZE OF CAR AND HOISTWAY OF ELEVATORS, Japanese Standards Association, Tokyo.

Jay, G. M., and Willis, S. L., 1989
INFLUENCE OF DIRECT COMPUTER EXPERIENCE ON OLDER ADULTS' COMPUTER ATTITUDES, Paper presented at the Gerontological Society of America Annual meeting, November.

Jeffers, J. S., 1977
BARRIER-FREE DESIGN: A LEGISLATIVE RESPONSE, in M. J. Bednar (Ed.), *Barrier-Free Environments,* Stroudsburg, Pa.: Dowden, Hutchinson and Ross.

Johnson, B., 1983
EVACUATION TECHNIQUES FOR DISABLED PERSONS, Springfield Environmental Research Ltd. for National Research Council of Canada, Contract 13SR-31155-2-3204.

Jones, M., 1980
ACCESS TODAY, *Progressive Architecture,* September.

Juillerat, E., Jr., 1962
THE HARTFORD HOSPITAL FIRE, *NFPA Quarterly,* National Fire Protection Association, January.

Juillerat, E., 1981
PREVENTION AND PLANNING AVERT HOTEL DISASTER IN EVANSTON, ILLINOIS, *Fire Journal,* National Fire Protection Association, July.

Kahana, E., 1982
A CONGRUENCE MODEL OF PERSON-ENVIRONMENT INTERACTION, in M. P. Lawton, P. G. Windley, and T. O. Byerts (Eds.), *Aging and the Environment: Theoretical Approaches,* New York: Springer.

Kennett, E. W., 1982
PROCEEDINGS OF THE 1980 CONFERENCE ON LIFE SAFETY AND THE HANDICAPPED, Report NBS-GCR-82-383, U.S. Department of Commerce, National Bureau of Standards, Washington, D.C.

Kerschner, P. A., and Hart, K. C., 1984
AGED USERS AND TECHNOLOGY, in R. E. Dunkle, M. R. Haug, and M. Rosenburg (Eds.), *Communication Technology and the Elderly: Issues and Forecasts,* New York: Springer.

Kimura, M., and Sime, J. D., 1988
EXIT CHOICE BEHAVIOUR DURING THE EVACUATION OF A LECTURE THE-
ATRE, in *Fire Safety Science: Proceedings of the Second Symposium,* International
Association for Fire Safety Science, Washington, D.C.: Hemisphere Publishing.

Kirby, R. E., 1988
APARTMENT BUILDING FIRE EAST 50TH STREET, NEW YORK CITY, Report
019, U.S. Fire Administration, FEMA.

Kop, Y., and Factor, H., 1985
CHANGING CHARACTERISTICS OF THE ISRAELI POPULATION AND THE
UTILIZATION OF HEALTH CARE SERVICES, *Israeli Journal of Medical Sci-
ences,* vol. 21.

Kose, K., and Nakaohji, M., 1989
DEVELOPMENT OF DESIGN GUIDELINES OF DWELLINGS FOR AN AGING
SOCIETY: A JAPANESE PERSPECTIVE, in *Proceedings of CIB 89,* Theme I,
CSTB, vol. 1.

Krauss, I. K., and Hoyer, W. J., 1984
TECHNOLOGY AND THE OLDER PERSON: AGE, SEX, AND EXPERIENCE AS
MODERATORS OF ATTITUDES TOWARD COMPUTERS, in P. K. Robinson, J.
Livingston, and J. E. Birran (Eds.), *Aging and Technological Advances,* New York:
Plenum.

Kubey, R. W., 1980
TELEVISION AND AGING: PAST, PRESENT, AND FUTURE, *The Gerontologist,*
vol. 20, pp. 16–35.

Lam, K. P., 1988
HIGH-RISE PUBLIC HOUSING DEVELOPMENT IN SINGAPORE, in *Second Cen-
tury of the Skyscraper,* Proceedings of Conference held in Chicago, Ill., January 1986,
Council on Tall Buildings and Urban Habitat, New York: Van Nostrand Reinhold.

Lang, J., Burnett, C., Moleski, W., and Vachon, D. (Eds.), 1974
DESIGNING FOR HUMAN BEHAVIOR: ARCHITECTURE AND THE BEHAV-
IORAL SCIENCES, Stroudsburg, Pa.: Dowden, Hutchinson and Ross.

LaRocca, J., and Turem, J. S., 1978
THE APPLICATION OF TECHNOLOGICAL DEVELOPMENTS TO PHYSICALLY
DISABLED PEOPLE, Washington, D.C.: Urban Institute.

Lathrop, J. K. (Ed.), 1985
LIFE SAFETY CODE HANDBOOK NFPA, 3d edition, National Fire Protection Association, Quincy, Mass.

Laurie, G., 1977
HOUSING AND HOME SERVICES FOR THE DISABLED, New York: Harper and
Row.

Lawton, M. P., and Simon, B. B., 1968
THE ECOLOGY OF SOCIAL RELATIONSHIPS IN HOUSING FOR THE ELD-
ERLY, *Gerontologist,* vol. 8, pp. 105–115.

Lawton, M. P., and Nahemow, L., 1973a
ECOLOGY AND THE AGING PROCESS, Psychology of Adult Development and Aging, C. Eisdorfer and M. P. Lawton (Eds.), Washington, D.C.: American Psychological Association.

Lawton, M. P., and Nahemow, L., 1973b
ECOLOGY AND THE AGING PROCESS, The Psychology of Aging, C. Eisdorfer and
M. P. Lawton (Eds.), New York: Van Nostrand Reinhold.

Lawton, M. P., 1975
PLANNING AND MANAGING HOUSING FOR THE ELDERLY, New York: Wiley.

Lawton, M. P., 1980
ENVIRONMENT AND AGING, Monterey, Calif.: Brooks-Cole.

Lawton, M. P., 1985a
  HOUSING AND LIVING ARRANGEMENT OF OLDER PEOPLE, in R. H. Binstock
  and E. Shanas (Eds.), *Handbook of Aging and the Social Sciences*, 2d edition, New
  York: Van Nostrand Reinhold.

Lawton, M. P., Moss, M., and Grimes, M. 1985b
  THE CHANGING SERVICE NEEDS OF OLDER TENANTS IN PLANNED HOUS-
  ING, *Gerontologist*, vol. 25, pp. 258–270.

Levin, B. M., (Ed.), 1980
  FIRE AND LIFE SAFETY FOR THE HANDICAPPED, Reports of the Conference on
  Fire Safety for the Handicapped, November 26–29, 1979. Workshops on Life Safety
  for the Handicapped, Washington, D.C., and Sacramento, Calif., August/September
  1979. U.S. Department of Commerce, National Bureau of Standards NBS Special Publication 585.

Mann, R. W., 1978
  TECHNOLOGIES FOR HUMAN REHABILITATION, *Technology Review*, vol. 81,
  pp. 44–53.

Miller, G. A., 1976
  THE MAGICAL NUMBER SEVEN, PLUS OR MINUS TWO, *Psychological Review*,
  p. 63.

Mills, J., 1983
  THE MILFORD PLAZA FIRE...A POST FIRE CRITIQUE, *W.N.Y.F.*, New York
  City Fire Department, 1st issue.

Ministry of Health and Welfare, 1987
  SURVEY REPORT ON CONDITIONS OF PHYSICALLY HANDICAPPED CHIL-
  DREN (in Japanese).

Ministry of Municipal Affairs, Province of British Columbia, 1984
  HANDBOOK ON BUILDING REQUIREMENTS FOR PERSONS WITH DISABILI-
  TIES INCLUDING ILLUSTRATIONS AND COMMENTARY, Victoria, B.C., Can-
  ada, Section 3.7.

Ministry of National Development, 1985
  DESIGN GUIDELINES ON ACCESSIBILITY FOR THE DISABLED IN BUILD-
  INGS, Development and Building Control Division, Public Works Department,
  Singapore.

Ministry of Social Affairs, 1983
  TOWARDS A BETTER PROFILE OF THE DISABLED IN SINGAPORE, in *Proceedings of Workshop on National Definition of Disability*, Singapore, August.

Ministry of Welfare, Health and Culture, 1984
  MAY I COME IN...? FUNCTION-MODEL FOR LIVING FOR PHYSICALLY
  HANDICAPPED (Mag ik binnenkomen? Funktiemodel gezinsvervangende tehuizen
  voor lichamelijk gehandicapten), Ministerie van Welzijn, Volksgezondheid en Cultuur,
  Den Haag.

Morgan, M., 1976
  BEYOND DISABILITY: A BROADER DEFINITION OF ARCHITECTURAL BAR-
  RIERS, *AIA Journal*, May.

Morton, D., 1978
  BEARING DOWN ON BARRIERS, *Progressive Architecture*, April.

Myers, A. H., 1989
  FALL-SAFE, Paper presented at Gerontological Society of America Annual Meeting,
  November 18.

Nahemow, L., Lawton, M. P., and Howell, S., 1977
  ELDERLY PEOPLE IN TALL BUILDINGS: A NATIONWIDE STUDY, in D. J.
  Conway (Ed.), *Human Response to Tall Buildings*, Stroudsburg, Pa.: Dowden,
  Hutchinson and Ross.

National Organization of the Handicapped, 1983
REQUIREMENTS FOR ACCESS: MANUAL FOR BUILDING ENTRANCIBLE AND USABLE FOR HANDICAPPED PEOPLE (Geboden toegang: handboek voor het toegangkelijk en bruikbaar ontwerpen en bouwen voor gehandicapten mensen), 7th edition (Nationaal Orgaan Gehandicaptenbeleid; in samenwerking met de Gemeenschappelijke Medische Dienst a.o.), Utrecht.

National Population Institute, 1986
REVISED ESTIMATE OF JAPANESE FUTURE POPULATION (Nihon no shourai jinkou shin suikei ni tsuite, in Japanese), Ministry of Health and Welfare, 38 pp.

National Research Council of Canada, Johnson, B., 1983
EVACUATION TECHNIQUES FOR DISABLED PERSONS: RESEARCH SUMMARY AND GUIDELINES, NRCC 23932, Ottawa, Ont., Canada, March.

National Research Council of Canada, 1985
NATIONAL BUILDING CODE OF CANADA, NRC 23174, Ottawa, Ont., Canada.

National Swedish Board of Planning and Building, 1981
HANDICAP ADAPTATION OF BUILDINGS, 70 pp.

Neno, M., Nachison, J., and Anderson, E., 1986
SUPPORT SERVICES FOR FRAIL ELDERLY OR HANDICAPPED PERSONS LIVING IN GOVERNMENT-ASSISTED HOUSING: A PUBLIC POLICY WHOSE TIME HAS COME, Public Law Forum, vol. 5.

Newman, O., 1973
DEFENSIBLE SPACE: CRIME PREVENTION THROUGH URBAN DESIGN, New York: Macmillan.

NFPA, 1981
INN ON THE PARK HOTEL FIRE, Fire Journal, National Fire Protection Association, May.

NFPA, 1982
INVESTIGATION REPORT ON THE LAS VEGAS HILTON HOTEL FIRE, Fire Journal, National Fire Protection Association, January.

NFPA, 1983
A COMPILATION OF NFPA TECHNICAL COMMITTEE REPORTS FOR PUBLIC REVIEW AND COMMENT PRIOR TO NOVEMBER 4, 1983, AND CONSIDERATION AT THE NFPA ANNUAL MEETING, RIVERGATE, NEW ORLEANS, LA, MAY 21–24, 1984, TCR-84-A, Cat. 12M-8-83-SM, National Fire Protection Association, Quincy, Mass.

NFPA, 1988
SMOKEY FIRE KILLS FOUR IN NEW YORK CITY HIGH RISE, Fire Journal, National Fire Protection Association, September/October.

Nolte, E., 1983
SUGGESTIONS FOR SAVING HOUSING FOR THE HANDICAPPED (Bezuinigingsvoorstellen huisvesting gehandicapten ondoordacht), Woningraad, no. 13, p. 12.

Oranje, G., 1984
OVERVIEW OF ADAPTABLE CONSTRUCTION (Beschouwingen over aanpasbaar bouwen), Introduction to Symposium aangepast wonen en aanpasbaar bouwen, Provinciale Raad voor het Gehandicaptenbeleid, Arnhem, pp. 15–17.

Passini, R., 1984
WAYFINDING IN ARCHITECTURE, Toronto/London: Van Nostrand Reinhold.

Passini, R., 1986a
VISUAL IMPAIRMENT AND MOBILITY: SOME RESEARCH AND DESIGN CONSIDERATIONS, in J. Wineman, R. Barnes, and C. Zimring (Eds.), The Cost of Not Knowing, Proceedings of the 17th Annual Conference of the Environmental Design Research Association, Atlanta, Ga., April 9–13.

Passini, R., Dupre, A., and Langlois, C., 1986b
  SPATIAL MOBILITY OF THE VISUALLY HANDICAPPED ACTIVE PERSON: A
  DESCRIPTIVE STUDY, *Journal of Visual Impairment and Blindness,* vol. 80, no. 8,
  pp. 904–909.

Pauls, J. L., 1980
  BUILDING EVACUATION: RESEARCH FINDINGS AND RECOMMENDATIONS,
  in D. Cantor (Ed.), *Fires and Human Behaviour,* Chichester: Wiley.

Pauls, J. L., 1984
  THE MOVEMENT OF PEOPLE IN BUILDINGS AND DESIGN SOLUTIONS FOR
  MEANS OF EGRESS, *Fire Technology,* vol. 20, no. 1, pp. 27–47.

Pauls, J. L., 1987
  ARE FUNCTIONAL HANDRAILS WITHIN OUR GRASP? in J. Harvey and D.
  Henning (Eds.), *Public Environments,* Environmental Design Research Association
  Annual Conference, May 29–June 2, Ottawa, Ont., Canada. EDRA Inc., Washington,
  D.C.

Pearson, R. G., and Joost, M. G., 1983
  EGRESS BEHAVIOUR RESPONSE TIMES OF HANDICAPPED AND ELDERLY
  SUBJECTS TO SIMULATED RESIDENTIAL FIRE SITUATIONS, Report NBSIR-
  83-429, National Bureau of Standards, Washington, D.C.

Preiser, W. F., et al., 1981
  GUIDANCE SYSTEMS FOR THE VISUALLY HANDICAPPED—PROGRESS RE-
  PORT NO. 1, Institute for Environmental Education, University of New Mexico, Al-
  buquerque.

Preiser, W. F., et al., 1982
  GUIDANCE SYSTEMS FOR THE VISUALLY HANDICAPPED—PROGRESS RE-
  PORT NO. 2, Institute for Environmental Education, University of New Mexico, Al-
  buquerque.

Preiser, W. F., 1985
  A COMBINED TACTILE/ELECTRONIC GUIDANCE SYSTEM FOR VISUALLY
  IMPAIRED PERSONS IN INDOOR AND OUTDOOR SPACES, in *Proceedings, of
  the International Conference on Building Use and Safety Technology,* Los Angeles,
  March 12–14, National Institute of Building Sciences (NIBS), Washington, D.C.

President's Commission in Housing, 1982
  REPORT OF THE PRESIDENT'S COMMISSION ON HOUSING, Washington, D.C.

Prinsen, J., Guffens, Th., and Kropman, J., 1984
  EVALUATION OF FOKUS CLUSTERS (Evaluatie van ADL-Clusters), Instituut voor
  Toegepast Sociologie, Nijmegen.

Provinciale Revalidatie Stichting, Gelderland, 1982
  GUIDELINES FOR RESEARCH ON ACCESSIBILITY (Een handleiding voor
  toegangkelijkheidsonderzoek), Arnhem.

Provinciale Revalidatie Stichting, Gelderland, 1984
  REQUIREMENTS FOR ACCESSIBILITY, ENTRANCE, AND USEFULNESS OF
  OFFICE BUILDINGS (Eisen voor bereikbaarheid, toegangkelijkheid en
  bruikbaarheid voor *Kantoo*rgebouwen), Winkels E. D., Bedrijfsgebouwen, Arnhem.

Provinciale Revalidatie Stichting, Limburg, 1984
  GUIDELINES FOR ADAPTABLE HOUSING (Leidraad woningaanpassing),
  Roermond.

Public Works Canada, 1982
  LIFE SAFETY AND DISABLED PERSONS, Seminar Summary/March 1981, Cat. no.
  W63-4/1983E, Ottawa, Ont., Canada.

Public Works Canada, 1985
  BARRIER-FREE DESIGN: ACCESS TO AND USE OF BUILDINGS BY PHYSI-
  CALLY DISABLED PEOPLE, Ottawa, Ont., Canada.

Public Works Canada, 1988a
LIFE SAFETY FOR PEOPLE WITH DISABILITIES: LITERATURE REVIEW, Ottawa, Ont., Canada, January.

Public Works Canada, 1988b
LIFE SAFETY FOR PEOPLE WITH DISABILITIES: A STATE-OF-THE-ART SUMMARY WITH AN EMPHASIS ON CODES AND STANDARDS, Ottawa, Ont., Canada, January.

Public Works Department, 1983
DESIGN GUIDELINES ON ACCESSIBILITY OF THE DISABLED IN BUILDINGS, Singapore.

Public Works Department, 1990
CODE ON BARRIER-FREE ACCESSIBILITY IN BUILDINGS, Singapore.

Raschko, B. B., 1982
HOUSING INTERIORS FOR THE DISABLED AND ELDERLY, New York: Van Nostrand Reinhold.

Rehab Group, Inc., 1980
DIGEST OF DATA ON PERSONS WITH DISABILITIES, Falls Church, Va., under contract to the Congressional Research Service.

Robert Scharf Associates, 1981
THE COST OF ACCESSIBILITY, Access Information Bulletin, National Center for a Barrier-Free Environment, Washington, D.C.

Rodgers, E. M., 1983
DIFFUSION OF INNOVATIONS, Free Press, New York.

Rubin, A. I., and Elder, J., 1980
BUILDING FOR PEOPLE, Environmental Design Research Division, Center for Building Technology, National Engineering Laboratory, National Bureau of Standards, Washington, D.C.

Salmen, J., 1987
DISCUSSIONS AT ARCHITECTS INSTITUTE OF AMERICA.

Sanford, J. A., 1985
DESIGNING FOR ORIENTATION AND SAFETY, in Proceedings of the International Conference on Building Use and Safety Technology, Los Angeles, March 12–14, National Institute of Building Sciences (NIBS), Washington D.C.

Schwartz, J., 1988
THE COMPUTER MARKET, American Demographics, 10 (9), pp. 38–41.

Scientific American, 1983
PHYSICAL DISABILITY AND PUBLIC POLICY, vol. 248, no. 6, June.

Sheehan, N. W., 1986
AGING OF TENANTS: TERMINATION POLICY IN PUBLIC SENIOR HOUSING, Gerontologist, vol. 26, pp. 505–509.

Shtarkshall, M., 1985
SHELTERED HOUSING FOR THE ECONOMICALLY DISADVANTAGED ELDERLY, Brookdale Institute of Gerontology and Eshel, Jerusalem.

Shtarkshall, M., 1987
SHELTERED HOUSING FOR THE ELDERLY IN ISRAEL—DEVELOPMENT OVER THE PAST FIVE YEARS AND PRESENT STATUS, Eshel and Brookdale Institute of Gerontology, Jerusalem.

Sime, J. D., 1983
AFFILIATIVE BEHAVIOUR DURING ESCAPE TO BUILDING EXITS, Journal of Environmental Psychology, vol. 3, no. 1, pp. 21–41.

Sime, J. D., 1985a
DESIGNING FOR PEOPLE OR BALL-BEARINGS?, Design Studies, vol. 6, no. 3, pp. 163–168.

Sime, J. D., 1985b
MOVEMENT TOWARDS THE FAMILIAR: PERSON AND PLACE AFFILIATION IN A FIRE ENTRAPMENT SETTING, *Environment and Behaviour*, vol. 17, no. 6, pp. 697–724.

Sime, J. D., 1986a
PERCEIVED TIME AVAILABLE: THE MARGIN OF SAFETY IN FIRES, in C. E. Grant and P. J. Pagni (Eds.), *Fire Safety Science: Proceedings of the 1st International Symposium*, International Association for Fire Safety Science, Washington, D.C.: Hemisphere Publishing.

Sime, J. D., and Gartshore, P. J. 1986b
ASSISTED ESCAPE OF A WHEELCHAIR USER: AN EVACUATION STUDY. Building Use and Safety Research Unit, School of Architecture, Portsmouth Polytechnic, unpublished.

Sime, J. D., 1987a
RESEARCH ON ESCAPE BEHAVIOUR IN FIRES: NEW DIRECTIONS, *Fire Research News, News of Home Office Fire Research for the Fire Service*, issue 9, Spring.

Sime, J. D., and Gartshore, P. J., 1987b
EVACUATING A WHEELCHAIR USER DOWN A STAIRWAY: A CASE STUDY OF AN "ASSISTED ESCAPE," in J. Harvey and D. Henning (Eds.), *Public Environments*, Environmental Design Research Association Annual Conference, EDRA 18, May 28–June 2, Ottawa, Ont., Canada, EDRA, Inc., Washington, D.C.

Singapore Council of Social Services, 1981
ACCESS SINGAPORE: A GUIDEBOOK OF ACCESSIBLE PLACES IN SINGAPORE FOR THE PHYSICALLY DISABLED.

Singapore Institute of Architects, 1979–1980
BARRIER-FREE DESIGN FOR THE PHYSICALLY HANDICAPPED IN SINGAPORE, Research and Documentation Committee Publication.

Singapore Institute of Architects, 1982
DESIGNING FOR THE HANDICAPPED, *Journal*, November/December.

Snyder, J. K., Jr., 1983
TESTIMONY BEFORE THE SUBCOMMITTEE ON COMMERCE, Acting Under Secretary for Travel and Tourism, Department of Commerce, Transportation and Tourism of the Committee on Energy and Commerce, House of Representatives, 98th Congress First Session, December 5.

Social Welfare Bureau, 1987
SURVEY REPORT ON CONDITIONS OF PHYSICALLY HANDICAPPED PERSONS (in Japanese), Ministry of Health and Welfare.

Spradlin, W. H., Jr. (Ed.), 1982
THE BUILDING ESTIMATOR'S REFERENCE BOOK, 2d edition, Chicago, Ill.: Frank R. Walker.

Standards Association of New Zealand NZS4121, 1985
CODE OF PRACTICE FOR DESIGN FOR ACCESS AND USE OF BUILDINGS AND FACILITIES BY DISABLED PERSON.

State Traffic Netherlands, 1982
ACCESSIBILITY, ENTRANCE AND USABILITY (Bereikbaarheid, toegangkelijkheid en bruikbaarheid), Hilversum: Veilig Verkeer Nederland.

Statistics Canada, 1985
HIGHLIGHTS FROM THE CANADIAN HEALTH AND DISABILITY SURVEY 1983–84, Cat. no. 82-563E, Ottawa, Ont., Canada, June.

Steinfeld, E., 1980
DESIGNING ADAPTABLE HOUSING TO MEET BARRIER-FREE GOALS, *Architectural Record*, March.

Stephens, S., 1978
HIDDEN BARRIERS, *Progressive Architecture*, April.

Struyk, R. J., and Zais, J. P., 1982
PROVIDING SPECIALIZED DWELLING FEATURES FOR ELDERLY WITH HEALTH AND MOBILITY PROBLEMS, Urban Institute, Washington, D.C.

Suggs, P. K., Stephens, V., and Kivett, V. R., 1986
COMING, GOING, REMAINING IN PUBLIC HOUSING: HOW DO ELDERLY FARE?, *Journal of Housing for the Elderly,* vol. 4, no. 1, pp. 87–104.

Teaff, J. D., and Lawton, P., 1978
IMPACT OF AGE INTEGRATION ON THE WELL-BEING OF ELDERLY TENANTS IN PUBLIC HOUSING, *Journal of Gerontology,* vol. 33.

The Ottawa Citizen, 1985
COMPLAINTS SWAMP ONTARIO RIGHTS BODY, Ottawa, Ont., Canada, October 31.

Timoney, T., 1984
HOWARD JOHNSON'S HOTEL FIRE ORLANDO, FLORIDA, *Fire Journal,* National Fire Protection Association, September.

Todd, C. S., 1985
INTELLIGENT FIRE ALARM SYSTEMS, *Fire Surveyors,* vol. 14, no. 2, pp. 5–15.

Treasury Board of Canada Secretariat, 1985
ACCESSIBILITY IMPROVEMENT, Circular 1985-41, Ottawa, Ont., Canada, July.

Turner, G., and Collins, B. L., 1981
PEDESTRIAN MOVEMENT CHARACTERISTICS ON BUILDING RAMPS, Report NBSIR 81-2310 National Bureau of Standards, Washington, D.C.

Turner, L. F., and Mangum, E., 1982
HOUSING CHOICES OF OLDER AMERICANS, National Council on Aging, Washington, D.C.

UFAS, 1984
UNIFORM FEDERAL ACCESSIBILITY STANDARDS, *Federal Register (49FR31528),* Washington, D.C., August 7.

U.S. Bureau of the Census, 1980
STRUCTURAL CHARACTERISTICS FOR THE HOUSING INVENTORY, Vol. 3, Subject Reports, HC80-3-4, U.S. Bureau of the Census, Washington, D.C.

U.S. Bureau of the Census, 1980
GENERAL SOCIAL AND ECONOMIC CHARACTERISTICS, PART 1, U.S. Summary PC 80-1-C1.

U.S. Department of HUD, 1977
HOUSING FOR THE ELDERLY AND HANDICAPPED: THE EXPERIENCE FOR THE SECTION 202 PROGRAM FROM 1959 TO 1977, Office of Policy Development and Research, Division of Policy Studies, Washington, D.C.

U.S. Department of HUD, 1979a
HOW WELL ARE WE HOUSED?: THE ELDERLY, Washington, D.C.

U.S. Department of HUD, 1979b
MANAGEMENT OF HOUSING FOR HANDICAPPED AND DISABLED PERSONS, Instructors' Guide, Office of Policy Development and Research, February.

U.S. House of Representatives Subcommittee, 1983
TRAVEL PROBLEMS OF THE HANDICAPPED, Subcommittee on Commerce, Transportation, and Tourism of the Committee on Energy and Commerce, 98th Congress First Session, December.

U.S. Senate and AARP, 1980
AGING IN AMERICA—TRENDS AND PROJECTIONS, U.S. Senate Special Commission on Aging in Conjunction with the American Association of Retired Persons, Washington, D.C.

U.S. Senate Special Committee on Aging, 1980
AGING AMERICA: TRENDS AND PROJECTIONS, in conjunction with the American Association of Retired Persons.

United Nations, 1982
AGING IN ISRAEL, Israel National Report to the U.N. World Assembly on Aging, Vienna.

United Nations, 1983
DESIGNING WITH CARE.

Ven, van, and Kruyne, 1984
THE ADAPTABLE ONE-FAMILY HOUSE (De aanpasbaar eengezinswoning), *de Architekt,* vol. 9, no. 15, p. 62.

Voordt, D. J. M. van der, 1983
BUILDING FOR EVERYONE INCLUDING THE DISABLED (Bouwen vboor iedereen inclusief gehandicapten), Centrum voor Architectuur Onderzoek, Delft.

Watrous, L., 1972
FATAL HOTEL FIRE NEW ORLEANS, *Fire Journal,* National Fire Protection Association, July.

Weihl, H., Azaiza, F., King, Y., and Goldsher, E., 1986
LIVING CONDITIONS AND FAMILY LIFE IN THE RURAL ARAB ELDERLY IN ISRAEL, Brookdale Institute of Gerontology, Jerusalem.

Willey, A., 1973
FIRE BAPTIST TOWERS HOUSING FOR THE ELDERLY, *Fire Journal,* National Fire Protection Association, May.

Williams, A. W., and Hopkinson, J. S., 1986
FACTORS DETERMINING LIFE HAZARD FROM FIRES IN GROUP-RESIDENTIAL BUILDINGS, PART 1: HOTELS AND BOARDING HOUSES, Building Research Establishment Report, Fire Research Station, Garston.

Wong, E., Aline, K., and Yeh, S. H. K., 1985
HOUSING A NATION: 25 YEARS OF PUBLIC HOUSING IN SINGAPORE, Maruzen Asia for Housing and Development Board.

Working Commission Report, 1989
AD-HOC WORKING COMMISSION ON THE KANAGAWA PREFECTURAL GOVERNMENT ADMINISTRATIVE SERVICE FOR BARRIER-FREE BUILDING DESIGN (in Japanese).

World Health Organization, 1980
CLASSIFICATIONS OF IMPAIRMENTS, DISABILITIES AND HANDICAPS, Geneva, Switzerland.

Yehudai, J., 1985
NEEDS OF THE ELDERLY POPULATION IN THE KIBBUTZ, League of the Kibbutz Movement, Tel-Aviv.

Zais, J. P., Struyk, R. J., and Thibodeau, T., 1982
HOUSING ASSISTANCE FOR OLDER AMERICANS, Washington, D.C.: Urban Institute Press.

Contributors

The following is a list of those who have contributed manuscripts for this Monograph. The names, affiliations, and countries of each author are given.

Richard M. Aynsley, University of Auckland, Auckland, New Zealand
Thomas O. Blank, University of Connecticut, Storrs, Connecticut, USA
Alexander Chen, Seabrook, Maryland, USA
G. Day Ding, California Polytech State University, San Luis Obispo, California, USA
Reuben Eldar, Ben Gurion University, Beer Sheva, Israel
Yona Friedman, Paris, France
Th. M. G. Guffens, Sociological Institute, Nijmegen, Netherlands
Gilda M. Haber, University of Maryland, Silver Spring, Maryland, USA
James D. Harrison, National University of Singapore, Singapore
Donald N. Henning, Public Works Canada, Ottawa, Ontario, Canada
Leonard F. Heumann, University of Illinois, Illinois, USA
Satoshi Kose, Building Research Institute, Ibaraki, Japan
Khee Poh Lam, National University of Singapore, Singapore
Bill P. Lim, Queensland University of Technology, Brisbane, Australia
James N. Macdonald, Travelers Insurance Company, Hartford, Connecticut, USA
Wolfgang F. E. Preiser, University of Cincinnati, Cincinnati, Ohio, USA
Miriam Shtarkshall, Association for the Planning and Development of Services for the Aged in Israel, Jerusalem, Israel
Jonathan D. Sime, Portsmouth Polytech, Portsmouth, UK
James G. Small, Hughes Aircraft Company, Los Angeles, California, USA

Building Index

The following index enables the reader to identify the page number on which a particular building is mentioned. Numbers in italics designate page numbers for figures.

Name Index

The following list cites the page numbers on which the indicated names are mentioned. The list includes the authors as well as other individuals or organizations named in the text.

Names followed by years refer to bibliographic citations that are included in the appendix entitled "References/Bibliography."

Subject Index

access, 21, 33, 50, 119, 120, 153–164, 206, 207, 210
  definition, 155
access/egress problem, 156
accessibility, 36, 40, 43, 69, 72, 106, 108, 113
accessibility standards, 29, 42
accessibility versus adaptability, 28
accessible environment, 33
accessible housing, 95
accidents, 18
  on stairs, 172
acoustic-path concept, 185
acoustic sensing, 186
Acre, 91, 94
activity limitation, 32, 33
adaptability, 34, 35
adaptable building, 79, 80, 81
adaptable environment, 35, 44
adapted housing, 77, 79
adjusted apartments, 98
administrative policies, 110
admission priority criteria, 91
age group integration, 93
age segregation, 91
aging housing stock, 36
aging in place, 90, 125–135, 192, 210
aging process, 27
alterations, 46
ambulant disabled, 103, 104, 110, 115, 120
Americans with Disabilities Act, 204
Arab, 85
architects, 46, 202
Architectural Barriers Act, 41, 153
architectural provisions, 70
areas of refuge, 54
atrophy, 195, 197
attitudes toward disability, 101
audible alarms, 169
audible signals, 39

auditory handicap, 16
automatic doors, 22
autonomy, 78
awareness of handicapped, 200

balustrades, 24
barrier-free access to public transportation, 149
barrier-free design, 7, 15, 27, 30, 33, 39, 49, 108, 120, 143, 203, 204, 206, 209
  guidelines, 20, 33, 210
  legislation, 153
barrier-free egress, 162
barrier-free environment, 28, 44, 115, 148
barrier-free requirements, 21
barriers, 157
bathroom, 145, 207
bathtubs, 35
behavior, 46, 160, 199
  in fires, 157, 159, 161
bilingual country, 61
blind, 6, 88, 160, 183, 184
braille flooring finishes, 21
braille blocks, 22
braille signs, 22
British standards, 153, 154, 161
building codes, 53
building design, 2, 36, 63–83, 101–122
building directories, 179
building image, 157
building layout, 69
building regulations, 154
Building Standard Law of Japan, 18
building technology, 201
building users, 158
  end user, 206
built environment, 140, 203, 209
buses, 119
button height, 22

Canada, 49–62, 68, 204, 206